Staying with Conflict

Staying with Conflict

A Strategic Approach to Ongoing Disputes

Bernard Mayer

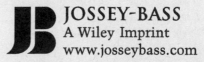

JOSSEY-BASS
A Wiley Imprint
www.josseybass.com

Published by Jossey-Bass
A Wiley Imprint
989 Market Street, San Francisco, CA 94103-1741—www.josseybass.com

Jossey-Bass books and products are available through most bookstores. To contact Jossey-Bass directly call our Customer Care Department within the U.S. at 800-956-7739, outside the U.S. at 317-572-3986, or fax 317-572-4002.

Jossey-Bass also publishes its books in a variety of electronic formats. Some content that appears in print may not be available in electronic books.

Library of Congress Cataloging-in-Publication Data
Mayer, Bernard S., date.
   Staying with conflict : a strategic approach to ongoing disputes / Bernard Mayer. —1st ed.
     p. cm.
   Includes bibliographical references and index.
   ISBN 978-0-7879-9729-8 (cloth)
     1. Interpersonal conflict. 2. Conflict (Psychology) 3. Conflict management.
   I. Title.
   BF637.I48M396 2009
   303.6'9—dc22
                                        2008043474

Printed in the United States of America
FIRST EDITION
HB Printing   10 9 8 7 6 5 4 3

Contents

To Julie, who stays with conflict with courage, integrity, wisdom, and compassion

Preface

Why should we commit to resolve disputes? Maybe we need to deepen them?

Environmental activist

Participants in a project I was assisting with were having doubts about advocating consensus-based solutions to environmental conflicts. As part of the Common Sense Initiative, sponsored by the U.S. Environmental Protection Agency in the mid-1990s, conflict specialists and a variety of others were working to produce a manual for industry, government, workers, environmentalists, and citizen groups about participation in collaborative processes, but a number of the participants were not buying the premise.

After considerable discussion, participants came up with the term *constructive engagement*, and the resultant *Constructive Engagement Resource Guide* (Mayer, Ghais, and McKay, 1999) details criteria for deciding whether a collaborative effort makes sense and how best to engage in one if it does. This was not the abstract formulation of conflict specialists, but the best take of experienced environmentalists, community activists, industry leaders, and government officials on how to characterize their aims for dealing with what they understood to be long-term conflicts.

They were onto something and my colleagues and I needed to listen.

As usual it was not the experts who broke new ground but the participants in conflict, who knew what they needed. According to their understanding, they did not necessarily need conflict specialists to help them resolve their disputes—because many of their conflicts were either not ripe for resolution or had to be understood in the context of deeper and further-reaching struggles. Instead, they wanted the conflict experts to understand the essence of what people in each conflict need and then to figure out how to meet those needs.

Given their inclination, values, and skill set, most conflict professionals are oriented to respecting client autonomy and leadership. But we also have to carve out our own identity and develop a market niche to make a living. And we are bound by the structures of our own practice. As a result we have not really embraced the concept of constructive engagement. Instead, we have gravitated toward conflict resolution as our defining goal. When resolution is the phase of conflict that parties need to address, we are in business. But this is a very limited and limiting view of what disputants want and need in the broad range of conflicts that they face in their lives. As a result our efforts have been more constricted than they need to be.

I have written previously about our need to move beyond identifying our work solely with third-party efforts to resolve conflicts (Mayer, 2004). But as I have considered the heart of what people struggle with in conflict, I have come to believe there is an additional dimension to our challenge. The most significant conflicts people face are the enduring ones—those struggles that are long lasting and for which a resolution is either irrelevant or is just one in a series of partial goals in service of a long-term endeavor.

Everyone knows that not all conflicts get resolved. Many of the conflicts that people experience today in their families, workplaces, and communities have probably been present in some form or another for a long time and are likely to continue for many years. But we in the conflict intervention field often act as if resolution is our entire purpose and focus. What we overlook is that there is work to be done—constructive, hopeful, and valuable work—in dealing with conflicts that are ongoing and likely to be around for a long time.

As I look back at the most challenging and meaningful work that my colleagues and I have been part of, almost all of it has been about assisting in some way with enduring conflict. Our role may have been specific and time limited, but the thrust of our efforts was to help people make progress in the ways they engaged in the long, deep, and intensely meaningful conflicts they faced. This has been true no matter what the system, focus, or context of the conflict—interpersonal, group, organizational, communal, societal, or cross-cultural.

Despite the comparatively narrow focus and self-definition that we conflict specialists have generally adopted, I am convinced that we have a great deal to offer participants in enduring disputes if we can broaden that focus and definition. We need to start by revising our sense of purpose. As articulated by the participants in the Common Sense Initiative resource manual project, our overriding goal ought to be to promote a constructive approach to engagement in the significant issues that disputants face, and very often that means working on enduring conflicts.

And just what does *constructive engagement* imply? Constructive engagement requires disputants to accept the conflicts in their lives with courage, optimism, realism, and determination. It means learning to engage with both the conflict and the other disputants with respect for each person's humanity, if not his or her behavior or beliefs. It means articulating the nature of the conflict in a way that opens the door to communication and understanding rather than slamming it shut. It means developing durable avenues of communication that will survive the ups and downs of a long-term conflict. Constructive engagement requires using one's power and responding to others' use of power wisely—upping the level of conflict when necessary but doing so in a way that promotes desired behavior rather than becoming destructive. It means negotiating and problem solving within the context of the long-term challenge, and it means developing support systems that can sustain and energize individuals throughout a conflict.

When disputants avoid important issues, polarize problems, look for quick fixes to long-term issues, cut off all intentional communication or communicate to shut others down, use power or respond to power with the intention of hurting others or beating them into submission, they are not engaging constructively. When they escalate their use of power way beyond what is necessary to encourage constructive behavior, sacrifice important concerns to avoid unpleasant or even dangerous interactions, or alternate between obsessing about a conflict and denying its existence, they are not engaging constructively.

Everyone, no matter how sophisticated he or she is about conflict dynamics and communication, struggles with maintaining a constructive approach to long-term conflicts. Everyone needs help with this critical challenge, and conflict specialists are one important resource. But to offer this help we have to recognize the nature of the challenge—which is at its core about assisting people in finding a way to stay engaged and committed to working on problems that are going to be around for the foreseeable future.

When faced with enduring conflict, we need to ask a new question. Instead of asking, "What can we do to resolve or de-escalate this conflict?" we need to ask, "How can we help people prepare to engage with this issue over time?" As we seek to answer this new question, our focus will begin to change and significant new avenues of intervention will become apparent. The basic challenge is strategic—it is the broad approach to the conflict that has to be altered. There are no simple steps or tactics that can change the whole dynamic, but the overall way in which parties approach the conflict can make a big difference in how constructive or destructive the conflict process is for them. This means that we have to start by understanding the nature of enduring conflict, and especially what makes it enduring. Once we achieve that understanding, I believe we have six strategic challenges:

1. To confront the pervasive and destructive power of conflict avoidance

2. To work with disputants to construct conflict narratives that encourage an effective approach to long-term disputes

3. To assist in developing durable avenues of communication

4. To help disputants use power and respond to power wisely

5. To understand and recognize the proper role of agreements within the context of long-term conflict

6. To encourage the development of support systems that can sustain disputants over time

In this book, I look at the nature of each of these challenges and the strategic considerations that conflict specialists need to employ in meeting them. I examine this from the perspective of the three primary roles that conflict professionals play—as conflict allies, third parties, and system interveners. The tools that the conflict intervention field has developed over many years are a rich resource for helping with enduring conflicts. We have developed approaches for dealing with poor communication, the destructive use of power, polarizing approaches to negotiation, cultural variations in approaches to conflict, and destructive group dynamics. We have honed our skills as mediators, coaches, advocates, negotiators, dispute system designers, and conflict trainers. We have learned a great deal about the nature of conflict, communication, collaboration, and decision making. And we have certainly found ourselves in the middle of many ongoing, enduring disputes. This is a firm foundation upon which we can build effective approaches to dealing with long-term conflict.

I believe that good practice derives from a clear understanding of the nature of the challenge and the essence of the intervention that is needed. Although there are many specific intervention tools that we can use (and I will discuss a number of these), the essential challenge is to reorient our thinking and the strategic approach we take. That is the focus of this book.

HOW THIS BOOK WORKS

For many years as a conflict intervention trainer, I said that the growth of individuals, communities, organizations, and societies is dependent on two variables in the conflict equation, knowing how and when to initiate a conflict or raise it to a higher level of intensity on the one hand and knowing how to resolve conflict wisely and thoroughly on the other. I have now come to believe there is a critical third variable as well, knowing how to stay with conflict over time—steadfastly, effectively, and responsibly. The experiences I have had over the past thirty and more years as a conflict practitioner and student of conflict and conflict intervention (and also my earlier work in mental health, child welfare, and substance abuse treatment and as a social activist) have led me to this conclusion and have informed the concepts and approaches described in this book.

In the first chapter I discuss the essential challenge and opportunities that enduring conflict presents and what it will take for conflict specialists to address these. In Chapter Two I start with a discussion of how we can help disputants understand the nature of enduring conflict and what it takes to engage constructively over time. I also examine the reasons why people need enduring conflict, and I introduce the concept of creative nonresolution. In the subsequent chapters I offer specific approaches to helping people stay with conflict.

In Chapter Three I discuss what may be the biggest obstacle to constructive engagement—conflict avoidance. Specifically, I look at why and how people avoid conflict and how we can help them deal with their avoidant tendencies. I also consider what to do when the wisest course may be to avoid a dangerous conflict. In Chapter Four I discuss how we can help disputants frame an enduring conflict constructively, which usually means altering the conflict narrative.

Chapter Five focuses on communication, with an emphasis on establishing durable approaches to communication and responding over time to dysfunctional patterns of communication. Chapter Six deals with power and escalation. Power differentials, the inappropriate and oppressive use of power, and the desire to maintain power are key factors in perpetuating conflict. Helping people learn how to develop constructive sources and applications of power and how to respond to the power of others is often the key to helping them stay with conflict. This sometimes requires that we guide people in escalating a conflict appropriately.

Chapter Seven focuses on the role of negotiation and agreements in enduring conflict. Agreements are viewed as tools for ongoing constructive conflict engagement rather than as the end point of a conflict process. Chapter Eight takes on the question of how people can sustain themselves over the long haul in an enduring conflict. I discuss how to help people develop the substantive and emotional resources necessary to stay with conflict, and then I consider how we can help disputants to encapsulate conflict so that they do not avoid it but they do not allow it to take over their lives either.

Chapter Nine looks in more detail at the different roles that conflict specialists can play in assisting disputants engaged in enduring conflict. I revisit our sense of our purpose and look specifically at the relationships among conflict resolution, transformation, and engagement. I then look at how conflict specialists can work in enduring disputes as third parties, allies, and system interveners. I also consider the challenge of marketing this approach. The Epilogue revisits the fundamental challenge of enduring conflict, summarizes the essential approach I am advocating, and ends with a consideration of the dynamic nature and potential of enduring conflict.

Throughout I rely on examples drawn from a broad variety of conflicts from interpersonal to international. I do this in the belief that the challenge presented by enduring conflict and the skills that staying with conflict requires are not specific to one type or arena of conflict and that the lessons we learn from one area can be adapted and applied to other circumstances.

Note also that I have changed the specifics of some of these case examples considerably, and in a few instances I have combined several cases into one, both to protect confidentiality and to consolidate the presentation. Although the specific facts have been altered, the dynamics and essential stories have not. In examples drawn from events that were open to public and media participation (for example, the Alaska Wolf Summit), I have tried to present what occurred as accurately as possible.

I have tried to maintain a focus on the conflict field, the role of conflict specialists, and the goal of conflict engagement. I have avoided referring to the field of *conflict resolution* or *alternative dispute resolution*. I believe that one way to begin to change our sense of purpose is to change the way we refer to who we are and what we do. When we fall into identifying our role as agents of conflict resolution and our approach as third-party intervention, we do not adequately describe our potential and often our practice, and we limit the scope of our services. I also focus on conflicts that are *enduring, ongoing,* or *long term* rather than ones that are *intractable* or *irresolvable*, because I think the latter terms suggest that conflict duration is itself a problem or that progress is hopeless. I believe that enduring disputes are important and necessary expressions of individuals' struggles as social beings and that their enduring nature is not itself the problem.

I have addressed this book specifically to conflict specialists. But the ideas and approaches are relevant to anyone who is faced with an enduring conflict, which of course means everyone. The challenge of staying with conflict is a fundamental one, and I hope that discussing how we can help others with this challenge will also help us consider how we can face it for ourselves.

ACKNOWLEDGMENTS

In the thirty-plus years I have worked as a conflict practitioner, I have been privileged to have wonderful, creative, supportive, and wise colleagues, first as a partner at CDR Associates and now as a professor at the Werner Institute for Negotiation and Dispute Resolution at Creighton University. One of the things I most appreciate about CDR is the degree to which reflective practice is valued. Theory and practice are seen as equally important, as coevolving, and as inseparable. CDR has provided me many wonderful opportunities, across a broad variety of conflicts and settings, to try out new approaches and ideas—and the development of these tools and concepts has taken place in the context of a collaborative approach to practice and management so that it has often been hard to say exactly where ideas originated.

For the past several years I have been privileged to be part of the Werner Institute, where I have been associated with an immensely creative, innovative, and dedicated set of colleagues and capable students who were willing to challenge me and to grapple with new approaches to practice and thinking. At Werner I have been encouraged and assisted in reflecting on my experiences as a practitioner, and I have been provided with a terrific laboratory for trying out new ways of looking at those experiences. The energy and enthusiasm that I experience at the Werner Institute reminds me of the excitement that I and many of my colleagues felt in the early years of building a conflict practice and a conflict field.

But my greatest teachers have always been the disputants who have let me into their lives and who have been willing to tell me exactly what they think of the approaches I have taken in order to assist them with serious conflicts. They have always guided my practice and development, and I have grown tremendously through my contact with them.

I also specifically want to thank my wonderful colleagues at Werner—especially Arthur Pearlstein, Jacqueline Font-Guzman, and Debra Gerardi—for their support, encouragement, and insights and my long-term partners and colleagues at CDR Associates—Mary Margaret Golten, Christopher Moore, Louise Smart, Susan Wildau, Peter Woodrow, Jonathan Bartsch, Judy Mares Dixon, Suzanne Ghais, Julie McKay, and many others.

Joan Kathol, my research assistant at Creighton, provided invaluable help in checking references and offering insight and support throughout this effort. Suzanne Ghais provided deeply insightful feedback and suggestions and saved me from several significant errors. Jonathan Bartsch, Howard Cohen, Chip Hauss, Christopher Honeyman, Edy Horwood, John Manwaring, Mark Mayer, Peter Salem, Don Selcer, Arnie Shienvold, and Louise Smart reviewed various parts of this manuscript and provided valuable feedback (any remaining folly is my own responsibility).

My editor at Jossey-Bass, Seth Schwartz, was a model of patience, honesty, and clarity and a pleasure to work with. Alan Rinzler helped me to develop this book's concept and kept me focused on the essence of my message. Elspeth MacHattie proved again to be a superb copyeditor. I thank everyone at Jossey-Bass/ Wiley for being willing to take a chance, as J-B also did with *Beyond Neutrality*, on publishing a work intended to challenge, stimulate, and push rather than to resort to simple formulas or easy answers to difficult questions.

My family was patient and supportive while I was engrossed with this project, and I particularly want to acknowledge the role of all my children, stepchildren, and grandchildren in keeping me centered and in keeping work in perspective—thanks to Ellie, Elona, Ethan, Henry, Hopey, Mark, and Sibyl. Molly and Lucy were my constant, nurturing four-legged companions as I wrote this.

My most special thanks go to my wife, Julie Macfarlane, to whom this book is dedicated. Julie gave me both unvarnished critiques and unstinting support throughout the writing of this book. She read and reread my work and provided exceptionally valuable insights, observations—and corrections. She also helped me to remember that life is not just about work, and she supported me totally in my work. She is a model of intellectual integrity and self-reflective practice.

Staying with Conflict

A New Direction for the Conflict Field

Divorced parents returning yet again to court have been referred to mediation because of disputes about child rearing. They have profound differences about religious upbringing, parenting practices, and education for their children. One of the parents now wants to move to a different state, partly in the belief that this will finally resolve their conflict—but it won't.

The principal partners in an engineering firm are embroiled in conflict about how to compensate themselves. Some argue that all profits should be shared equally, others that allocation should be based on billable hours, on dollars earned, or on business generated. Some believe that special credit should be given for enhancing the firm's profile or for providing public service. This dispute has been going on in various versions for many years and has led to the departure of a number of key staff.

An electricity generating facility has a long history of labor relations problems, including highly publicized job actions, threatened facility closures, lawsuits, and multiple grievances. Union leadership and management have an antagonistic relationship, and the membership has just issued a vote of no confidence in the management over a plan to outsource certain plant maintenance functions.

Traffic in an attractive and prosperous midsized city has grown tremendously over the past ten years, and downtown parking has become especially challenging. Every time there is a proposal to increase parking capacity or engage in major transportation infrastructure development, conflict erupts between those who feel that automobile traffic should be limited and discouraged and those who feel that unless more parking is made available the local economy will suffer.

Most of us who have worked in the conflict field have faced situations such as these throughout our careers. They are emblematic of the most challenging disputes we face, as both individuals and practitioners—the ones that won't go away. These conflicts are unlikely to be resolved, and they therefore call for long-term engagement strategies. This presents a terrific opportunity for conflict professionals, but one that we have largely neglected.

We can make progress in the management of these conflicts. We can help the parties to arrive at interim or partial agreements, we can guide them in escalating or de-escalating them, but we typically can't help them to end these conflicts because the disputes are rooted in the structure of the situation (for example, limited resources or conflicting organizational roles), core values (for example, the kind of community people want to live in or the life they want to lead), personality traits (for example, being quick to anger or conflict averse), or people's sense of who they are (for example, committed social activists or realistic business people).

As conflict professionals we exhibit a strong tendency to ignore the *ongoing* (or *enduring*, *long-term*, or *endemic*) aspect of these conflicts and to focus only on those aspects that can be resolved. In doing this we fail to address people's most important conflicts and miss out on a major opportunity to increase the role and relevance of the work that we do. In each of the previous examples, if we limit our focus to the immediate conflict, we may provide some value but we overlook the underlying challenge that confronts the individuals, organizations, and communities involved. For example, if the only assistance we offer to the struggling parents relates to the proposed move, we leave them adrift with the ongoing conflict they are likely to experience for the duration of their coparenting years, if not longer. And although it is no doubt worthwhile to mediate an immediate solution to the outsourcing issue, if we cannot help the union and the management to develop a more productive framework for confronting their ongoing conflicts, we have failed to address the most important challenge facing the electricity generating facility.

In each of these conflicts, whatever the terms of our involvement, our outlook will expand dramatically if instead of asking our customary question, What can we do to resolve or de-escalate this conflict? we ask, How can we help people prepare to engage with this issue over time? As our outlook grows, significant new avenues of intervention become apparent, and our potential to help parties with their core struggles will grow as well.

Our challenge as conflict specialists is to meet people and conflicts as they are genuinely experienced and to help disputants deal with each other and their conflicts realistically and constructively. When we focus only on those elements that are resolvable, we are neither meeting people where they truly are nor offering them a realistic scenario for dealing with the most serious issues they face. Instead, we marginalize our role, limit the reach of our work, and fail to realize the full potential we have to help disputants. In the process, we also constrain the growth of our field and our economic viability as conflict professionals. We have the tools, the experience, and the capacity to do better than this, but too often we don't have the vision.

Intuitively, we know that important conflicts don't readily end. Each of us can think of a conflict that was present in an organization, community, or personal relationship when we entered it and will likely be there, in some fashion, when we leave. This is not necessarily a sign of organizational or personal pathology—it is rather a reflection of the human condition. That does not mean, however, that there is nothing to be done about these long-term conflicts. People can deal with these conflicts constructively or destructively. They can face conflicts or avoid them. They can escalate or de-escalate. They can let conflicts destroy important relationships or see them as the context for deepening these connections.

There is of course a role for mediating agreements or finding ways to de-escalate dangerous or destructive interchanges, and there are times when our focus must be on the immediate and the short term. But we ought always to do this with a full appreciation for the enduring nature of most significant conflicts and with a clear view of how what we do in the immediate circumstances needs to be informed by the long-term struggle that disputants face.

CHALLENGING OUR CONFLICT NARRATIVE

Perhaps the hardest challenge enduring conflicts present to conflict professionals is that they ask us to alter the assumptions we have about conflict and the narratives we construct to explain our approach. The story we often tell is that conflict is a problem in human interactions that might be inevitable but can usually be fixed. Conflict can be fixed by *prevention*, *analysis*, and *intervention*. We say that we can anticipate and prevent conflict by effective communication and decision-making processes. We can understand conflict by analyzing the interests, needs, values, and choices of all the players. We can intervene in conflict by bringing the right people together to engage in a collaborative problem-solving process. Most important, by doing this, we can end a conflict. We can address the key interests of the people involved and thereby solve the problems that led to the dispute.

This is a heartening story. It offers a simple and optimistic approach and suggests a clear and appealing role for conflict professionals. And sometimes an intervention works in just this way, producing constructive results that are welcomed by parties who had thought their conflict was unsolvable. But where profound conflict is concerned this story is incomplete and unrealistic, and people know it. The real course of the most significant conflicts people face is muddier, less predictable, and more impervious to intentional change.

Conflict professionals can anticipate conflict up to a point, but the more significant the conflict—the deeper its roots and the further reaching its impact—the more likely it is that we will not be able to prevent it, only prepare for it. Conflicts involve chaotic and ever changing systems. The idea that we can find the key to solving a conflict by deploying ever more systematic tools of analysis is misleading. Understanding the nature of a conflict is an ongoing challenge, and our best hope is to gain enough insight to help us make good choices at a given time.

Rarely will analysis itself reveal a magic key that will transform the nature of a deep or complex conflict. We can contribute to a better understanding, but seldom can we offer the blinding insight that will alter the course of a conflict. And whether we are talking about the long-term struggle between divorced parents, warring business partners, ethnic or racial groups in a community, workers and managers in a troubled organization, environmentalists and energy producers, or religious and secular worldviews, such core conflicts do not get resolved cleanly, completely, or quickly—if at all.

The basic choice that each of the four situations described at the beginning of the chapter and countless others like them present to us is one of purpose. Should our intention be to identify those elements of conflict that are resolvable and focus on these or to devise ways to assist people to *stay with conflict* in a powerful, constructive, and effective way?

THE CHALLENGE FOR THE CONFLICT FIELD

As conflict professionals we gain something and lose something by limiting our range of services to the resolution process. When we make resolution our focus, we are better able to explain our purpose and role definition, presenting them clearly to the public (and to ourselves). At the same time, we lose a great deal of relevance and opportunities for intervention, because disputants come to view our services as relevant for only a narrow range of conflicts. And this is why we are sometimes viewed with a certain amount of mistrust, why people often feel that conflict specialists—mediators, facilitators, conflict coaches, and collaborative practitioners—are offering a formula that is too easy, too clear cut, and just plain naïve. We often feel that way ourselves.

People want help with conflict, but they also want realism. When we offer to help them prevent, resolve, or in some way fix conflicts that they are experiencing as inevitable, intractable, or deeply rooted, we are not seen as credible. This is not to say that the worst aspects of long-term conflict cannot be ameliorated, that complex and destructive interactions cannot be made more constructive, or that progress toward a more positive approach is impossible. But when we focus on preventing or settling conflicts that are not likely to be resolved, we lose credibility and forego the opportunity to help people in realistic and meaningful ways.

I am not suggesting that conflict professionals have created this problem out of either naïveté or hubris. We have responded to a clear need as we have seen it, and we are often asked to take on impractical goals—to resolve a long-term, deeply rooted conflict or fix a complex and entrenched problem. But if we buy into such unrealistic hopes or expectations, we are in the long run likely to disappoint our clients, and perhaps ourselves. Taking a request for assistance that may be unrealistic and negotiating appropriate and realistic terms for our work is often our first big challenge. In doing so, we need to maintain a clear view of the dispute and the possibility that it is an enduring conflict.

Sometimes the challenge of helping people face long-term conflict is obvious, either because the dispute cannot be mediated or because the disputants are clearly entrenched in their positions. Efforts to mediate disputes about abortion provide an interesting example of this. The fundamental conflict between the "pro-choice" and "pro-life" camps about abortion rights is clearly irresolvable—but that does not mean the conflict cannot be engaged with in a more constructive way. Ancillary issues (such as ground rules about picketing outside abortion clinics or information that should be provided to teenagers about contraception, abstinence, and pregnancy termination) have also proved to be enduring because they cannot be disconnected from the core values and identity issues involved in the abortion issue itself.

Sometimes we have the choice of whether to look at the enduring aspects of a conflict or to focus just on the immediate and the resolvable features. For example, when mediating a high-conflict divorce we are occasionally presented with seemingly short-term disputes that are manifestations of intractable conflicts. A hiring conflict among business partners may seem like a short-term conflict, and we may chose to treat it as such, but it may also be a manifestation of a long-term struggle about organizational mission or direction, fair hiring practices, or power over decision making.

Sometimes our role in enduring conflict is short term, if for example we have been called in to mediate a conflict about a proposal to build a new parking facility rather than to address overall concerns about traffic and development. At other times we may find ourselves having a role to play over time, as when we are asked to work with organizations over a period of years or to set up and participate in ongoing systems for dealing with ethnic violence. But regardless of the specific circumstances of our involvement, the challenge is the same. Can we help people deal constructively with long-term, enduring conflict, and what tools can we bring to this task?

We have reached a stage in the development of the conflict intervention field where we are comfortable and often adept at working as third parties in time-limited, resolution-focused approaches. But if our field is to realize its full potential to assist with the key challenges conflict presents, we need to move beyond this zone of comfort, beyond this fairly circumscribed and limited role we have generally defined for ourselves.

We are therefore at a crossroads in the work we do as conflict professionals. We can take on the important challenge and opportunity that enduring conflict presents, or we can continue to see ourselves primarily as agents of resolution. If we take on the challenge, we can increase our relevance and reach; if we do not, we will continue to limit ourselves to working at the margin of the most serious conflicts that people face.

NEW ROLES FOR CONFLICT RESOLUTION PROFESSIONALS

In *Beyond Neutrality: Confronting the Crisis in Conflict Resolution* (2004), I suggested that conflict professionals move beyond an exclusive focus on conflict resolution and look at how we can help disputants throughout the entire life cycle of a conflict—prevention, anticipation, management, escalation, de-escalation, resolution, and healing. I also called for an expansion in how we think about the roles we play in conflict, beyond our traditional focus on third parties. I identified three types of roles for us to consider fulfilling—*third-party roles, ally roles,* and *system roles.* In order to encourage this expanded view, I proposed that we think of ourselves as conflict specialists or conflict engagement professionals. Whatever specific names we use for identifying what we do, our basic challenge is to think more broadly about our purpose and our function.

I am now suggesting a further expansion of our roles in order to encompass the important work necessary to help people take a constructive approach to enduring and entrenched conflict. In this book I look at the specific skills and approaches that conflict professionals can bring to this challenge. I do this in the belief that we are well situated to take on this task. We have much of the necessary experience and many of the required skills and values, but we have to learn how to direct these qualities to the particular challenges that enduring conflict presents. In this book I discuss how we can understand these challenges, hone our skills, and refine our approach in order to address enduring conflict.

We have to start this process by taking on a new mission—we have to embrace the challenge of helping people *stay with conflict*.

STAYING WITH CONFLICT

When people stay with conflict, they engage in the ongoing struggles of their lives directly, clearly, respectfully, without avoidance, and with a full realization that these are issues that will be with them over time. They do not run away from conflict, resort to destructive escalation, or attempt to find a grand resolution for a conflict that is by its nature ongoing and deeply rooted. When business partners are willing to engage over time with their most divisive issues without vilifying one another or resorting to superficial remedies, they are staying with conflict. When a divorced couple confront each other about their different views on child rearing, advocate for their points of view, arrive at whatever intermediate agreements are possible, and do all this without attacking the integrity or personality of the other, they are staying with a conflict. When community activists address local government officials directly, repeatedly, and powerfully, but without denigrating the competence or commitment of those officials and with an awareness that their concerns are unlikely to be completely addressed soon, and maybe not ever, they are staying with conflict.

The need to stay with the most enduring and emblematic conflicts is more than simply an inevitable and unfortunate reality in people's lives. Staying with conflict is what allows all of us to lead life to the fullest. By staying engaged with the enduring conflicts in our lives we involve ourselves in core questions of identity, meaning, values, and personal and systems change. Staying with conflict requires courage, vision, resources, skills, and stamina, and all of us need help and support in this effort. Our satisfaction with our lives may be more determined by our ability to stay and evolve with enduring conflicts than by the success we have in resolving those conflicts.

We can see this on the many different levels at which enduring conflict is experienced. For example, the success of an intimate relationship is determined less by the parties' resolving conflicts than by their productively and continuously engaging with conflicts—be they about child-rearing practices, communication styles, time together and apart, or power in decision making. At work, the more people avoid potentially conflictual issues of responsibility, direction, decision making, and strategy, the more they disengage and alienate themselves from an important part of their experience. For this reason the union activist is generally much more engaged in his or her working life than is the cooperative but passive worker. On a larger stage, those who embrace the challenge of struggling for a better world—whether they see this in terms of social justice, environmental sustainability, economic strength, or family integrity—are likely to lead full and rich (if not always easy) lives.

Enduring Conflict

To face the challenge of staying with conflict, conflict professionals have to start by understanding and accepting the role of ongoing conflicts in people's lives. Whether we refer to these conflicts as ongoing, intractable, entrenched, long term, or enduring, we are basically talking about struggles that do not go away. They stay with people over time. If they die down in one form, they reappear in another. Disputants may resolve particular issues, but the essential conflict does not get resolved, it endures.

When I first moved to Boulder, Colorado, in 1972, the city was struggling with a variety of views on how to deal with traffic, transportation, open space, and affordable housing. Today, more than thirty-five years later, the community is still struggling with those same issues, and they continue to generate conflict. There have been all sorts of master plans, citizen task forces, public dialogues, and specific agreements over the years. I have facilitated several such efforts myself, and they have seemed to be worthwhile endeavors. But the fundamental conflicts have not, likely cannot, and probably should not be completely resolved because they reflect the necessary and often healthy competition of a variety of values and the reality of limited resources.

Are all such conflicts irresolvable? Not necessarily. Some long-term, deeply entrenched conflicts do get resolved for all practical purposes (perhaps that is what is happening now in Northern Ireland) or they transform into virtually unrelated conflicts (an adolescent's power struggle with his parents may eventually transform itself into struggles with other authority figures, for example). But these conflicts are fully resolved only after their structural underpinnings undergo fundamental change, and this does not often happen through direct resolution efforts.

We can think of enduring conflicts as those struggles that are embedded in people's lives, relationships, and institutions because they stem from their most deeply held values, their sense of who they are, and the structure of the organizations and communities that they are part of. The circumstances that give rise to these conflicts might change, and personal development might eventually move a person to a place where an enduring conflict is less toxic or relevant to her experience. But enduring conflict normally stays with people over the long haul, and so the challenge is to learn how to stay with it.

What Staying with Conflict Looks Like

All of us face the challenge of dealing with ongoing conflict in our lives. At our best we handle enduring conflict effectively—that is, we learn to stay with it. But what does it look like when we stay with conflict in a constructive and effective way?

When we stay with conflict, we remain engaged with the core issues that we care about, we continue to work on the problems or concerns that are important to us, and we continue to relate to the people with whom we are in conflict. We also continue to communicate about the conflict and to advocate for what is important to us, and we always try to deepen our understanding of how others think and feel about the issue. We develop the emotional and intellectual capacity to live with our enduring differences but also to continue to work on them, even though we know that the core conflict will likely continue for a long time. We look for areas where general progress can be made, but we do so with the full knowledge that progress does not mean final resolution.

For example, consider this conflict, one that is typical of many situations faced by teachers and parents working with special needs children:

John is an eleven-year-old with severe learning disabilities and behavioral problems. He has been diagnosed at various times with attention deficit disorder, Asperger's syndrome, and various developmental disabilities. John has been tested repeatedly, seen many specialists, and been provided with individual assistance from teacher's aides and a special education teacher. But despite these efforts, he is reading at barely second-grade level, has very poor social relations, and often seems extremely anxious or unhappy in the classroom.

His teachers and the school principal are recommending that John be referred to a different school, one with classes especially designed for children who cannot function in regular classroom settings. John's parents, Frank and Dorothy, want John to remain in the neighborhood school and in his regular classroom and have asked that a specially trained teacher work with him individually for half of each day and that a teacher's aide be assigned to him the rest of the time.

This is the latest manifestation of a conflict that has been going on for several years about the resources the school should commit to John's education, the appropriate educational setting for John, and whether John should be in a regular school at all. At times the relationship between the parents and school personnel has been testy, volatile, and litigious. But at other times the parents and school staff have been able to talk about the concerns they share about John's falling further behind and becoming increasingly stigmatized and isolated.

Can Frank and Dorothy continue to negotiate with school personnel when they believe their child's needs have not been properly addressed? Can the school staff continue to remain flexible and open-minded about what to do for John, even while believing that no matter what the school offers it won't be enough? Can everyone remain optimistic about the possibility of making progress and the potential for working together when the conflict history does not support this? Can everyone approach each new negotiation in a constructive spirit, knowing that in one form or another, negotiation will have to occur repeatedly over the years, as John's needs change and innovations in treatment and special education programming are made? It is people's response to these kinds of challenges that determines whether a long-term conflict process can be productive or whether it will degenerate into pointless and harmful confrontation or, perhaps even worse, a pattern of avoiding the most significant issues that need to be addressed.

At some point taking legal action to argue for more resources for John might be helpful, but no matter the outcome of litigation, the essential conflict is likely to continue in some form. No single remedy will solve the problems faced by John and his parents or by the school as it struggles with resource allocation decisions. Instead, the parties will need to reengage frequently to set, review, and revise baseline standards and expectations and to modify their approach as John develops and as new information and ideas emerge. They will need to work together but also to struggle with each other as they learn to function with the stress and doubts characteristic of this situation of enduring conflict.

The critical point about this level of engagement with enduring conflict, whatever the context, is that the most important result of disputants' best efforts is constructive interaction with incremental progress, rather than final resolution.

Challenges for Staying with Conflict

Staying with conflict requires us all, whether disputants or interveners, to communicate even when we believe communication will not produce solutions and even when little trust exists to facilitate communication; to be prepared to negotiate, even on issues we consider nonnegotiable; and to remain flexible about the ways we are willing to approach a conflict even as we remain true to our core values. It is especially challenging for disputants to do this when negotiating or communicating feels not only difficult but pointless because no end to the conflict is in sight.

We need to stay with conflict and meet these challenges on issues that range from those that can appear to be trivial (how we divide up housework) to fundamental societal issues (global warming, racism) and on any issue that represents something important about who we are or how we want to be in the world. We must try to do this with both optimism (believing that we can make progress on even the most serious conflict and the most painful personal differences) and realism (understanding that we can't find easy solutions to basic problems and that enduring conflicts do in fact endure).

Staying with conflict also requires that we gather and use power wisely and constructively. Many enduring conflicts play out against a background of serious power differentials and the misuse of power. The challenge is to respond to others' power and to use (and increase) our own without allowing a situation to devolve into a destructive exchange and without violating our values about human relations. This challenge is seen every time one party to a conflict ups the ante by threatening to use a particularly destructive alternative, whether it be legal action, a strike, public exposure, dissolving a business partnership, pulling out of a negotiation, or military force.

In order to advocate effectively for our interests, we sometimes have to be prepared to be less cooperative or collegial than we usually are, and we sometimes have to escalate a conflict in order to move toward a more constructive engagement. At most times, however, these tactics do more to sour the atmosphere and impede communication than they do to leverage others to behave differently. For example, in the special education situation discussed earlier, Frank and Dorothy likely have legal alternatives they could pursue, and school staff are certain to be aware of these. But repeatedly threatening to resort to those alternatives will not create the long-term leverage that will help Frank, Dorothy, and the school staff stay with this conflict effectively. In enduring and protracted conflicts, making threats to up the ante may feel like a necessary exercise of power, but it often fails to produce a powerful and constructive step forward—because the parties have to be able to continue to engage with one another in order to make any progress at all.

In essence, staying with conflict means engaging with the issues most important to who we are, what we value, whom we care about, and how we understand ourselves—and doing so without seeking quick fixes to serious problems or final resolutions to entrenched problems and without throwing our hands up and walking away or burying our heads in the sand. Staying with conflict calls on all involved to develop their capacity to fully engage in life, with all its perplexities and challenges.

THE ROLE OF THE CONFLICT SPECIALIST

We who have chosen the role of conflict specialist are not the only professionals with an important role to play in helping people stay with conflict—in their own ways, therapists, lawyers, police officers, community organizers, diplomats, organizational development specialists, and others face the same challenge. However, we may be especially well situated by experience and skills to assist people involved in long-term conflict to develop the capacity and outlook that can sustain them and guide them in a more constructive direction. Indeed, staying with conflict builds on many of the same skills and tools that we use in a resolution model and involves challenges we have already faced. For example:

- When we encourage government officials to open up a public hearing to genuine dialogue and disputation, rather than sticking to a pro forma input process, we are working to help them face the reality of a conflict and consider the consequences of avoidance, and we are encouraging a genuine effort to bring different voices to the discussion and to frame a conflict more authentically.

- When we work with divorcing parents with profoundly different beliefs about religion, discipline, and education in order to help them maintain a clear sense of their own values but also be open to a variety of ways of honoring those values and when we help them to find an authentic voice, and to reexamine their approach and beliefs, our goal is to help them stay with conflict.

- When we work with highly conflicted workplaces where there is a history of mistrust between management and workers, we often find it essential to assist in the development of effective channels of communication, coach individuals to use their power effectively and wisely, work on agreements when appropriate, and find appropriate arenas for interaction.

- When we work with child protection disputes, with ethnic conflicts, or in restorative justice programs, we not only assist in developing an immediate or short-term solution but we also ask people to consider how to develop the resources and approaches that will sustain them over time, often paying special attention to safety considerations.

These are interventions that we may apply to any conflict, but they are especially valuable in relationship to ongoing and enduring conflicts. When we mediate a plan that guides disputants in communicating around the inevitability of future conflict and when we facilitate dialogues between opposing sides in a long-term conflict, part of what we are doing is helping people stay with conflict. However, this kind of help is usually a tacit or unrecognized purpose. We don't explicitly recognize, embrace, and articulate this element of our efforts as part of our core purpose. Nor do we develop the specific strategies and approaches that would enable us to more knowingly and effectively pursue this goal.

This means that the challenge of helping people to stay with conflict requires us to take on a significantly new role. Before we can apply our skills and experience to this difficult challenge, we need to break through the limits we place on ourselves with our current assumptions about our role and with the conflict narrative we promote. We have to develop a new frame of reference for our goals in conflict and for the ways we can achieve those goals. We also need to develop and hone tools specifically oriented to helping people deal with enduring conflict.

From both a personal and a business perspective it may sometimes appear far more attractive and indeed far simpler to emphasize our role in the prevention or resolution of conflict rather than our role in creating productive engagement in conflict. But if we are committed to addressing the most important challenges that conflicts present and if we want to open up significant avenues for our work, then we will have to take on the most difficult and daunting elements of conflict, not just those that are most rapidly and easily addressed and encapsulated. This requires us to develop additional skills and tools and further avenues of service. How we can do this is the subject of this book.

The first requirement of any effective—and durable—approach to conflict is clarity about purpose, goal, and role. I am proposing that conflict specialists adopt a new overall goal: assisting disputants to develop a constructive approach to engaging in enduring conflict. In the next chapter I look at what this new goal means and its implications for the way conflict specialists approach their work.

2

Conflict and Engagement

Conflict flows from life. . . . Rather than seeing conflict as
a threat, we can understand it as providing opportunities
to grow and to increase our understanding of ourselves, of
others, of our social structures. Conflicts in relationships
at all levels are the way life helps us to stop, assess, and
take notice. One way to truly know our humanness is to
recognize the gift of conflict in our lives. Without it life
would be a monotonously flat topography of sameness and
our relationships would be woefully superficial.
                                      John Paul Lederach, 2003, p. 18

Staying with conflict begins with an understanding and appreciation of the nature and significance of enduring conflict in everyone's life and a clear sense of what is required to engage in a sustainable conflict effort. Part of our job as conflict specialists is to explore this with the individuals or groups we are working with, but all of our work needs to be informed by this understanding.

THE ROLE OF CONFLICT IN PEOPLE'S LIVES

Conflict is essential to everyone's growth and survival. It is the vehicle all of us use to face our most significant challenges. Conflict is our stimulus to attack problems and gives us the energy to overcome our powerful inclinations toward passivity. Because conflict can push us to face what we would rather ignore and because it can be scary and dangerous, we avoid it, deny it, or think of it as abnormal and transient. But the most important conflicts in our lives, the enduring ones, can be avoided only at great cost. We may be able to suppress these conflicts, but they do not go away. Instead they almost always reappear in various forms, and in one way or another, we are forced to deal with them.

This is not a bad thing, because enduring conflicts help us to define who we are and the path we need to follow. During this journey we may reach the true heart of these conflicts. We may achieve the wisdom and courage to deal with them in all their complexity and power, but we will not resolve or end them because they are deeply rooted in our personalities and our relationships. Our biggest life challenge is to learn to embrace these conflicts, accept their central role in our lives, and find an effective way to engage them.

The ongoing struggles that people experience even in well-functioning families offer the most universal examples of enduring conflict. Each of us can think of conflicts that have endured in his or her family with a spouse, children, siblings, or parents. The struggle between adolescents and their parents if not universal is extremely widespread, and even though people typically grow past the specifically adolescent characteristics of these struggles (at least most do), the underlying struggle between autonomy and belonging that is characteristic of adolescence has manifestations throughout their lives as they struggle with the balance between separateness and intimacy, family and work, individual recognition and group loyalty, independence and interdependence. This broad but essential conflict has manifestations in life relationships (family time versus personal time versus work time), work life (accountability versus individual initiative, flexibility versus consistency, clear lines of authority versus participatory management), and communal life (insularity versus openness to newcomers, dedication to the good of the whole versus a focus on one's individual well-being). Enduring conflict is part of our everyday lives.

THE SIX FACES OF CONFLICT

Significant conflicts generally have both enduring and time-limited aspects. When we as conflict specialists make a decision (or assumption) about which aspect to address, that may be our key strategic choice in how we approach a conflict—a choice we don't always recognize that we are making. However, recognized or not, this choice is critical to how we (often unconsciously) frame the nature of the conflict and therefore to how we intervene and what we can do to help. I find it useful to think about conflict as having six overlapping categories, or faces. These categories are low impact, latent, transient, representational, stubborn, and enduring.

Low-Impact Conflict

This is the most frequent face of everyday conflict. Conflicts over where to eat dinner, who folds the laundry, who gets to go on break first, who interrupted whom, and how to allocate limited parking are, for example, disputes ordinarily viewed as low impact, as not having significant consequences. However, even though these conflicts may appear trivial or inconsequential to some, they are often important to those involved in them and may become more serious if mishandled—especially if they become symbolic of deeper issues.

Sometimes low-impact conflicts fester because they do not seem serious enough to warrant the energy it would take to deal with them. Sometimes they are long lasting because they are reflections of personal characteristics that people cannot easily change (for example, I have tried for years, with varying degrees of success, to become less of an interrupter because my interrupting is a behavior that often leads to conflicts with family and colleagues). Sometimes low-impact conflicts mask other, more serious concerns and may get in the way of dealing with those concerns, as when business partners fight about the name for their enterprise rather than about their differing visions of purpose and strategy (this situation is addressed further in the discussion of representational conflict later in this chapter).

Latent Conflict

Latent conflict exists when the conditions out of which a conflict could arise are present, but there has as yet been no crystallizing event or issue. Latent conflicts are always present but vary greatly in the degree to which they are primed to erupt or to which they are already affecting behavior, decisions, and relationships. Greater tension in workplaces, growing racial separation in schools, rising resentment over economic disparity, and increasing differences in worldviews between religious and secular states suggest latent conflicts that may become manifest when a crystallizing event occurs.

The disintegration of Yugoslavia after the death of Tito and its rapid degeneration into warfare, ethnic cleansing, and brutality seemed surprising at the time. This society had appeared to be a peaceful one in which Croats, Serbs, and Bosnians (Catholics, Eastern Orthodox, and Muslims) were coexisting quite successfully. But the region's centuries-old religious and nationalist tension had only been suppressed by the authoritarian rule of the Tito regime, not resolved or eradicated. The latent conflict was always present, and after Tito's death it did not take long for it to erupt.

Transient Conflict

Transient conflicts are those that can be resolved and are time limited, although this does not necessarily mean that they are not serious or do not have any long-term implications. A grievance about a promotion or pay raise, a collective bargaining dispute, or a disagreement over the location of a landfill or a plan to annex a neighborhood are all significant and sometimes extremely intense conflicts but also usually time-limited ones. The conditions that give rise to the conflict are not permanent and can be changed or eliminated by an appropriate decision or solution. Of course such conflicts often represent much deeper issues, but to the extent that they are expressions of time-limited problems that can be addressed by specific outcomes, they are transient disputes.

Contractual disputes—for example, over a time-limited commercial relationship—are often transient. Concerns about where to build a new thoroughfare through a community can be resolved with a decision, although the consequences may continue to raise conflicts, especially in the eyes of the dissenters. Decisions about how to allocate marital assets or divide up parenting time in a divorce may be transient to the extent that they do not reflect more deeply rooted conflicts.

Representational Conflict

Perhaps all aspects of conflict to some extent represent disputants' deeper issues, but some expressions of conflict can be fully understood only in terms of these deeper issues, which they epitomize. Even though a representational conflict is usually time specific, it is fundamentally a manifestation of an enduring or core conflict. When Rosa Parks refused to get up from her bus seat for a white man, the specific issue, segregation on buses, could be and in fact was resolved. But that conflict also had a deeper significance; it was representative of a long-term pattern of discrimination that was very resistant to change and that to some extent is still ongoing, many years after the end of bus seating discrimination.

Similarly, when parents struggle over the division of child-care responsibilities, this may represent their fundamental differences about roles, commitments, and values or on a deeper level, differences in their senses of who they are, what gives meaning to their lives, self-esteem, and the need for control. They may resolve the immediate issue with a new arrangement, but the conflict is likely to recur unless the underlying issue is identified and addressed.

Stubborn Conflict

Stubborn conflicts are those that are challenging, difficult to resolve, and resistant to resolution, but still potentially time limited—especially if handled appropriately. We may sometimes confuse stubborn conflicts with enduring ones because of the difficulty of bringing them to closure, but a stubborn conflict is difficult because of the complexity of the issues, the intensity of the emotions, or the communication styles of the disputants and not because of the enduring nature of the conflict's fundamental dynamics. The most dramatic moments in mediation may come when we break through an impasse or find a solution to a stubborn conflict, but this is not the same as solving the enduring elements that are manifestations of deeper issues.

When a divorced parent decides that he or she needs to move to a different geographical region, it can lead to a stubborn conflict. Even when both parents share important values about parenting and respect each other's roles, the relocation presents them with stubborn practical challenges. A contractor on a large construction project who is in dispute with a subcontractor about cost overruns, delays, and defects in workmanship may be in a stubborn conflict, one that could take quite a while to resolve. Different understandings of contractual obligations and past communications, personality clashes, and different predictions about legal alternatives may all contribute to stubbornness. So may the very complexity of the issues involved.

Enduring Conflicts

As discussed earlier, enduring conflict is that aspect of a dispute that is embedded in structures, systems, values, or identity and will therefore not be resolved through short-term, resolution-oriented conflict interventions. Enduring conflict is long lasting because of its nature, not because of ineffective or inappropriate efforts to resolve it. Until the roots of the conflict change, the system evolves, or the identity- or value-based elements are profoundly transformed, the conflict will remain, although how it is manifested may vary over time.

Enduring conflict is unlike stubborn or transient conflict because it is by nature long lasting and not amenable to resolution efforts. It is unlike low-impact conflict because it represents core issues in the lives of individuals, families, groups, communities, and organizations. Although all conflict has representational aspects, enduring conflict—once clearly identified—can be seen as a foundational or essential struggle in itself. Struggles over chores, child-care practices, or money, for example, may be representational conflicts that can be resolved; however, the conflicts underlying these struggles may involve values, power, or gender roles, and are most likely to be enduring.

WORKING WITH THE SIX FACES OF CONFLICT

Most of the significant conflicts I have been involved in have manifested a number if not all of the six faces of conflict, and I have had to chose, in partnership with the parties involved, which elements to address. Sometimes this *meta-negotiation* (negotiation about a negotiation) was the heart of the process and determined the success or failure of an effort. This was the case at the "Alaska Wolf Summit":

> In 1993, my partner Christopher Moore and I were asked to facilitate the Alaska Wolf Summit (an effort to bring together a broad range of groups with widely different views about appropriate policies for controlling the Alaska wolf population). We were thrown into a situation in which every issue was representative of the deepest identity concerns and values of all the parties (First Nations participants, other Alaska residents, hunters and trappers, environmentalists, biologists, animal rights activists, government planners, political leaders, and more). We were continually faced with choices about which element of the conflict to take on—the basic values and beliefs, immediate or long-term policy decisions, short-term questions about how the summit should be organized, or fractured personal relationships.

For some, dealing with anything other than the most fundamental issues involved was avoidance and capitulation. For others, tackling "yet again" these issues was a big waste of time ("although good midwinter entertainment in Fairbanks," as one participant put it to me) unless the summit could make concrete progress on immediate policy questions. Negotiating with the participants about which aspect of the conflict to focus on at which time proved to be our greatest challenge. In the end the summit focused on the broader value and policy questions, encouraged a dialogue about the principles that ought to govern wolf control, and allowed a great deal of communication among people who normally never directly communicated with each other. No concrete agreements were reached, but this context eased the way for the ongoing policymaking process to occur in a less destructive and acrimonious way than previously.

However, what the summit did not (and in the context probably could not) address were the enduring elements of the conflict and how the problem could be engaged with over time. To this day (over fifteen years later), the conflict about wolf control in Alaska remains intense, high profile, and often extremely acrimonious. Many of the same arguments heard in 1993 are still being put forward by people on all sides of this issue. The conflict continues to be carried out in many arenas (courts, legislatures, and the media). I suspect that this will continue to occupy an important place in Alaskan discourse for many years to come.

Frequently, the key decision that conflict professionals make (consciously or intuitively) is which face of conflict to tackle. Often I am asked to go into an organization to deal with a specific conflict or issue—for example, about job assignments or compensation policies. Upon further inquiry I often find that the real concern is that "people aren't communicating" or "there is no trust" or "relationships with management suck." This poses an interesting dilemma—do I focus on the presenting conflict and hope that working on it will contribute to a more favorable overall climate, or do I go for the deeper problems, knowing that unless these are discussed the toxic climate is likely to continue?

The appeal of focusing on the transient, representational, low-impact, or stubborn faces of conflict is that they lend themselves to the resolution processes that we conflict professionals are most familiar and comfortable with. And sometimes that is the best we can do and the most we are asked to do. But focusing on these aspects of a conflict dynamic often takes us away from the real work to be done, which is to help people understand and develop a strategy for coping with the enduring aspect. Sometimes *beginning where the client is* requires us to start with the nonenduring aspects of conflict, but as we work with these we will inevitably be led to the enduring dimensions. To be effective, conflict professionals have to stay attuned to all the faces of conflict and to think strategically about which aspect to work on.

THE CHARACTERISTICS OF ENDURING CONFLICT

Enduring conflicts are an essential part of the human struggle. They define who we are as individuals and as societies. Many of the key philosophical and psychological theorists of the past two hundred years have focused on the enduring or developmental conflicts that inform our lives. Freud talked about our intrapsychic conflict, Marx about class conflict, and Darwin about our evolutionary adaptation to the struggle for survival. Sociologists such as Coser (1956) have identified the key role of conflict in organizing society and building community.

When we talk about what defines the purpose or challenge of our time in history, we are largely discussing enduring conflicts— for example, those involving global climate change, human rights, limited resources, differing worldviews, north-south tensions, or values about families. We can look at almost any level of human organization from the individual to the global and see the central role that enduring conflicts play in the formation and expression of identity and worldview.

Earlier I introduced the characteristics of enduring conflict, traits that both define and explain its ongoing nature. We can assess the degree to which enduring conflict is a critical component of a dispute by considering the presence of these traits. So let's look at these defining characteristics of enduring conflict in more detail.

Enduring Conflict Has Deep Roots

A conflict may seem trivial but be genuinely enduring if it is connected to deeply rooted issues in the lives of the people or the structures of the organizations involved. Enduring conflicts are not superficial. A couple may struggle throughout their marriage about housework or frugality. Perhaps these are simply low-impact conflicts, but if they are ongoing sources of significant tension, then they are almost certainly connected to deeper issues such as differentials in power, privilege, and responsibility.

Enduring Conflicts Reflect Identity Issues

One reason conflicts do not get readily resolved is that they reflect core concerns about meaning, community, intimacy, and autonomy—in other words they involve questions of identity. Sometimes a person's identity is wrapped up in the conflict experience itself, as may happen with the union activist whose life has been devoted to the struggle against management. For many such activists the goals and outcome of any specific struggle or issue may be less important than their own long-term participation in a struggle against the power of corporations or managers. One of the most famous statements of principle in U.S. labor history—made in the early part of the twentieth century by Eugene Debs—exemplifies this: "While there is a lower class I am in it; while there is a criminal element I am of it; while there is a soul in prison, I am not free" (Andrews and Zarefsky, 1989).

At other times it is the content of the enduring conflict that is rooted in identity issues. For example, religious conflict is often related to the desire among a group of people to defend both the beliefs that give them meaning and the community with which they identify. Religious conflict throughout history—whether between Catholics and Protestants during the Thirty Years War, between Islam and Christianity during the Crusades, or among Shias and Sunnis today—has been more about the communities that different people identify with and struggles in defense of those communities than about theological differences.

Identity conflicts cannot easily be resolved by time-limited negotiations or by the exercise of either rights or power. These conflicts can be suppressed, but genuine progress requires time, work at a deep level, and the emergence of a new sense of identity. Northern Ireland appears to be experiencing this process as people there are gradually accepting that their needs regarding identity and survival can perhaps be achieved in partnership with long-term adversaries, but this has been a long, slow process with lots of detours. Many Protestant and Catholic activists in Northern Ireland have risked their lives, gone to jail, sacrificed careers and normal family lives, and in some cases lost their lives to carry on a struggle that has both given them meaning and promoted the values and community that are core to their identity. Now that the struggle has entered a new phase in which the conflict is redefined and the arena is more political and less violent, they face the difficult challenge of adapting their sense of who they are. This personal challenge can also be a challenge to the peace process.

Enduring Conflict Involves Values

One reason people hold on to a conflict over time is that it expresses values important to them. Although temporary accommodations can be made, the long-term issue strikes to the core of participants' belief systems. Values and identity are wrapped up in each other of course. The abortion debate, although significantly related to identity, is conducted almost entirely in the context of values. The hardest conflicts to mediate are the ones that are genuinely about values (not the ones where values are used as a cover for other concerns). In several mediations I have conducted involving animal rights activists, hunters, trappers, and ranchers, the policy issues were almost always overwhelmed by basic differences in values about nature, wildlife, hunting, guns, and individualism.

Enduring Conflicts Are Embedded in Structure

The structure that surrounds a conflict is a key element of the conflict. What people experience as conflict over natural resources and environmental values is deeply embedded in the nature of both economic and political systems. The economic system and the lifestyles it has enabled and on which its continued growth rests require the ever more intense use of limited resources, and this inevitably results in certain kinds of environmental degradation (Diamond, 2005). There is no simple or even complex resolution to this. This is a conflict that will inevitably endure over time, and a society's success in sustaining a constructive engagement with this conflict is critical to its survival (the conflict over global warming is discussed further later in this chapter).

Other kinds of structural conflict involve roles, geography, limited resources, power, the tension between the needs of an organization overall and the needs of its parts, and the constraints of the legal environment (see, for example, Mayer, 2000; Moore, 2003). The common denominator is that conflicts rooted in structure cannot be resolved unless the structure is changed, and this is often extremely difficult if not impossible.

Enduring Conflicts Are Systemic and Complex

Enduring conflicts are not easily encapsulated but involve the whole system of interactions among the people involved. What may manifest itself as a conflict between a minority community and a police department (for example, the Rodney King riots in Los Angeles in 1992 or the outrage after Amadou Diallo was killed in New York in 1999) can be understood only in terms of the larger system of political, social, economic, and power relationships of which it is part. Furthermore, such systems are complex and adaptive in that they are constantly reorganizing themselves in response to new circumstances and new inputs. This also means that enduring conflicts are not amenable to linear, straightforward approaches to resolution. (Coleman, Bui-Wrzosinska, Vallacher, and Nowak, 2006, have described protracted conflicts as "dynamical systems," which can be understood only in terms of the participants' patterns of communication and interactions.)

Enduring Conflicts Are Rooted in Distrust

Enduring conflicts both arise from and breed distrust. Communicating, problem solving, and negotiating are made more difficult by this lack of trust. Interventions in enduring conflict frequently have to deal with the issue of trust, either through trust-building activities or through developing some way of interacting in the absence of trust. Many conflicts (for example, high-conflict divorces, disputes in hostile working environments, racially based community conflicts) display the phenomenon of reactive devaluation (Ross, 1995), meaning distrust is so high that whatever offer or suggestion is made by one party, it is automatically discounted by the other. Although this is a problem in many conflicts, it is especially characteristic of enduring conflict. (See Lewicki and Weithoff, 2000, for a discussion of different forms of trust and distrust.)

Enduring Conflicts Involve Fundamental Issues of Power

Power is a currency in all conflict, but in enduring conflict it is fundamental to the struggle itself. Enduring conflict almost always involves efforts by individuals or groups to secure a more favorable long-term power position. This may be a primary goal or a goal in service of other concerns, but the struggle for power is an important part of the picture. Furthermore, enduring conflicts often involve concerns about survival or safety in the face of power. For some participants, therefore, enduring conflict involves a long-term effort to find a way of contending with the untrammeled use of coercive power.

All enduring conflicts exhibit some of these characteristics, and often all of them are present. For example, consider the nature of many labor management conflicts. The essential goals of labor are often at odds or out of sync with those of management—making a good living versus making a profit, autonomy and equality versus accountability and control. Labor and management generally have different *values* about work, authority, and distribution of benefits. Workers' *identity* is often centered on their affiliation and solidarity with each other, whereas for leaders identity is embedded in their roles in the organizational hierarchy. These conflicts stem from the *structure* of the workplace and have *deep roots* in the *economic and political systems* and the history of labor management relationships. *Mistrust* is often extremely high or at least close to the surface, and almost all negotiations between labor and management have *power* as a subtext.

None of this is to say that nothing can be done about enduring conflicts. They can be addressed constructively or they can be made worse. The challenge that conflict specialists face is how to help people engage in these conflicts in a wise and effective way.

FACING ENDURING CONFLICT: TWO KEY CHALLENGES

What does it mean to take a constructive approach to enduring conflict? Even when we are faced with the most intractable and intense conflicts, it is important that we understand there are alternatives to either immediate resolution or despair, to victory or defeat, or to dominance or submission.

One of the biggest challenges we face in helping people through enduring conflict is to provide an alternative vision that is less polarized and more sustaining. This requires that we develop what John Paul Lederach (2005) calls a "moral imagination," an ability to see beyond the polarities that people so easily fall into when hopeless, frustrated, and fearful. We gain this ability, I believe, by confronting two related challenges: we and those we help need to accept, even embrace, certain paradoxes that are almost always present in enduring conflict, and we all need to be able to live with uncertainty.

Embracing the Paradox of Enduring Conflict

Enduring conflict presents a significant paradox. To successfully engage with it, people have to approach it with hopefulness, optimism, and a will to make things better—but also with realism and an awareness that the conflict will not be resolved and that the situation may improve only slowly and with many setbacks. We have to act confidently or at least decisively on the basis of the information and choices we have at any given time—but with the knowledge that we don't really know all that is involved and that we are often plunging into uncharted seas. We need to embrace the conviction and beliefs that give us the courage to move forward at the same time as we recognize that these beliefs cannot be based on absolute truth and that opposing beliefs and convictions also have to be honored. This paradox poses a challenge that none of us is always able to meet.

Let's consider the challenge of what to do about climate change—a widely discussed example of an enduring conflict that must be engaged but won't be resolved for a long time (if ever).

Global climate change poses a challenge that will be around for the rest of our lives. There is no more critical international issue, and no definitive solution to this problem can be achieved through negotiation. We have already seen the limits of several negotiated accords, which even though representing important steps in the development of dialogue around global warming were far from decisive answers to this challenge (even if they had been universally accepted and implemented). In fact it is hard even to imagine what a solution would look like or entail. But remaining locked in a hopeless conflict around this issue is also inconceivable, given the enormity of the consequences of not taking decisive action. We therefore have to face three paradoxes, or contradictions, in dealing with climate change:

- There is no comprehensive solution that will fix this problem, but taking action directed to the comprehensive nature of the problem is critical.

- Many different players with profoundly different viewpoints will have to engage in a long-term struggle about what to do to deal with climate change, but cooperation on a global basis is essential.

- We have to act decisively and with conviction, but we must do so before we are completely certain of the ramifications of our actions.

If we get stuck in a mode of thinking that equates progress with solutions and that suggests we have only two choices—to come together in agreement as a world community about how to proceed or to face disaster—then our ability to cope creatively with this challenge will be significantly, possibly fatally, impaired. Instead we have to embrace these paradoxes. We have to engage in a long-term struggle, continue to keep the dialogue open, and seize partial (but not necessarily small-scale) solutions, agreements, and directions as they emerge, knowing that no one of them will fix the problem and that some may eventually prove counterproductive.

Our very survival depends on this, and yet the obstacles are enormous. This conflict is rooted in the structure of the society we have built and the global population we have propagated. Core values and beliefs are involved. Sacrifices are needed (currently, everyone agrees that others need to sacrifice). Distrust among key players is enormous. The system in which this conflict is rooted involves the entire planet—ecologically, politically, and economically. Furthermore, time is of the essence.

If we believe that the solution to climate change necessitates a grand negotiation leading to a comprehensive treaty, we are significantly limiting our options and most likely pursuing an elusive or impossible goal. What we do need to do is develop a robust system for communication, negotiation, partial agreements when possible, and ongoing struggle. The three paradoxes, the enormity of the problem, and the complexity of the issues are disincentives for facing this challenge, but face it we must and with the same energy and commitment that we would muster if we had complete clarity and certainty about the correct path to take.

But we need not look only at global issues to see the challenges of enduring conflict. Divorced parents raising a special needs child and experiencing profound and heartfelt disagreement about how to deal with that child's needs face exactly the same three paradoxes. They too need to prepare for a long-term conflictual engagement about this process and for the reality that although partial agreements will be important, no comprehensive solution is likely. The same is true in a business when its managers and its employee organizations are facing the challenges of changing technologies and market conditions.

And only when conflict specialists face the reality of these paradoxes can they begin to help their clients develop the moral imagination and courage necessary to cope with enduring conflict.

Living with Uncertainty

To stay with conflict, people have to move beyond despair, rage, false confidence, and bravado and develop a willingness and capacity to live over time with uncertainty. This may be the key to dealing with the paradoxes and challenge of enduring conflict.

In the face of conflict and stress, people want something to hang onto, such as clarity about the "correct" outcome, a simple view of right and wrong, a belief in the inevitability of victory, or even a conviction that one is part of a noble if doomed struggle. Sometimes hopelessness and cynicism offer the best prospects for some solid ground. If things are never going to get better, only worse—well, that at least offers some certainty, or as Kurt Vonnegut (1969) said, "so it goes." But hopelessness, bravado, false optimism, and cynicism are all ways of avoiding dealing with vital conflicts.

To stay with conflict, all of us, disputants and conflict specialists alike, need to develop the capacity to deal with several dimensions of uncertainty or irresolution. We need to develop the capacity to live with

Anxiety. False certainties can be reassuring but misleading. Staying with conflict requires living with a certain amount of anxiety, without being debilitated by it.

Moral ambiguity. No one has to give up beliefs or commitment to stay with conflict, but to remain constructive we do need to get beyond the simplistic view that enduring conflict is all about good versus evil.

Emotional turmoil. Accepting a conflict's uncertain and enduring nature—instead of distancing ourselves from it—means facing the ongoing emotional impact that the conflict will have on us.

Identity confusion. Most enduring conflicts are to some degree about issues of identity. We have to live with these issues that are important to our identity but that are not going to be resolved readily or neatly.

Cognitive dissonance. To stay with conflict we usually have to accept certain contradictory realities—for example, that someone whom we think is behaving badly is a good person, that we can communicate and work with people whom we view as untrustworthy, and that our beliefs and views are open to challenges just as we are challenging the views of others.

Intellectual uncertainty. Believing something does not make it true (or as my favorite bumper sticker says, "don't believe everything you think"). If our views about a conflict do not change over time, then we are probably locked into a rigid stance that will not serve us well. Furthermore, the more complex and important the issue, the more likely it is that we will have to act without having all the information we would like and without complete intellectual clarity.

Individuals involved in a long-term struggle need to develop the capacity to live with these paradoxes and uncertainties. Moreover, they need to accept these dilemmas without sacrificing their commitment, involvement, or energy. This is no easy task. No one is continually capable of living with these ambiguities while maintaining his or her courage and focus. Sometimes the only way for someone to stay committed is to claim more certainty, assert greater clarity, and adopt a more defined identity than is warranted. But this also makes it harder to engage in enduring conflict effectively.

In order to stay with conflict effectively, people need energy and motivation to sustain them, and these vital resources are fostered by moral certainty and a polarized framing of the conflict. But in order to remain constructive in the face of enduring conflict, people also need to challenge such sustaining certainties and polarities. Accepting this task is perhaps the primary hurdle conflict professionals must jump if they are going to be effective at helping people with enduring conflict.

THE BUILDING BLOCKS OF EFFECTIVE ENGAGEMENT

To help people stay with conflict, conflict professionals need to understand the characteristics of an effective and constructive approach to enduring conflict. Our essential goal here is to encourage people to focus on how they can engage in conflict constructively, rather than on how they can end it. In *Beyond Neutrality* I defined conflict engagement as "accepting the challenges of a conflict, whatever its type or stage of development may be, with courage and wisdom and without automatically assuming that resolution is an appropriate goal. Effective engagement requires finding the right level of depth at which to engage. It also means being fully aware of the many different ways we could choose to avoid conflict, including trying to resolve it prematurely" (Mayer, 2004, p. 184).

The challenge of engaging in enduring conflict requires that we accept the importance of dealing with a conflict constructively over time, knowing that it may evolve but is not likely to end. Taking a constructive approach to enduring conflict involves attending to conceptual, ethical, behavioral, and sustainability factors.

Conceptual (Cognitive) Factors

Success in staying with conflict requires that people develop an effective way to think about their situation, one that allows them to be realistic, hopeful, flexible, and focused. The way in which our clients make sense of a conflict and the narratives they construct about it determine how they will approach it. Staying with conflict poses challenges of focus, definition, context, and flexibility. We need to help disputants with the following four approaches.

Keeping a Focus on What Is Essential

What confuses or distracts people more than anything else is to lose sight of what is essential about a conflict. Disputes may be turned into power struggles, morality plays, or campaigns for personal vindication. Disputants may maintain animosities even when they cannot remember the origin of a dispute. A constructive approach to enduring conflict requires maintaining a focus on what is essential about the conflict—why people are in it or what their most important goals are. It's easy to lose sight of this in the face of intense interactions or dramatic events, but disputants need to be able to step back from time to time and ask themselves what is really important here, to do what William Ury (1991, 2007) calls "going to the balcony" to regain one's perspective.

Finding the Appropriate Level of Depth and Breadth

Conflicts can be viewed too narrowly or too broadly, too superficially or too abstractly. Therefore one challenge is to understand and articulate the conflict in a way that is broad enough to encompass disputants' core concerns without trivializing them but not so broad as to make it impossible to take a meaningful approach to those concerns. A second is to frame the conflict in terms of the core needs that drive it, without going so deep into the human psyche that people become immobilized. (Effective framing of enduring conflict is discussed further in Chapter Four.)

For example, if on the one hand a struggle between managers and workers is defined very narrowly as centering on decision-making prerogatives in contractual issues (as it often happens in collective bargaining), then the additional key issues of management style, worker involvement, and resource allocation can be readily lost. If on the other hand the conflict is defined as an ideological struggle over management philosophy, these key issues can also be lost. If the important issue is worker involvement in resource allocation decisions, then it is important to frame the issue accordingly. Of course the frame for a conflict also needs to evolve over time—an inflexible framing, no matter how effective at one point, will eventually become an impediment to constructive engagement; frames need to be modified to reflect changing circumstances.

Putting the Conflict in a Historical, Cultural, Economic, and Political Context

No conflict occurs in a vacuum, and understanding the larger context is enormously important. At the same time, although history, economics, culture, politics, and other systemic factors are important, a balance is required here as well in order to avoid both hopelessness and determinism.

For example, on the one hand the Israeli-Palestinian conflict cannot be understood without considering the relatively recent history of colonialism in the Middle East; the Holocaust; the strategic location of Israel, Gaza, and the West Bank; the politics of the Middle East; and the politics of oil. On the other hand, viewing the conflict as a 2,000-year-old struggle is basically inaccurate and leads to hopelessness rather than perspective. History is a factor to keep in mind, but it is not destiny. When we place a conflict in the context of the larger picture and forces involved, we can better understand why it is enduring, but that does not mean that the nature of the conflict cannot change, evolve, or improve (or get worse).

Allowing for the Possibility That Adversaries Can Change

We don't want to promote a naïve view of human motivations or capacities to change, but it is always helpful to assume that people can change their views, their behaviors, and their attitudes. One's former adversary can become one's future ally or at least a person with whom one can communicate and negotiate. Even if this seems unlikely, just maintaining the view that this could happen can guide disputants' behavior in more productive directions. Of course this implies that every disputant can change.

The way people characterize or treat those with whom they are in conflict ought to reflect a belief that they might some day need to work together. People sometimes feel empowered by demonizing an enemy and defining a conflict as residing in the evilness or maliciousness of a particular person or group. But enemies become friends, and friends become enemies. If disputants always treat each other as potential allies, they are less likely to burn bridges that they may someday need to cross or to find themselves behaving in a way not congruent with their values. To stay with conflict effectively, even while knowing that resolution is highly unlikely, people have to be open to the possibility that those with whom they can't work at present may one day be sitting across the table from them.

This does not mean that consequences for destructive behavior are inappropriate. Finding the balance between defending oneself against aggressive tactics or unprincipled behavior and leaving the door open to constructive change is important though not easy. It requires holding people accountable for their behavior, withholding trust if necessary, and developing reasonable consequences for destructive behavior but not demonizing any one person. This is not about "separating the people from the problem," because in enduring conflict they are often not separable. It is about recognizing that all of us are fallible and all of us can change. It's also about recognizing that being involved in a long-term conflict with someone does not mean that discussions are impossible or that one's adversary is evil.

This challenge is particularly dramatic when deeply held values are involved or when a history of oppression and domination is present. Struggling to end apartheid in South Africa required that long-term enemies with a history of serious conflict talk. Nelson Mandela had to be willing to talk with the leaders of the National Party, even though this governing party had imprisoned him for twenty-five years and killed many of his colleagues. On a smaller scale, unless people who have profoundly different views about race relations are willing to talk, racism and racial tension can never be confronted in communities, schools, and organizations.

Ethical Factors

People are best able to stay with conflict when acting in an ethical way. When a person's beliefs and behaviors are congruent, it is easier for him to stay centered, focused, and engaged over time. Often we see people use rigid adherence to a set of beliefs as a justification for harsh, rigid, punitive, and destructive behavior. This is usually a reflection of a bifurcated value system in which one set of values and behavioral precepts is applied to enemies or subservient groups and another set to allies, friends, or oneself. To stay with conflict and remain constructive, people need to be operating from a set of values that can be applied to both themselves and their adversaries. The most important ethical factors are value congruence, authenticity, accountability, and reflection and reexamination.

Maintaining Congruence Between Values and Behavior

Clarity and steadiness of values and beliefs are an immense source of strength and resilience. When people are acting in accordance with their most important and deeply held values, they are most likely to approach a conflict constructively. How does this square with the many destructive actions taken in the name of an ideology, religious dogma, or system of belief? Many of the most horrendous acts of violence and oppression are done in the name of deeply held beliefs. But these acts almost always involve suppressing one set of values (human dignity, respect, kindness, and so forth) in order to further another, and thus congruence between values and behavior is sacrificed. Sustaining enduring conflict requires honoring basic commitments and beliefs without violating values about relationships, communication, or interpersonal interaction. Nonviolent approaches to social change derive much of their power from their commitment to value congruency and from their insistence that the goals of a struggle must be reflected in the means by which the struggle is conducted.

Being Authentic

Finding an authentic voice in conflict, a voice that allows a person to speak her truth with power and to power while remaining true to her values about human relations and communication is critical to maintaining a sustained presence in conflict. People often adopt a face or a mask in conflict that is not congruent with their values or self-image. Although this may protect them or help them feel more powerful in the short run, over time it makes it harder to be both consistent and flexible and to approach a conflict with constructive power. When community activists demonize a government employee despite realizing that he is not responsible for the policies they are opposing nor able to deliver the results they desire, they are likely to be undercutting their ability to stay with conflict constructively. The activists may in the short term achieve the goal of mobilizing support and highlighting a conflict. But in the long run this approach can weaken their ability to stay with conflict because it is not authentic and leads them to direct their anger and protest toward the wrong target.

Being Accountable

Ethical behavior requires some sense of accountability to others, such as to one's community, partners, or family. Having a clear commitment to being accountable and a method for implementing this commitment provides an important mirror and check on one's actions over time. As counterintuitive as it may seem, working with people to identify to whom they are accountable for their behavior in conflict can empower them over time, because it will connect them to the larger systems or groups that can sustain them through a long-term conflict.

The mediator or advocate who helps a very angry parent think through what her own values are about pursuing her goals and to whom she ultimately needs to answer for her behavior (her children, church, family, or herself) is at the same time establishing some limits around acceptable behavior and empowering the parent for what may be a long-term struggle. Furthermore, when disputants fully understand the importance of developing reciprocal norms for the conduct of long-term conflicts, then they realize that in an important sense, they are accountable to each other.

Engaging in Reflection and Reexamination

Unless disputants periodically reflect and reconsider their views, ethical behavior becomes a matter of rigidity. Staying with conflict requires that people have the courage to rethink their views and behavior regularly. This is not about wavering or self-doubt—it is about having the clarity and confidence to think about doing things differently from time to time. Otherwise people are acting in a particular way because they always have. When they can be reflective, they can also be more grounded and powerful in their approach to conflict. A process of ongoing reflection also assists disputants to live with the uncertainties and ambiguities of enduring conflict that were discussed earlier.

Behavioral Factors

Behaving constructively in enduring conflict requires finding a way to be powerful and flexible, to stay both realistic and optimistic, to provide appropriate incentives and consequences, to keep open lines of communication even when talking seems counterproductive, and to use short-term goals and agreements in the service of a long-term presence in conflict. We can think of this in terms of power, communication, negotiation, use of agreements, and approaches to the conflict cycle.

Using Power Constructively

All conflict involves power exchanges of some sort. But power is often used ineffectively or destructively. The key to using power constructively is to be clear about the purpose, the consequences, the alternatives, and the sustainability of the approach being used, and to ensure that both the type of power used and the way that power is employed are consistent with long-term goals. Part of the challenge here is to develop and use consequences, rewards, and alternatives intentionally and wisely. The greater the number of realistic and effective alternatives that a party has for attaining his most important goals, the more powerful he is. This is a familiar concept, most notably discussed by Fisher and Ury (1981) when they introduced the concept of the BATNA (best alternative to a negotiated agreement). For example, divorcing spouses in a long-term struggle over financial issues are in a much better position to maintain that struggle when they are not desperate for whatever resources they can get. Workers who have no alternative but to work in a particular industry are much more vulnerable than those who have realistic and acceptable alternatives.

The ability to apply appropriate and measured consequences and incentives that are consistent with long-term goals and values is also essential to staying with a conflict. If there are no consequences for destructive behavior or rewards for cooperation, then there is no reason for adversaries to do anything but escalate. Part of helping people to stay with conflict involves helping them to develop more effective ways of standing up to oppression. However, if the only rewards or sanctions available are draconian or costly, they will be ineffective as well. Consider, for example, the limited practical power of having nuclear weapons. The degree to which legitimate, constructive, and ethical power is being used is the most important measure for determining whether conflict is being carried out constructively.

Building and Maintaining Lines of Communication

Refusing to communicate directly may sometimes be a reasonable stance (for example, when ending an abusive relationship or responding to the manipulative use of communication), but it is naïve to think that this refusal means no communication is occurring. Governments that have ostensibly broken off all contact (as the United States has at times with, for example, Cuba, North Korea, and Iran) find ways of sending signals, such as using third parties, the media, covert channels, or other approaches to deliver messages or maintain communication. Individuals who are alienated or who have broken off contact but who continue to be involved in an enduring conflict do the same.

If conflict exists over time, so will communication, and it is therefore important to build and nurture multiple channels of communication. Breaking off all contact or putting too many conditions on contact is often tempting as a way to show determination and to exercise a bit of power, but it is seldom effective and often dangerous. So the challenge is to create avenues of communication that don't in themselves enable destructive behavior, convey an inappropriate message, or exacerbate a problem but that do give people a means of engaging in an ongoing discussion and carving out whatever agreements or *rules of engagement* may be appropriate. The many efforts to find quiet third channels through which Catholic and Protestant leaders in Northern Ireland could talk, for example, were an essential prelude to changing the nature of that conflict. The ongoing debate about when and how to open negotiations between Western powers and Iran, North Korea, or Libya is airing different views about the best way to begin such talks.

Negotiating (Even When Refusing to Negotiate)

As with communicating, people embroiled in long-term conflict are negotiating even when they say they are not. When hostages are taken, governments almost always say that they will not negotiate. Unions and managements put forth nonnegotiable demands all the time. Parents often assert that they do not negotiate with their children over any number of rules (for bedtime, curfew, chores, and the like). But in all these situations negotiations occur all the time.

If negotiation means a communication that is intended to produce an agreement or a resolution, then all of us are in negotiations all the time, even when we say we are not. When someone says she will not negotiate, she's delivering an important message, but it's not that there will be no negotiation. Usually, people are saying, "I will not enable your behavior by letting it leverage my behavior," "I am not willing to compromise on my essential needs or values," or even, "I do not feel like talking to you and will let you stew for a while." Each statement still amounts to engaging in a form of negotiation. Important if coded information is being conveyed that is relevant to the conflict.

Whether it's called negotiation or not, a constructive approach to long-term conflict requires avenues through which parties can try to resolve, ameliorate, or contain intermediate problems. An effective approach to sustainable conflict involves an intentional and wise use of negotiation—one that allows all parties to save face, advocate for their interests, address their legitimate needs, take time out from direct discussion, look for creative solutions, and contain the ongoing destructive consequences of conflict. Furthermore, the more people succeed in engaging in negotiation on intermediate issues, the more they develop their capacities to dialogue about broader and more far reaching concerns. This leads us to the next factor in constructive engagement, which concerns agreements.

Using Agreements Strategically

Even when we are engaged in a conflict that will not end quickly or easily and for which there are no "agreement fixes," we may still benefit from solving problems and reaching agreements. Environmental conflicts, for example, typically involve long-term struggles. Along the way, however, it is extremely important to find areas of agreement that solve specific problems and refocus the conflict in a constructive way. The Kyoto Treaty would by no means have ended the conflict about climate change, but it did (even without U.S. participation) advance the conflict to a new level.

There will be times over the course of an enduring conflict when all parties share an interest in reaching partial, temporary, or conditional agreements. As discussed earlier, communication always occurs in conflict. Negotiation of some kind is usually present. In addition, agreements are occasionally reached. Disputants often view their choices in absolute terms—clear, open, and honest communication or no communication; negotiation on the fundamental problems or no negotiation; agreements that settle the big issues or no agreements. The reality is more complicated. Intermediate agreements may allow a respite for all concerned, and they can establish a new and perhaps better platform from which to engage in the ongoing struggle.

Attending to the Conflict Cycle

Conflict is not a linear process that begins, escalates, de-escalates, and ends. Conflict may de-escalate and then escalate again. Agreements occur and the conflict continues. Prevention and healing are all wrapped up in each other. Conflict is a chaotic process. However, it is a *process*, and at different times it poses different challenges. The key challenge, for example, might be on prevention, healing, management, naming, escalating, de-escalating, resolving, encapsulating, or broadening (see Mayer, 2000, 2004). A constructive approach to enduring conflict requires an ability to discern which aspects of the conflict process require attention at any given time and how to engage in them while keeping the long-term goals in mind.

Sometimes escalating a conflict is necessary to ensure that essential concerns are noticed, to bring in more players, or to enhance a disputant's legitimate power. Sometimes, de-escalation is necessary. The important and often counterintuitive point is that our goal should be not always to lower the level of the dispute but to take whatever action is necessary in a way that does not prevent future constructive developments or compromise essential needs or values.

The most effective political movements are characterized by appropriate uses of escalation (in the form, for example, of sit-ins, boycotts, work stoppages, demonstrations, or petitions to recall elected officials) alongside the wise use of agreements, compromises, de-escalation, and negotiation. Groups, organizations, nations, and movements that are stuck in only one mode tend to be less effective or more destructive. Often, different organizations within the same general movement will focus on different aspects of the conflict process. In the environmental arena, for example, groups like the Natural Resources Defense Council or the Audubon Society are more likely to focus on negotiation and searching for agreements, whereas groups like Greenpeace and Friends of the Earth are focused on escalating conflicts, or at least maintaining them at a relatively high level of intensity, in order to raise public awareness and pressure.

Sustainability Factors

If a conflict is truly enduring, then the challenge for all participants is how to sustain themselves—as individuals and as groups, communities, and organizations—to participate over time in an effective way. This means attending to resources, energy, emotions, and safety. It also means finding a way of encapsulating a conflict.

Developing Resources

Finding allies, support systems, and the emotional, personal, structural, and material resources to participate over the long haul is essential to staying with conflict. For example, political movements that sustain themselves over time require effective organizational structures, ways to accommodate the life needs of activists, and an ongoing inflow of new energy.

At high points of struggle or conflict, participants may not focus on the sustainability of their approach, but if they put this aside for too long, the effort will falter or participants will pay too great a price to endure. Building sustainable organizational frameworks has been critical to the sustainability of the labor movement, the environmental movement, and the civil rights movement (even though the bureaucratization of a movement carries its own risks). Many other social movements have faltered because they did not attend to this (for example, the antiwar, student rights, and welfare rights movements).

This is also true for individuals in a long-term conflict. A parent who faces the prospect of dealing with a contentious ex-spouse for many years needs to develop the support systems to endure. Business partners in a highly conflictual relationship need support systems if they are to continue to stay in business with each other.

Maintaining Energy

A conflict that occupies all of one's energy is probably not sustainable over time without incurring great personal costs. People need to learn ways to concentrate their energy on a conflict when necessary but also to maintain or develop other activities or resources that replenish and nourish them.

I have often been asked to work with organizations on the verge of disintegration ostensibly because of a long-term conflict. Unless the conflict is resolved, I am told, the organization will not endure. But often the conflict is not resolvable because it reflects structural issues or value differences that are intimately related to the organization's purpose. The problem is not the existence of a necessary and inevitable conflict but the fact that it is occupying all the available energy and resources of the organization. The real challenge in these circumstances is to help people and organizations find ways of accepting and carrying on the conflict without having it occupy all their energy all the time.

Managing Emotions

In order to stay with conflict effectively, disputants need an effective approach to managing their emotions. Usually, this involves finding a way to experience, articulate, understand, and sometimes release the conflict-related emotions. This can be done in the context of the conflict itself or apart from it. Even for people who typically suppress their emotions or maintain a stoic front (and maybe especially for them), when there is no safe place to express and release emotions that inevitably go along with conflict, staying with conflict becomes very difficult.

Encapsulating the Conflict

Conflict should not be the dominant feature of anyone's life. Sometimes organizations let conflicts become more important than fulfilling the organizational mission. Sometimes a parent becomes so focused on a conflict with an ex-spouse that he or she loses sight of the needs of the children or his or her own needs. Sustainability almost always requires putting boundaries of some kind around a conflict. This does not mean denying it, ignoring it, or avoiding it—it simply means not letting it become the reason for one's existence. I once asked a retiring government employee involved in an age discrimination dispute what his retirement plans were. The sum total of his plans, he told me, was to continue to pursue his grievance. That did not sound to me like a very rewarding approach to retirement. The challenge is to encapsulate a dispute, keep it in perspective, and engage with the rest of life without avoiding the conflict or failing to do the work that it calls for.

Attending to Safety

Conflict is often dangerous—sometimes extremely so. Engaging constructively in enduring conflict is sometimes unsafe. It would be naïve to assert that effective engagement means ensuring that all participants are safe. What is important and possible, however, is to address issues of personal, physical, and psychological safety realistically and not ignore or deny them. Unless people find a way of facing the real challenges to safety without overstating, denying, or ignoring them and without becoming debilitated in the face of them, staying with conflict constructively is not possible.

CREATIVE NONRESOLUTION

Staying with conflict relies on the ability to remain productively, creatively, and even serenely in a state of nonresolution (not to be mistaken for irresolution). Many of us who help others with conflict are not particularly good at living with nonresolution. If there is a problem we want to fix it, if there is a conflict we want to resolve it, and if there is uncertainty we want to find the answer. Staying with conflict, however, requires us to live with unsolved problems, unresolved conflict, and more questions than answers. A need for certainty and closure often gets us into trouble; it impels us to act as if we know more than we do and to solve problems superficially or ill advisedly, and it limits our ability to think creatively and broadly about difficult issues.

Instead, if we are to stay with conflict ourselves and work with others to help them stay with conflict, we need to develop the ability to tolerate ambiguity, uncertainty, and contradictory needs and realities and to live with cognitive dissonance. We need to be able to make the most of nonresolution, and this calls for a special kind of creativity.

We are often taught that an important component of wisdom is knowing the difference between what we can fix and what we cannot. Indeed, a prayer about this—"God, give us grace to accept with serenity the things that cannot be changed, courage to change the things which should be changed, and the wisdom to distinguish the one from the other"—has become popular enough to reach bumper sticker status. (Reinhold Niebuhr is often cited as the author of this prayer; see, for example, "Serenity Prayer Attributed to Niebuhr, Reinhold," 1942.) The lesson some draw from this (not necessarily Niebuhr's meaning) is that we should concentrate our energies on what can be fixed or resolved.

I am suggesting something quite different, particularly for those of us who work as conflict specialists.

We should indeed develop the wisdom to know which conflicts can be resolved or ameliorated and which cannot. But that does not mean that our energy should be concentrated only on the more easily resolved disputes. Working on the enduring conflicts in people's lives may be the most important work that we have to do. This requires that we do the personal work that allows us to live and even prosper in conditions of nonresolution. Part of this work requires that we learn to accept a story that has no neat or foreseeable ending as an essential reality and that we find a way to help those we work with accept this as well. We also need to maintain a sense of what can be accomplished, of the constructive potential that exists in a conflict that continues, and of the ways in which we can lead our lives and help others to lead their lives productively and even to flourish in the face of nonresolution.

We face many obstacles in helping others stay with conflict creatively. Perhaps the greatest challenge we face is the powerful pull to avoid dealing with conflict at all. To help people stay with conflict we must confront the problem of avoidance. This is what I consider in the next chapter.

3

Escaping the Avoidance Trap

I was angry with my friend:
I told my wrath, my wrath did end.
I was angry with my foe:
I told it not, my wrath did grow.

William Blake, c. 1792

Dealing with conflict avoidance may be the most important challenge that conflict specialists face. The pull to avoid conflict is ubiquitous, powerful, and understandable. Why would anyone want to engage in a process that is difficult, emotionally draining, relationship threatening, and uncertain in outcome? Yet the cumulative costs of avoidance are enormous for relationships, productivity, morale, and the quality of decision making. As conflict specialists we can contribute to a pattern of avoidance, or we can help people begin to move past avoidance, to escape the avoidance trap.

People are endlessly inventive in how they avoid conflict, even though the consequences of doing so can be extremely debilitating. If we are going to help people engage in enduring conflict effectively, we have to understand both why they avoid conflict and how they do so. Then we have to help them begin to move past their avoidance strategies into more constructive patterns of engagement.

The entire course of our work in helping people stay with conflict involves contending with the power of avoidance. As hard as it can be to face an immediate conflict, developing the wherewithal and the skills to engage constructively over time with an enduring conflict can be even more daunting. So whether we are helping people to face the long-term elements of a conflict, work on maintaining communications where communicating seems futile, or respond to coercive power wisely, we are also contending with conflict avoidance.

I explore these methods of helping people to engage in enduring conflict in subsequent chapters of this book. In this chapter I focus specifically on why people avoid conflict, how they avoid it, and some of the specific responses to avoidant behaviors that we will find ourselves using over and over again as we work with people on staying with conflict.

THE URGE TO AVOID CONFLICT

Sometimes avoiding a conflict is wise and even essential. Not all conflict can be safely or productively approached, and sometimes nothing good will come from engagement. Although one message of this book is that conflict avoidance is a major obstacle to long-term healthy relationships and growth, we must always remember that sometimes conflict needs to be avoided, or at least the timing of engaging conflict needs to be carefully thought through. The first question, however, is why the urge to avoid conflict is so pervasive, even when that avoidance appears to be ineffective or destructive.

Why Disputants Avoid Conflict

There are some very powerful incentives to avoid conflict that everyone experiences from time to time. They include fear, hopelessness, uncertainty, energy conservation, relationship preservation, powerlessness, shame, inadequate skills, and resource depletion.

Fear

People often fear the consequences of engaging in conflict, consequences that may affect their relationships, reputation, self-image, emotional well-being, or physical safety. This fear is often well placed but can also become a self-fulfilling prophecy. That is, if someone avoids a conflict because of fear of the consequences (such as arousing someone's wrath), the dispute may escalate and the feared outcome may be realized to a greater extent than it would have been if the conflict had been addressed earlier. However, there are also circumstances in which there is no safe way for people to engage in a conflict, and we must always respect people's own assessment of the genuine dangers they face.

Hopelessness

People are frequently pessimistic about the chances of engaging successfully or the prospect for things to get better. If the consequences of taking on a conflict are disrupted relationships, insecurity, or increased vulnerability, and if the chances of things improving are minimal, what is the point? In part this hopelessness flows from a lack of confidence in one's own ability to handle conflict, but it also stems from pessimism about the personality, skills, or intentions of others; the ability of organizations or systems to change; the potential for making progress on fundamental problems; or the possibility that people can change and conditions improve.

Uncertainty

When one is uncertain about what one thinks, about being able to defend or justify one's own behavior or beliefs, or about what has happened, should happen, and is likely to happen, avoidance can seem more attractive than engagement. There is an irony here. For a person to engage in conflict successfully, uncertainty is essential. Uncertainty about outcome (and about the rights and wrongs of a situation) is what allows sufficient open-mindedness and willingness to engage in a meaningful dialogue. When people are certain, their dialogue is usually more about persuasion, prescription, or propaganda than about listening, sharing, and considering. But uncertainty can also discourage engagement, particularly when a person lacks self-confidence.

People often wait to bring up an issue or concern until they feel they have developed all their alternatives, mobilized all their potential power, gathered all the facts they need to make their case unequivocally, and lined up all the potential support they can. As we shall see, some of these resources are necessary for engaging in sustained conflict, but this degree of preparedness has to be weighed against the dangers of escalating a conflict unnecessarily, making it harder for others to engage, letting problems fester, and failing to deal with important issues. So although uncertainty is a key to successful engagement, it is also an obstacle to it.

Energy Conservation

Engaging in conflict takes a different type of energy than avoidance does (for example, communicating takes a different kind of energy than stonewalling does). Moreover, even though in the long run it may take more energy to avoid conflict, it often feels as though avoidance is the less demanding route. People are often accustomed to the level of exertion that they have been making to avoid conflict and do not want to expend more or different types of energy. Effective engagement can be very energizing, but it can also be tiring, time consuming, and demanding of personal resources that are not easily mobilized.

Systems or Relationship Preservation

Avoidance often serves, at least in the short run, to maintain the appearance of harmony and to preserve relationships that cannot handle overt conflict. Over time, relationships maintained through conflict avoidance may not endure or progress beyond the superficial, and systems that depend on the appearance of harmony or the suppression of conflict may not remain robust and effective. But all of us occasionally decide that the appearance of harmony is the best we can hope for in a relationship and is some-times of value.

Many people maintain a somewhat superficial contact with certain family members, friends, and coworkers and work very hard to avoid raising conflictual issues with them because they want to have some relationship, albeit a limited one. People usu-ally want to minimize stress in their interpersonal relationships and to be liked (and feel likeable) if at all possible, even if the cost of this is allowing themselves to be taken advantage of or having superficial relationships.

Powerlessness

People often have little confidence in their power to engage constructively or to protect themselves from the negative con-sequences of engagement. There is a self-fulfilling prophecy here too. The more disputants learn to take a constructive approach to engaging in conflict, the better they are able to do so and there-fore the more powerful they become in the face of enduring conflict. The less they do so, the less able and therefore the less powerful they are.

But powerlessness is not just about what one believes. Sometimes, the structure of a relationship or system leaves peo-ple genuinely and even dangerously without power. The child in an abusive family learns to avoid conflict at all costs, as does an abused spouse or a vulnerable member of any coercive system. Of course, if no one ever takes on the conflict, the power differential becomes further entrenched and more severe.

Shame or Embarrassment

Acknowledging a conflict is usually the first step to engaging in it, and disputants are often ashamed to do so. People hide their con-flicts because they want to maintain a public image that is consis-tent with their self-image or with the norms of their community. For example, I hate to argue in public (which gives a great deal of power to people with whom I am in conflict who don't mind doing so). But there is a deeper form of shame as well. Disputants are often fearful of the feelings and actions that engaging in conflict can release. They fear that they will lose their temper, say things they will regret, engage in behavior they will be ashamed of, and in general show a side of themselves that they do not like to experience or even admit to themselves, much less to anyone else.

Inadequate Skills

Conflict engagement requires a skills that many people do not have or don't feel that they have. These are basic life skills such as the abilities to communicate, manage emotions, negotiate, and problem solve, and everyone has to develop these capacities to some extent simply to function. But almost everyone at times feels that his or her skills are either underdeveloped or inadequate to meet a particular challenge.

Resource Depletion

Sometimes people do not have the time, fortitude, support, or energy to take on a conflict process. People have to choose their battles because it takes personal and material resources to engage in conflict. Of course, failing to engage in conflict and allowing it to continue and even grow depletes resources as well.

The Path of Least Resistance

These factors in avoidance play out in many different ways, and they reinforce each other as well. The more powerless and depleted someone feels, for example, the more likely he or she is to feel hopeless and fearful. These are obstacles that everyone experiences, and they operate together to induce individuals and systems to conspire to avoid conflict.

All of this adds up to the fact that it is often easier, in the short run at least, to avoid conflict than to engage in it. The modes of interaction, communication, energy expenditure, and intellectual focus that engagement requires are all very different from what avoidance requires. The crossover from avoidance to engagement is therefore often very difficult and demanding. Many people feel as though they are two entirely different individuals when they are involved in a conflict and when they are not, and they are often not at ease with the type of person they might be when they engage in conflict.

For all these reasons, the pull toward avoidance is strong and pervasive. But the ways in which people avoid conflict are also varied, creative, and ever changing. A second key element of understanding avoidance is being able to recognize it in its many different forms.

HOW PEOPLE AVOID CONFLICT

Individuals and organizations bring an immense array of creativity to the avoidance of conflict. They deny the existence of a conflict, cut off contact, escalate to intimidate, scapegoat, minimize, distract, promise action, pretend to agree, feign ignorance, lie, focus on minor issues, use surrogates, and find many other ways to avoid actually having to engage a conflict. Perhaps the most common approach is simply to remain passive or nonresponsive in the face of provocation (to "bite one's tongue," "remain above the fray," or "count to ten"). (See Mayer, 2000, chap. 2, for additional discussion of the ways people avoid conflict.)

Many approaches to avoidance can look like taking on a conflict even though they are in fact mechanisms for shutting down a conflict engagement effort. For example, if I am confronted by someone who challenges my behavior (perhaps I was rude, inattentive, or curt) and I respond by yelling at him to mind his own business or by slamming a door in his face, I have escalated the conflict by my behavior, but I have also tried to avoid the interaction and shut the conflict down. Another tactic is to apologize immediately and agree to do something different, and this too can be an effort to avoid genuine engagement.

Even though the cost of avoidance may be great, conflicts may fester and relations may sour, people will go to great lengths to evade actually saying what they think or listening to what others may think about difficult issues.

Conflict Avoidant Behaviors

Four distinct behaviors seem particularly characteristic of entrenched avoidance patterns: minimization, misdirection, escalation, and premature problem solving.

Minimization

Perhaps the most common approach to avoidance is to deny or minimize the seriousness of a conflict ("we are not fighting, we are discussing"; "there is no real conflict here"; "aside from a few chronic malcontents and troublemakers, everyone in this company is happy"). People minimize the depth of the disagreement, the seriousness of the issue, or the extent of the problem. Sometimes they minimize the number of people who are in conflict. For example, when Richard Nixon was president, he claimed to represent the "silent majority" who supported the war in Vietnam and other policies, and he argued that those protesting the war were really a tiny if vocal minority. Whatever the division of opinion by numbers, the issue was not isolated and the protestors were not a marginal sector of American society. The divisions apparent in those years were never really addressed, and they continue to have an impact on American political culture to this day.

If there really is no conflict or it is of no consequence, then ignoring a problem, remaining passive, or carrying on business as usual may be a reasonable response. But if a serious dispute is present, the approach of minimization can be extremely destructive and shortsighted.

Misdirection

People are endlessly inventive at defining a conflict in ways that cloud the real issue or problem. One way to do this is to change a relationship issue into a monetary issue or legal issue or to define it in some other way that avoids the genuine conflict. For example, when relationships in a workplace are problematic, trust is low, and people feel abused or misused in some way, complaints about essentially tangential issues tend to get raised. People make procedural complaints about hiring, promotion, performance reviews, or job assignment practices. Or they take what is a pervasive problem throughout an organization and blame it on one particular person, unit, or procedure—in other words, they identify a scapegoat as a way of avoiding the genuine problem.

People often focus on the more tangible and behavioral aspects of conflict rather than on the more difficult, often relationship-based aspects. Most of us in this field have at one point or another heard something along these lines: "I don't want to get into any of that Kumbaya, touchy-feely stuff." Sometimes the important message behind such statements is that people want to deal with concrete issues and seek measurable progress rather than talk about relationships or emotions. But at other times the message seems to be that people don't want to work on the more intangible and uncomfortable problems in the workplace—which they know they can't solve anyway.

Another way to misdirect is to construct a narrative about conflict that eliminates people's personal responsibility for trying to understand or deal with it. To explain, understand, and avoid conflict simultaneously, people often use one of three causal crutches, assigning a conflict to

- *Evil.* They say that the source of the conflict lies in the sociopathic, sadistic, immoral, manipulative, or untruthful personalities of others.

- *Stupidity*. They say that the conflict arises out of low intelligence, cluelessness, stubbornness, or unwillingness to face the facts.

- *Craziness*. They say that the conflict is caused by mental illness, inability to understand the consequences of behavior, "living on another planet," or extreme emotional volatility.

People use these explanatory crutches to account for behavior that makes no sense to them, but they also use them to dismiss the potential legitimacy of other points of view. Once someone describes a conflict in one of these ways, she's no longer expected to engage with the conflict because the corollary assumption is that there is no effective way to engage with others who are evil, crazy, or stupid.

Moreover, once the cause of conflict is relegated to one of these crutches, no further effort is made to understand its root causes. But of course even if we are dealing in part with evil behavior, mental health issues, or cognitive impairment, we still have to deal with the conflict as effectively as possible. Furthermore, although these issues may often be factors, they are never the whole story.

Escalation

In all profound disputes, upping the level of conflict is at times a necessary part of engaging, but escalating to promote engagement is very different from escalating to prevent it. The first is intended to lead to more communication and interaction (not always direct), the second to limit or end communication about an issue. When bullies threaten, they are not trying to encourage engagement; they are trying to force retreat or submission. This is not a tactic restricted to bullies—all of us on occasion get aggressive, loud, angry, positional, or demanding, partly in the hope that we can get another person to back off, thereby freeing us from the obligation of having to engage in a conflict. Because escalation looks like jumping into a conflict, it is easy to overlook that it is essentially avoidant.

On occasion escalation is helpful and even necessary. Sometimes a parent, boss, leader, or other person in authority has to make it clear that a decision has to be respected or abided by even if there is disagreement and even without discussion, because not everything can be debated. But even this escalation is a conflict avoidant behavior and the cumulative effect of doing it repeatedly in regard to a serious conflict is that the problem will worsen or the relationship deteriorate. Escalation sometimes occurs because people feel powerless or fearful—believing that they have no ability to protect themselves (or gain traction) except by escalating an issue. At other times it happens because people believe they are so powerful that they can shut someone else down and not have to worry about the consequences of escalation.

Avoiding a conflict by upping the ante turns inward and destructive on occasion—for example, when people engage in self-destructive or addictive behaviors to avoid having to engage with the impact a conflict is having on them or others. When people increase the level of emotional intensity and redefine a conflict as a matter of fundamental values, they may be trying to enhance their own power and determination, but they may also hope to make a continuation of the interaction so unpleasant that others will back off. Of course, when escalation is met with counter-escalation, the situation can quickly deteriorate.

Premature Problem Solving

Problem solving at the right time and in the right spirit is an important part of constructive engagement, but often people rush to solutions out of a desire to run away from a conflict. An important example is the way that many workplaces have dealt with sexual harassment. They have created rules, reporting procedures, and intervention systems to contend with this problem, but seldom have they genuinely dealt with the underlying beliefs or attitudes that reinforce gender-based stereotyping and harassment.

In this case the rules, procedures, and systems, although important, are not enough to fully address the essential problem. They tend to represent bureaucratic responses to harassment rather than comprehensive efforts to address underlying issues. Sometimes, when organizations institute clear expectations and consequences for violating them, the underlying attitudes eventually change, but a long-term engagement with the core issues is usually necessary before the culture of discrimination and harassment shifts and normative assumptions about appropriate behavior can be altered.

Challenging Our Collusion in Avoidance

In most significant conflicts we can find all these elements of avoidant behavior present to varying degrees. People will minimize, misdirect, escalate, or problem solve in sequence or simultaneously to avoid having to deal with deep problems. For example, it is not unusual to see a conflicted workplace where managers are avoiding dealing with union representatives, who are in turn escalating a problem through threats, and all of them are proposing quick fixes to a problem that is embedded (for example) in relationships, resources, and power structures and that cannot be easily resolved but does need to be addressed.

The pervasiveness of avoidance, the energy everyone brings to it, and the often devastating long-term consequences of it are among the many reasons people need the help of conflict specialists. Unfortunately, by aligning ourselves as strongly as we have with the goal of resolution and by promoting "win-win" outcomes when no comprehensive solutions are currently achievable, we have sometimes unwittingly colluded in avoidance and fallen into the resolution trap. But there is an opportunity here as well, one that we can use if we develop the perspectives and the skills necessary to help people understand and overcome their avoidant tendencies and engage in conflict in a sustained and productive way.

RESPECTING AND CHALLENGING AVOIDANCE

If we are to help disputants to confront their avoidant behaviors, we must find ways to challenge their avoidance while always respecting the choices they make. We may believe that an avoidant approach to conflict is not productive or wise, but it is not for us to coerce or manipulate people into engaging in conflict when they have chosen not to do so. Nevertheless, there are usually opportunities to challenge avoidance, to discuss its consequences, or at the very least to suggest to parties that they are in fact choosing not to deal with important elements of a dispute.

Challenging avoidance usually involves two separate tasks: helping people become aware that they are making a choice to avoid conflict and helping them consider whether and how to move from avoidance to engagement. These two tasks apply whether we are talking about a transient or enduring conflict, but with enduring conflict, we face the additional task of helping people approach the long-term challenge of engagement and the ongoing appeal (and danger) of avoidance.

We have to do this in partnership with those with whom we are working, and we must always remember that avoidance is sometimes the best strategy. Furthermore, the decision about whether it is the best strategy is not in the end our decision—as I experienced in a tense mediation I conducted in a government agency several years ago:

Everyone in this large government agency knew about the long-standing problems between Paul and Bill, it seemed, but they themselves never dealt with their issues directly. Paul was the department manager and Bill was a supervisor who had worked for him for many years. There had always been a great deal of tension between them—tension that they were loath to acknowledge. Paul was Caucasian and Bill African American. The case was referred to me when Bill filed a grievance stemming from a poor performance evaluation that he felt was undeserved. Paul said that everyone had been dancing around the supervisor's inadequate performance and it was time to confront it, whereas Bill basically said, "Show me the facts."

The immediate conflict was readily resolved (clear performance guidelines, review procedures, agreed-upon rewording of the review), but the underlying issue was much more complicated. It seemed clear to me that there were considerable racial overtones in what was being said, but neither was speaking about this directly. I debated with myself about whether to raise this issue, knowing that it could lead to a tense and not necessarily productive interchange, or let it be, despite my view that it was likely an important factor in their ongoing work together.

In private meetings with each, I asked whether there were any concerns about the way racial issues were affecting their relationship. Paul (while insisting that he was acting completely without regard to race) said that he thought people had danced around the supervisor's performance out of fear of being accused of racism. Bill said that he suspected the manager thought Bill had gotten his job because of his race and never looked at his performance objectively, only through a racial lens. I encouraged both of them to put this issue on the table, but neither was willing to do this—feeling it would only open a can of worms—and so it was never directly dealt with. Their relationship continued to be shaky and eventually they both left the department.

I wondered then, and wonder now, how directive I should have been about raising the issue of race, but in the end, it was their call.

FACING AVOIDANCE

When people avoid conflict they know it, at least on some level. Furthermore, as we work with people we can often tell very quickly when a deeper conflict is being avoided, even if we don't yet know what it is. Often the parts of their conflict story just do not add up to a whole. Something does not make sense, or people keep reverting to formulaic accounts or patterns of interchanges. We see people rushing to solutions or storming out of a conflictual situation before any communication can occur. We observe them becoming furious at someone who does not seem to be the real source of their concerns, or refusing to engage in a discussion about a problem because "nothing can be done about it." We can't always nail down what is going on, but these cues should alert us to the possibility that avoidance is occurring.

In our normal interactions as mediators, coaches, facilitators, or advisers, we ought always to be asking ourselves (and often our clients) what is not being said or, alternatively, what is being said in a vague or circuitous way. When we see people rushing to resolve an issue that does not seem like the real problem; escalating a conflict in a nonproductive way; choosing to explain a situation in terms of the evil, crazy, or stupid behavior of others; or denying that a problem exists or is serious or widespread, we should ask ourselves, is this avoidant behavior, and if so, what is being avoided?

Usually, disputants are not in complete denial that a conflict exists. Mostly we find we are dealing with people who minimize, escalate, misdirect, or problem solve prematurely. Our challenge then is to work with these people to enable them to recognize their avoidant behavior and to make a conscious choice about whether to engage the conflict or not. The manager and the supervisor in the previous example may or may not have been making the right choice for themselves in staying away from the issue of race, but their conscious choice to do so was probably more productive for them than continuing to use other issues as a surrogate for this one would have been. Whether people choose to engage or not, there is still value in working toward a more intentional and constructive decision about engagement or avoidance.

Once we recognize that avoidance is occurring we need to find an effective way to respond. One guide to responding is first to identify the specific approach to avoidance that people are using—whether minimization, misdirection, escalation, or premature problem solving.

Minimization

Minimization, denial, and passivity in the face of conflict may be the hardest approaches to deal with. Most approaches to avoidance offer some opportunity to build on people's realization that there is a conflict or a problem, but when people deny that any serious conflict exists or that there is any reason to look at a situation differently, we have much less purchase around which to intervene. However, unless there is complete denial that any problem exists, we can still build on people's description of the situation as they see it. If a manager, for example, believes that complaints from workers are essentially just the grumblings of a few malcontents, we can start with a discussion about how to deal responsibly with these few individuals. This can lead to a discussion about how to assess the degree to which others may share these individuals' concerns. Furthermore, there are often manifesting events, incidents, or flare-ups that make conflict difficult to deny entirely. Two somewhat opposite approaches to dealing with minimization are often effective—we can align with it or challenge it.

Aligning with minimization means accepting it, working from within the denial framework, and helping people strategize about how to keep the conflict encapsulated, while remaining alert for signs that they may be ready to recognize the dispute's more enduring or deeper elements. People involved in a difficult divorce, for example, often take comfort in the idea that the conflict will soon be over. Sometimes the conclusion of a divorce negotiation leads to a significant and more or less permanent diminishment in conflict, and the hope of this can help people through a difficult period. It can also lead to considerable additional distress if the conflict continues to manifest itself well after the divorce is finalized.

Working with the separating spouses on their immediate concerns and supporting their hope that the intensity of the divorce process will be succeeded by calmer and happier times may be advisable. But it may also be useful to help them at least consider and prepare for the possibility that concluding the process will not put an end to significant conflict. Sometimes this means building ongoing dispute resolution mechanisms into an agreement, but it can also require helping people to develop the negotiation and communication skills they will need over time. It may also mean simply cautioning them against assuming that divorce means closure when we can see obvious signs that in this case it will not.

Aligning with the resistance is not always useful, effective, or even possible, however, and sometimes a more direct (but respectful) challenge to minimization is necessary. (Also see the section later in this chapter on "naming the elephant.") I have frequently had to tell managers and leaders that I believed the conflicts in their organizations were deeper, more extensive, and more intractable than they believed. Typically, those with positions of power and privilege in a system are not as aware of their power and the conflicts that go with it as the less powerful people around them are (Coleman, 2000). Telling people that we believe there is a significant amount of conflict in their settings does not mean that anything will change, that our version of the situation will be accepted, or that the denial will cease, but often such confrontation does give people permission to discuss something that has been bothering them.

When we do confront denial or minimization, we have to be careful not to make the opposite mistake of overstating the severity of the conflict. Although such exaggeration can get someone's attention, in the long run it will lead to a loss of our credibility and will not help people prepare for enduring conflict. Oftentimes

the best approach to minimization is to offer both some alignment with it and some respectful, moderated confrontation of it.
The more aligned we are with disputants' aspirations and goals,
including their hope that a conflict is less intense or toxic than
we might believe it to be, the better able we are to confront their
denial when it is especially destructive.

Misdirection

Misdirection may be the most common form of avoidance facing
conflict specialists. Frequently it goes along with premature problem solving—people avoid a significant conflict by pushing to
resolve a different, perhaps related issue. We are often called on
to help people resolve a conflict that does not seem to be at the
core of the problem—for example, working on Christmas plans
with divorced parents who are unable to communicate about
serious problems their children may be having. Misdirection can
occur around the issue, the people, the context, or the timing.
Sometimes, the misdirection may involve work on real conflicts
about which there are genuine concerns but that are still not the
primary conflict.

Perhaps the most serious form of misdirection we face in working with enduring conflict is the tendency to focus on the transient rather than enduring elements of a conflict. By framing a
conflict in terms of immediate and potentially resolvable issues we
avoid the more fundamental problems that need to be confronted.
An essential focus of this book is to help us and our clients move
past this very powerful form of misdirection and get to the conflict
at the heart of the problems people are having.

Conflict professionals can easily fall into the trap of reinforcing
avoidance through misdirection by taking a conflict at face value
and forging an agreement on the terms presented, thereby supporting the avoidance and perpetuating a problem rather than helping
to resolve it. We are of course not alone in facing this challenge.
Therapists can find themselves focusing on the treatment of an

acting-out adolescent when the real conflict resides in a dysfunctional family system. Lawyers may focus on contractual disputes when the real problems are relationship based.

Sometimes we have no choice but to work on the conflict as presented to us—when we mediate a grievance, for example, we not may have access to larger issues of a hostile work environment or ineffective labor-management communication processes. Sometimes helping people with their smaller, more accessible issues is an important service, but we ought to at least ask whether we are part of a system of avoidance of the more problematic aspect of a conflict.

I have often found it useful when entering into an organizational conflict to refer to the framework articulated by Robert Blake and Jane Mouton in their classic work *Solving Costly Organizational Conflicts* (1984). They argue that the most important conflicts in organizations are those that occur "at the interface" of organizational boundaries—that is between organizational teams, divisions, or levels. But these are also the most difficult conflicts to face and the least open to tangible solutions. People are therefore far more likely to focus on individuals or structures as the source of organizational conflict, rather than on interface issues such as relationships, communication, and trust.

Often, for example, when looking into an organizational conflict, I find people focusing on a particular manager or a single difficult employee. The implication is that if only that person would change or leave, all would be well. I will usually ask people to consider whether this really is the case. Sometimes it is. I once worked with a very troubled organization that was riddled with low morale, stress, and conflict. When the CEO left and a new one was hired, things rapidly improved, and stayed so for many years. Not that there were no conflicts or other issues, but the fundamental problems that had existed really had resided in the communication and decision-making approach taken by the then CEO. More often, however, conflict is widespread and systemic, and the problems with a particular individual are reflections of the systemic problems. Firing a particular supervisor or manager in a business or a particular teacher, principal, or superintendent in a school is not likely to deal with long-term problems of, for example, resources, race relationships, and morale.

Blake and Mouton argue that the second misdirection prevalent in organizations is a tendency to focus on structure rather than relationships. Organizations will go through massive attempts to restructure departments, accountability procedures, or managerial responsibilities in order to deal with conflicts that are in fact about trust, communication, and interpersonal interactions. This can be a very expensive approach to avoidance—restructuring organizations is neither simple nor cheap—and if it is undertaken in service of solving the wrong problem, it can also be an enormous exercise in futility.

When we point out this dynamic to organizations, we are not saying that problems with individuals or structure are unimportant or that they ought not to be dealt with. We are simply suggesting that the organization check out where the problem really lies. This approach can be applied in interpersonal and community contexts as well. Indeed, this tendency to look primarily at people or structures and at the short-term and tangible aspects of conflict can be found in almost any arena of human interaction.

Another concept that is helpful in dealing with misdirection comes from the work of attribution theorists (see Allred, 2000; Jones and Davis, 1965; Kelley, 1967). How people explain others' behavior can lead to the escalation of conflict or to its avoidance. Are others intentionally behaving in a way that is injurious to someone else? Is this part of a consistent pattern? Are they behaving this way because of dispositional factors (they are mean spirited, ill disposed to another, self-centered, cold, or as discussed previously, stupid, crazy, or evil) or situational factors (they had no choice, circumstances dictated their behavior, they had to make a no-win choice, and so forth)? We all have had experiences of choosing, sometimes wavering between, attributions. For example, if I keep you waiting at a restaurant for a luncheon date, you are likely to wonder whether I have done so because I don't care about you, am hopelessly disorganized, am always overcommitted, or have been caught in an unexpected traffic jam or had a genuine emergency to deal with. Your attitude toward my behavior will then reflect what you attribute my lateness to. If you see my behavior as intentional and within my control, you will likely be upset with me. If you believe it was not intentional and due to factors out of my control, you are likely to be more forgiving and even sympathetic.

We can ask clients to consider the attributions they are making. When we ask why someone believes an adversary is behaving in a certain way, we open up a discussion of attribution that we can then use to consider whether misdirection of some sort is occurring. Once a conflict is ascribed to the innate personality or characteristics of another person, it is easy to disclaim all responsibility for what happened and all hope for a constructive engagement. However, if a conflict stems from the circumstances of the interaction, then a different picture of possibilities and responsibilities is painted. It is always important to hear and to acknowledge the attributions that disputants are making, but it's also helpful to ask them to consider other or additional possibilities. In most conflicts, personal characteristics, circumstances, and interactions are all part of the picture.

The line between conflict avoidance and conflict engagement is not always clear, and to some extent all efforts to raise or engage a conflict require finding some issue or person to serve as a focus or representation of the problem. People talk about particular incidents, problem behaviors, specific people, or tangible issues not just because they are avoiding dealing with the core conflicts in their lives, but because it is hard to find the language, conceptual framework, or narrative that addresses these conflicts. So they think of incidents or issues that they can talk about. This may be all the engagement our clients can manage at the moment, but as conflict specialists part of our job is to broaden the scope of conflict that they are able to engage with.

The effort to deal with misdirection is in this respect similar to the challenge of understanding what the core issues in a conflict are (whether conflict avoidance is in play or not) and to articulate these issues in a meaningful and useful way. We do not confront misdirection, so much as explore it with people, consider it with them, and then work with them to understand the real nature of the conflict in which they are involved.

Escalation

The most important question we can raise with people who are escalating a conflict is to ask what kind of conversation or interaction they would like to be having with others. Escalation is sometimes critical to conflict engagement (and in Chapter Six I will discuss how to help people escalate). But escalation should be proportional to the problem and in service of engaging an issue productively rather than shutting it down. If people really want to end all contact, there are generally (though not always) better ways of accomplishing that than through escalation.

We can't always tell whether escalation is being used for avoidance or engagement, but we can always ask people what the situation would look like if a genuine conversation or interaction were to occur—what would be the subject, the focus, the tone, the behavior, and the hoped-for outcome. As with our approach to other forms of avoidance, the hope here is to start a conversation about the issues or feelings being avoided, what other approaches might work, what issues need to be engaged, and what the long-term nature of the challenge is.

In a sense what we are doing is accepting the escalation in terms of its intent, if not the behavior itself, and then asking the disputant to explore that intent and consider alternative approaches. Of course escalation is often emotionally driven.

People escalate because of an onrush of anger or other emotions, and they do so without using the cognitive and rational tools normally at their disposal (Goleman, 1995). In other words, people escalate because their emotions overtake them and not because they have made a conscious decision to escalate to advance their interests in some way (although they may be very well able to rationalize their actions later). They resort to escalation because they feel threatened, cornered, vulnerable, or attacked, and the flight or fight response that is sometimes a functional defensive mechanism when survival is at stake is triggered. But of course, people also escalate (or flee) when survival is not at stake, and in those circumstances it is seldom a useful response and often a harmful one. Escalation as a form of avoidance is fight as a means of flight.

Our challenge in these situations, one that mediators are very familiar with, is to accept and validate the emotion but at the same time bring people back to a more thoughtful approach and by doing this help them to consider what sort of conversation or behavior they would genuinely like to engage in. Disputants may want to minimize all communication and contact. This is often a legitimate goal that we can support, but we have to help them consider whether it is a feasible goal and whether it will genuinely serve their interests. And we need to do this with an eye both to the immediate challenge and the long-term nature of the conflict. Although the best immediate action might be to minimize interaction, we also have to help people think beyond their immediate choices to the longer-term implications of whether and how they escalate a conflict. Consider the following example.

Kirk was a successful businessman and reputed to be a shrewd negotiator. Louise, his ex-wife, was flamboyant and volatile. They shared parenting of their two children, who were about eight and twelve years old and who spent approximately equal time in each home. They were referred to me by their attorneys, who were frustrated that every single postdivorce decision seemed to cause histrionics and threats of court actions and restraining orders.

Any issue or decision could provoke an escalated interchange. A typical pattern was for Louise to request a variation in their normal routine and for Kirk to resist. Louise would then get very upset, and Kirk would threaten to end all communication or to file for a change that would give him full custody. Escalation would ensue, and direct communication would cease. For both Kirk and Louise, escalation was a means of control and of defense. They did not want to engage with each other, and I could well understand why—their conversations quickly devolved into shouting matches and threats. But they were facing at least ten more years of joint parenting. And they were taking a nonsustainable approach to conflict.

We agreed not to focus on immediate issues but to look at the long-term pattern of escalation (the enduring conflict). I asked them to describe what an effective conversation about a contentious issue (I gave an example) would look like. At first they focused on what the other person would need to do differently, but I encouraged them to talk about the nature of the conversation and how each of them could act differently. I then asked them whether there was part of such a discussion that they did not want to have. What came out, separately at first, but then in joint conversations, was that they did not want to experience reasonable conversations because they were afraid of the feelings this might generate and the questions it might raise about why they had separated. They needed to provoke each other into escalated behavior to justify their decision to separate.

Conversations like this don't once and for all end the use of escalation or completely prepare people to stay with conflict over the long term. But they are still important, and over time, with assistance when necessary, achieving this type of clarity about the particular function of escalation can be critical to helping people engage in constructive interactions about enduring conflicts.

Premature Problem Solving

Conflict specialists are particularly vulnerable to premature problem solving because we have made resolving conflicts our purpose and calling. Our language and much of our common wisdom is geared toward resolving conflict, and the idea that we should help people deepen and sometimes perpetuate conflict does not come naturally. However, as I have discussed, we often contribute to the perpetuation of a destructive conflict when we try to solve it too quickly and hence too superficially.

For all of us therefore, the first step in dealing with this type of avoidance is to raise our consciousness about our own tendencies in this area. Our biggest challenge is to learn to focus on the nature of the conflict, the underlying needs and values driving it, and its systemic and structural roots, before we focus on what can be done to fix the problem. This also provides us with our best opportunity to open new doors of intervention for ourselves and offer more meaningful service to our clients. We need an effective approach to slowing down people's urge to rush to a solution and refocusing their attention on trying to understand what is really going on.

I frequently ask disputants who are rushing to a solution three questions:

What problem is your proposal trying to address?

Is that the most significant issue that needs to be addressed (and if not, what is)?

How well does your proposal address that issue?

All these questions are asked from within the problem-solving mode—they are about solving a problem rather than exploring conflict. In other words, here too I am starting where the disputants are. But the impact of these questions is to slow the process down in order to understand the nature of the problem better. This is the great value of an interest-based approach—when it is done in a thorough and committed way, it moves the focus from outcome to understanding. Exploring the interests or the deeper level of needs behind proposed solutions can often open up this larger discussion (though not if interests are used primarily as a tool for fashioning attractive proposals).

One reason to ask these three questions is to ascertain the purpose of reaching a resolution. Once we are clear that the disputants' focus on problem solving is in essence a form of avoidance, we have to choose (again) whether to go with that avoidance or challenge it. We may choose to assist the problem-solving process, both because it will provide opportunities to open up a discussion about the real nature of the conflict and because of our commitment to client self-determination.

But another choice is to ask people to consider whether they are avoiding the real issue. We can do this with a deeper exploration of their needs (as discussed earlier), or we can ask them to envision an agreement along the lines they are proposing and to consider what issues will still remain along all three dimensions of conflict (behavioral, emotional, and attitudinal).

Sometimes the best advice we can give is simply to slow down. If a problem-solving process is effective today, it probably will work tomorrow. A situation that requires that we nail down an agreement or lose the opportunity may occur when there are structural time frames that can't be altered (a looming court date, elections, the expiration of an option to purchase, a school enrolment deadline), but this occurs far less often than people assert. In fact, when people emphasize the importance of an agreement in the absence of clear and inflexible deadlines, that is one clue that conflict avoidance may be in play. Even when there are clear deadlines (as may have been the case with, for example, President Clinton's rush to conclude a Palestinian-Israeli settlement in his final months in office), it is sometimes more important to delve further into a conflict than to seize the moment and arrive only at an ephemeral resolution.

NAMING THE ELEPHANT

Sometimes we can go with the resistance, sometimes we can engage people in a discussion of the enduring nature of the conflict by the kind of questions we ask, and sometimes we can wait for events to encourage the disputants' realization that avoidance will not end a conflict. But often we have no effective alternative but to be direct and to assert that we think people are avoiding a conflict and even to suggest what we think they may be avoiding. We have, in other words, to name the elephant that is on the table but that everyone is ignoring.

There is no magical approach to doing this, although short, direct, and with empathy is usually the most effective route to take. When we name what we think might be the elephant (the aspect of conflict being avoided), we usually accomplish two things: we help people begin to face the issue and we release energy that has been wrapped up in denial.

Consider some of these statements, each of which I have made in one form or another many times in conflicts. The most frequent response has been a relaxation of the tension in the room.

"You two profoundly disagree with each other, and you probably will continue to disagree after we finish."

"I don't think the two of you like each other very much right now."

"I think it is hard to agree on anything because you just don't trust each other."

"No matter what we agree about here today, relationships will continue to be tense, communication a challenge, and trust low."

"This is a far broader problem than we have the power to solve."

"I think you feel fairly hopeless about things getting better."

"Some of what may be going on could be about race [or 'gender' or 'age' or the like]."

"I think there is something that we are not talking about [or 'that we are avoiding' or 'dancing around'], and I wonder what it is."

The art is in how we say these things, because if these statements come out of nowhere, are posed as challenges, are made in a resigned or helpless fashion, or come across as patronizing, they will not help. But if we offer these remarks as observations that arise out of our interactions in a tentative, frank, realistic, empathic, and yet hopeful tone, in alignment with the people we are interacting with, then I think we will often succeed in giving people a choice to at least recognize their most troublesome concerns and to consider what they have been choosing not to deal with.

Alex was the president of the union local representing the police force in a midsized city. For several years he was embroiled in a series of conflicts with John, the police chief. The issues related to overtime assignments, promotions, shift rotations, and performance reviews, but they could have been anything. An inescapable part of the conflict was that the two men clearly disliked and distrusted each other, but they could not avoid each other.

After a number of rather fruitless sessions working on the identified issues they wanted to resolve, I looked at them both and said, "We are not making much progress here and I think I know why." They both looked at me, curious. "The problem is that the two of you don't trust each other or like each other, and no matter what goes wrong, your first instinct is always to blame each other." "It's not personal," Alex argued. "Seems pretty personal to me," I said, "although there are plenty of workplace issues you disagree about too. Each of you is very good at thinking about what the other person has to do differently, but not so good at thinking about what you have to do. If you want to make progress, that is where you have to start."

This did not lead to an in-depth interchange about their feelings toward each other. But they did acknowledge that they did not trust each other and that this was getting in the way—and could continue to get in the way—and they also acknowledged that they had to try to focus more on the task and less on each other. Only by getting to the level of conflict that was very personal could they put that level aside and struggle over what they really did have to fight about.

Naming the elephant can be a powerful tool, but we have to use it carefully. If we misfire, moving way beyond where people are ready to go, then we may increase anxiety rather than diminish it. I was once at a conference planning meeting in which there was considerable tension over how much emphasis to put on presentations from relative newcomers and to some extent unknowns and how much to put on presentations by recognized (predominantly white) leaders in the field who might draw people to attend but who were frequent presenters. A well-meaning but perhaps not very skillful participant stood up and said: "Let's just call this for what it is. This is about race and the racial tensions in this organization. That's OK, we can talk about it, but we all know that is why we are having such a hard time."

He did confront a problem that people may have been avoiding, but he did so by leaping into an issue that called for a more incremental approach, and he could well have been projecting his own issues onto the group. At that point some people just checked out of the conversation. Others got agitated, and no one was willing to talk about race. It took the very skillful intervention of two mediators to get the conversation back on track.

So we should not assume that naming the elephant we perceive is always appropriate, accurate, or effective. We always have to be sensitive to how people may respond to this kind of directness. Some people will want to challenge us. Some will need time to reflect about this alone. Some will want to fix the problem immediately—even though that may not be possible. We don't name the elephant or make any other intervention in a vacuum. Everything we do in dealing with conflict has to be interactive and iterative, and we should always approach the naming process carefully, incrementally, and with humility.

OPENING THE DOOR TO ENGAGEMENT

We cannot nor should we make people engage in a conflict (or any aspect of a conflict) that they have chosen to avoid. But we can open the door to constructive engagement very wide so that walking through it will be less daunting. Usually, this means finding an effective way to frame the conflict (discussed in the next chapter) and offering a series of smaller steps that people can take to begin to address their concerns. It also requires creating, to the extent that we can, a safe environment for taking these steps and helping people envision what engaging in the conflict might look like.

Where we believe there is avoidance, we can identify the nature of the avoidance and respond to it. Where there is denial or minimization, we can help people gradually address the larger and more serious nature of the conflict. Where there is misdirection, we can suggest that people consider a different focus or framing of the conflict. Where there is avoidant escalation, we can help people begin to use more appropriate forms of power and to understand this type of escalation for what it is—avoidance. And where there is premature problem solving, we can encourage people to delay problem solving or redefine it as a step toward engagement rather than an end point.

The key to moving parties from avoidance to engagement is to respect where they are, to meet them there, and to encourage them to take incremental steps—to name the conflict differently, to try bringing up the more difficult issues, and to practice the type of constructive and engaged conversation that they might want to think about having with others. We can help people think through the pros and cons of bringing up the most difficult issue or area of disagreement. Sometimes, as shown in the example of the racial issues between the manager and the supervisor, people will chose to stay away from the most sensitive part of the conflict. At other times, as in the instance of the police and union leaders, they may cautiously bring difficult issues up, and as they find they can talk about them, they may become increasingly encouraged (and emboldened) to go deeper into an area of conflict that they had been spending considerable energy to avoid.

AVOIDING AND ENGAGING IN ENDURING CONFLICT

When we work with people on staying with conflict, almost everything we do involves helping them to deal with various forms of avoidance and to accept the challenge of engaging with the enduring aspects of conflict on a sustainable basis. Over the life of a long-term conflict people will often choose an avoidant stance and perhaps only occasionally genuinely engage. Seldom is it possible to make a single lasting choice to engage in an enduring conflict. The decision to avoid or engage is one that will have to be made over and over.

Depending on our means of access to the problem, our challenge as conflict specialists can be individual (case based) or systemic or both. We can help people face the enduring elements of their conflict at a particular point in time, or we can assist in setting up systems for engagement that deal with the tendency toward avoidance over time. Many conflicts require both a case-based, time-specific approach to intervention and a systemic ongoing approach. For example when we look at the problem of sexual harassment in a workplace, the ongoing challenge is to see each individual case in the context of the larger workplace culture. As a result of our work on a given case, we may be able to help those in a decision-making capacity face the broader, deeper, and longer nature of this problem. There are also times when we are able to encourage and assist people in setting up ongoing processes, such as review, monitoring, or assessment groups that can regularly look at the issue of harassment in the workplace and provide feedback and recommendations for addressing it.

Everyone uses avoidance to deal with stress and difficulties in life, but an excessive reliance on avoidance gets in the way of dealing with enduring conflict. As people learn to stay with conflict, they become better at facing what they have been avoiding, understanding it, and naming it. In the next chapter, I will focus on how we can help people frame the enduring nature of conflict in a constructive way. When disputants include the enduring aspect of conflict in the conflict narrative that they build to make sense of their situation, they have taken an important step away from an avoidant posture and toward accepting the challenge of staying with conflict.

4

Working the Conflict Narrative

*People grow up amid a multitude of competing narratives
that help shape how they see themselves and others. They
tell stories about themselves and about others. They act
both out of and into these stories, shaping the direction of
the ongoing plot as they do so. Descriptions of problems are
typically told in narrative terms. Such problem narratives
have often been rehearsed and elaborated over and over
again by participants in a conflict.*
                          Gerald Monk and John Winslade, 2000, p. 3

How people approach conflict determines and is determined
by the narratives they use to describe and conduct conflict.
Polarized narratives promote polarizing interactions. Rigid narratives encourage rigid approaches to conflict. Narratives reflect disputants' understandings, assumptions, values, and fears, as well as
the social and cultural context of the dispute. Although narratives
can evolve, they can also be remarkably impervious to change.
Suggesting a new story can make an immense difference, but only
when people are ready to look at things in a different way and are
at the center of the narrative reconstruction process.

In this chapter I consider how conflict professionals can understand the nature of disputants' narrative frames and help disputants incorporate the most difficult and enduring aspects of the
conflict into their narratives. An essential part of this challenge is
to help people construct narratives that do not exclude the vital
elements of other disputants' stories. Our ultimate goal is to help
each disputant evolve his or her narrative in a way that fosters a
constructive and durable process of engagement.

THE NATURE OF CONFLICT NARRATIVES

Conflict narratives are constructs created to describe the events and characteristics of a dispute. People create or adopt conflict narratives to explain and give meaning to their conflict experience. Until a narrative of some kind is attached to a series of experiences, people's awareness of the experience is fragmented and even chaotic, but narratives are also limiting in that they guide our consciousness about events in a certain direction (see, for example, Monk and Winslade, 2000; Levi-Strauss, 1963; Berger and Luckmann, 1966; Lederach, 2005). At the same time, narratives are rooted in social experience and are socially constructed, and as such they can be reconstructed.

One of the most powerful elements of a narrative is the time frame implied and the dramatic flow invoked. A narrative that suggests a clear beginning, a natural and linear course of events, and a decisive conclusion frames people's thinking about their role and purpose in conflict in a particular way, one that can easily obfuscate the depth of an issue or the enduring nature of the conflict people face. But these are the type of narratives that people often cling to and that mediators generally adopt because there is something comforting and familiar about this kind of story.

Our task in enduring conflict is to help people develop and become comfortable with a story that is less clear and straightforward but that may guide people to a more productive approach to their problem. For instance, a tenured faculty member in a university academic department might offer various descriptions of a conflict he is having with another professor. Here are two examples:

1. Professor B is on a power trip. He delights in intimidating students and harassing new faculty, especially those who don't become his acolytes. He has been especially rude to me and his egregious attacks on my graduate students are unacceptable.

I am going to let him know once and for all that I will not accept this kind of behavior.

2. Professor B is on a power trip. I don't like the way he treats new faculty, and I really resent his attitude toward my graduate assistants. He and I really do not get along—we just don't like each other very much. Unless I luck out and he takes a position elsewhere, I am going to have to figure out how to deal with him because he and I are likely to be in this department for many years.

Neither of these stories is correct or incorrect. They just reflect different (although not inconsistent) ways of thinking about a problem, and these differences have implications for the approaches the speaker will take to the conflict. In the first narrative the key phrase is "once and for all." The implication is that by taking decisive action, this conflict can be brought to a conclusion. Maybe there is a way for the speaker and Professor B to go through a process (a facilitated dialogue perhaps) that can permanently change their relationship, and maybe over time their relationship will evolve into something different (and better, one hopes). Furthermore, there is nothing wrong with hoping for a change of this nature, but there are consequences to thinking of this conflict as transient, if stubborn.

The key phrase in the second statement is "figure out how to deal." The implication of this narrative is that the enduring aspect of this conflict has to be faced and that any approach that can diminish the immediate conflict will have to be part of an ongoing effort to manage what is by nature a forced, long-term connection so that perhaps the interaction will genuinely improve over time. In addition, even if the intensity of this conflict diminishes, or if Professor B leaves, dealing with difficult colleagues is a frequent reality of academic life requiring an approach to dealing with conflictual relationships over time. (A famous comment on this reality, attributed to Henry Kissinger, is that "university politics are vicious precisely because the stakes are so small.")

One narrative guides the disputants to a short-term, decisive intervention that might lead to an improved or to a severed relationship. The other narrative might lead them to an effort to negotiate ongoing guidelines for interaction, communication procedures, dispute resolution processes, and monitoring systems. When we consider narrative frames, we are not deciding which is "right" or "good," but we are very much interested in the implications of different narratives and the window they provide into the thinking of disputants.

One important task of conflict specialists is to help disputants arrive at an effective way to understand and deal with their conflict. This requires that we consider the narrative used to explain the conflict and that we help people work with the narrative to support constructive engagement. When dealing with enduring conflict, this means working to incorporate the enduring elements of the conflict into the narrative, in a hopeful (but realistic) way. This does not mean abandoning efforts to work on immediate conflicts or problems, but it does mean finding a way to understand and frame those immediate issues in terms of the long-term challenges that people face. We have to learn the art of framing the conflict for staying with conflict.

CONFLICT NARRATIVES AND CONFLICT BEHAVIOR

People experience and express conflict along three dimensions: behavioral, emotional, and cognitive (Mayer, 2000). We often describe the course of conflict as if it consists primarily of a set of behaviors, but the emotional and cognitive dimensions are also critical. Looking at the interaction among these dimensions is essential to understanding the dynamics of conflict. People behave in a certain way because of how they feel and how they understand a situation, but their feelings and understanding are influenced by the results of their behavior (and the behavior of others) and their need to make sense of their behavior and its consequences. So although we can approach conflict behavior directly, our intervention is likely to be superficial and short-lived unless we also address the cognitive and emotional dimensions. Our most direct route to dealing with the cognitive dimension lies with the narratives that people have constructed. Some of the most innovative approaches to conflict, notably narrative mediation (Monk and Winslade, 2000) and restorative justice (Johnstone and Van Ness, 2007), have been designed for this purpose. That is, they are intended to help people arrive at a fundamentally new way of understanding the nature of the conflict and themselves as disputants.

To help people stay with conflict we have to contend with very powerful narratives, promoted by social norms about conflict and by the conflict resolution field itself, that assume the outcome of a successful engagement with conflict is the end of the conflict. Conflict may end through agreement, cooperation, defeat, or victory, but the alternative to its termination is often viewed as stalemate, impasse, or deadlock. In other words, unless conflict ends, the assumption is something is wrong. The most popular conflict styles inventory, the Thomas-Kilmann instrument (Thomas and Kilmann, 1974), poses five styles (collaboration, compromise, competition, accommodation, and avoidance) and all are oriented toward either avoiding or ending a conflict. These narratives are not wrong, but they are limiting.

Our challenge, therefore, is to help people expand the scope of their narrative, which can in turn open new approaches to conflict. We do this by attending directly to the conflict narrative and also by helping people draw new and different lessons from their experiences in conflict and their interactions with each other. We work with individuals in reconstructing their personal narratives, and we also work with multiple parties to co-create a shared narrative, one that adequately incorporates enough of each person's narrative so that effective communication can take place. For example, we might work with the faculty member in the earlier illustration to tell a story that allows for the possibility that his relationship with Professor B might change for the better, while also understanding that conflicts will still arise. We might also work on helping him incorporate even a little bit of Professor B's story into his so that, for example, he recognizes that one source of the conflict is a genuine difference between them about appropriate expectations of junior faculty.

CHARACTERISTICS OF CONFLICT NARRATIVES

Conflict narratives can be constructed in ways that open or close the door to cooperation, communication, negotiation, empathy, problem solving, escalation, and engagement. Narratives typically follow a certain dramatic structure wherein people are assigned archetypal roles and action is seen as increasing in intensity, reaching a crisis of some sort, and then resolving. Not all narrative has to be constructed this way (see, for example, Le Guinn, 1998, 2004; Johnson, 2005), but this is the most common narrative form. To work with the way a conflict is framed and to assist disputants in finding a constructive approach to its enduring elements, we have to consider the nature of the operational narrative. Let's examine some of the key characteristics of narrative construction and framing.

Victim, Villain, and Hero Dynamics

An important clue to a narrative's construction can be found in the assignment of key dramatic roles. Typically, people in conflict see themselves as either a victim or a hero (or both) and their antagonists as villains. Questioning this characterization is often an important first step in changing how people think about conflict (Harper, 2004). Asking disputants, for example, how they view each other, can sometimes lead to an interesting discussion of dramatic roles and the conflict narrative. Often we can pose a question that in essence suggests there is enough of the victim role for everyone to share in it. Or we can cast the problem as the villain and all those who are struggling with it as either heroes or victims. Labor and management in a fading industry, for example, can sometimes understand that the source of their problems is not each other and that they are all in their own ways trying to combat a difficult reality.

Often in divorce mediations we see a struggle for the victim role, as each party strives mightily to cast himself or herself as the victim and the other spouse as the villain. Often the way through this involves bringing the children into the narrative. They can sometimes occupy a jointly defined *victim space* or at the very least challenge the simplistic victim-villain-hero story that has been presented. Of course, the fact that the structure of the narrative fits into this classic dramatic framework may also mean that one party is indeed acting in a more destructive manner than another.

Integrative and Distributive Approaches

Disputants tend to view conflicts through a distributive lens, particularly when emotions are high. That is, people view conflict in terms of what concessions they can wrest from others and what they will have to cede to others. The integrative elements—how mutual gains can be achieved—are often lost as a result. This insight is the foundation of the most popular contemporary schools of thought on negotiation and conflict analysis (Fisher and Ury, 1981; Lax and Sebenius, 2006; Thomas and Kilmann, 1974; Shell, 2000; Walton, Cutcher-Gershenfeld, and McKersie, 1994). Purely distributive stories can seem hopeless and can reinforce adversarial tactics. Purely integrative narratives can seem naïve and unrealistic. What's more, integrative narratives can seem less gripping and motivating (there are a lot of courtroom dramas centered on win-lose outcomes but virtually no mediation shows).

Working with people to develop a narrative that incorporates both the integrative and the distributive dimensions can prepare them to confront challenges in a more flexible way. An experienced divorce lawyer and mother of three once explained her approach to counseling clients to me in a way that reflected this: "People come to me and ask for sole custody all the time. They usually want to know how to cut the other parent out of any significant parenting role. I say to them, 'You gotta be kidding. Do you know what it's like to raise children alone? Beware what you ask for, you just might get it. You are going to want all the help you can get. We just have to make sure you don't drive yourselves or the kids crazy in the process.'"

Whether one agrees with this specific advice or not, the change of focus from "how much can I get and how little can I give" to "what kind of help can we give each other and how can we do it without driving each other or the kids crazy" clearly shows a shift from a distributive to an integrative framework. A narrative that focuses the problem entirely on the other person ("he never paid any attention to parenting before and then he left") and seeks an outcome based on one side's gaining at the expense of another ("I want the kids to live with me; she can visit as long as she does not disrupt their lives") is a distributive narrative. One that describes the problem in mutual terms ("we never learned how to communicate") and looks for progress in terms of mutual gains ("we have to learn how to work together to give our children what they need") is an integrative narrative. Once the integrative challenge is addressed, distributive decisions about the role each parent will play in child rearing will still have to be made. Constructive narratives need to incorporate the realistic challenges and hopes along both dimensions.

Internal and External Approaches

Does the conflict arise from within individuals or from the external environment or system? This question raises a distinction similar to the difference between a situational and a dispositional attribution (discussed in Chapter Three). People embroiled in an emotionally charged conflict are likely to see the problem as residing in the behavior, personality, and morality of those with whom they are in conflict. But this conflict might also be understood in terms of social, cultural, and systemic roots. Is a conflict over whether to build a huge retail outlet in a community about the people ("naïve, stuck-in-the-past community activists" versus "grasping, rapacious, corporate raiders") or is it about the economic and market forces that militate in one direction and the social and cultural values that promote another outcome and that are inevitably challenged by these forces?

Exclusive and Inclusive Approaches

Sometimes when listening to the different parties to a conflict, I wonder if they are both living on the same planet. Their stories seem so entirely different, and there is no room in one party's story for the reality or perspective of another's view. Monk and Winslade (2000) call this a "totalizing description." These exclusive narratives do not allow for the possibility that other histories, perspectives, or realities are possible or legitimate. We see this in the extremely different narratives continually propagated in the Middle East, for example. These exclusive narratives are present in most serious conflicts.

An inclusive narrative, one that allows for a variety of different perspectives or histories, is usually far harder to create than an exclusive one but is ultimately essential to a constructive engagement process. Working with people so they can allow even a little space for another's narrative can be immensely important in promoting a more effective approach to conflict. The development of inclusive narratives played a major role in a meeting a colleague and I conducted between a teacher's union and a school administration in preparation for an upcoming collective bargaining process:

The antagonism between the teacher's union and the district leadership was intense and had been growing for years. During the last contract negotiations the teachers felt that management had lied to them about the district's financial situation, in particular about projected revenues from real estate taxes, and as a result had manipulated them into accepting minimal raises. After the revenues had proven to be greater than expected, the teachers felt that the contract should have been reopened, but it was not. They now wanted to make up for what they thought were three years of being "jerked around." The main source of their anger was the school superintendent, whom they saw as weak and manipulative, and the financial director, whom they thought was arrogant and dishonest.

The district leaders had a different story to tell. They felt that given the tenuous financial situation the district was in, they had gone out of their way to avoid layoffs and salary cuts. They had been able to do this only by postponing extremely important capital improvement projects, and they felt they had made it clear that even if revenues were slightly better than projected, they would have to fund the delayed infrastructure improvements before salary raises. So when the revenues were better, they felt compelled to use the excess revenues for the improvement projects. They were hopeful that the economy in the district might improve further, but prospects for this were tenuous at best. Teachers were just going to have to face the realities of the situation.

My colleague and I asked both sides to tell their stories, and asked that the parties on each side try to understand the other side's story, even if they did not agree with it. We offered the people on each side a chance to react to what they heard, and each group proceeded to denigrate the other's version of what had happened. Then we asked two questions that changed the discussion: "Can you accept, whether you agree with this version of events or not, that those telling them do genuinely view the situation this way?" and, "What part of the other story can you accept?" Although these were potentially dangerous questions, the process of answering them began to focus the discussion on the shared narrative space rather than the exclusive space. This led to a discussion of how the two sides' different perceptions might have developed, what might be done to check perceptions in the next round, and an acknowledgment of the various sacrifices that had been made and pressures decision makers were under.

Fatalistic and Hopeful Approaches

Narrative structure can also be understood in terms of dramatic theory (Hale, 1998). The simplest distinction for our purposes is between tragic (or fatalistic) and comedic (or hopeful) narratives. This contrast is more complex than distinguishing between sad and funny. Fatalistic frames imply that the course of the conflict is something disputants have no control over. Either because of fate, fatal flaws, tragic errors, or the acts of higher powers, the primary actor in a tragedy is in some sense doomed and not in control of what happens. Hopeful frames imply more agency, more choice, and a greater potential for improvement through the decisions and actions of the participants.

We can gain insight into this aspect of the narrative frame by listening to whether people are telling a story that implies they have the ability to make things better or to determine the course of events or a story that implies they have no control over what happens. Constructive engagement does not require a purely hopeful frame, but when people are fatalistic and hopeless, engaging at all, much less staying with conflict over time, may seem impossible or pointless to them.

When conflicts are described as ancient (as those in the Middle East, Kosovo, and Northern Ireland have been), the implication is that they are deeply rooted in forces beyond anyone's control—a very fatalistic frame indeed. To suggest that efforts to deal with them must contend with their cultural and historical roots, implies that they may be difficult and enduring but they can be addressed—if not a completely hopeful frame, at least one with hopeful elements.

Outcome and Process Approaches

Traditional descriptions of the construction of dramas generally pose a five-stage structure: initial problem or conflict, rising action, crisis, falling action, and resolution. (Gustav Freytag, 1863, described a system of dramatic structure that became known as Freytag's pyramid, and Aristotle's Poetics, composed around 350 B.C.E., described the tragic genre.) This format is characteristic of many conflict narratives and implies a march toward an outcome. However, narratives can also be process focused, or nonlinear. That is, they can focus on how things transpire, how relationships take place, or the nature of the interaction rather than the direction and outcome of the action (Johnson, 2005). Consider two extremely successful and beloved musicals—Cats and West Side Story. Cats (based on the poetry of T. S. Eliot), although certainly having dramatic high points, does not result in a clear outcome or conclusion and has a story line that is more about interaction and personality than a linear plot. The key is the system of relationships that are evolving but ongoing and the interactions among the characters. In contrast, West Side Story (based on the story of Romeo and Juliet) offers a classically linear course of action that almost inexorably leads to a tragic outcome.

When we listen to the narratives of people in conflict, the degree to which they are outcome focused versus process focused or conflict centered versus relationship centered is a clue to the work that needs to be done to help these disputants with the enduring elements of conflict. If a narrative is to be a productive basis for staying with a conflict, the process, or interactive relationship, involved in the conflict has to be a significant part of that narrative, even if it also retains a focus on a positive outcome. It is understandable, for example, that people involved in conflict in the Middle East are looking for an end point, and specifically one that offers an end to violence, a resolution of all outstanding issues, and a peace treaty outlining how this is going to happen. But if people remain limited by or caught in that type of narrative, it may actually be harder than it would be under other narratives to diminish the violence and address some of the problems that the Middle East faces. A narrative that instead poses the challenge of creating more connections and engaging in productive long-term interaction is probably a healthier foundation for peacemaking efforts.

FRAMING VARIABLES

Our main goal when working with conflict narratives is to help people expand their stories to allow space for other narratives and to incorporate the enduring elements of conflict. We also want to help disputants develop some confidence that they can successfully stay with conflict and that this is not a negative or hopeless place to be but an empowering and hopeful way of understanding their circumstances. In order to do all this, we have to look in more detail at exactly how conflicts are framed.

Four variables in the way a conflict is characterized offer opportunities for framing conflict to help people stay with conflict. These variables are depth, breadth, length, and conflict dimension. We can work with each of these variables to help disputants get a handle on the enduring elements of conflict. Each variable can contribute to defining that zone in which engagement needs to occur—in other words, where the conflict really "lives."

Depth

Is the conflict characterized in a superficial way ("just a spat," for example) that avoids the significant issue or is labeled as such a profound issue ("basic philosophy of life," for example) that there seems no way to engage it? Questions that go beyond the parties' opening positions or superficial characterizations of interests and get at the deeper levels of motivation can help us explore this. Below every interest lies another interest and below every need lies a deeper need—at some level we will arrive at the place at which the conflict seems alive and real. We cannot determine this by ourselves, but exploring this in partnership with disputants can be extremely useful.

Consider the following dialogue from a mediation between two neighbors concerning a fence that one had erected, blocking the other neighbor's view. The mediator is talking with the neighbor who erected the fence:

MEDIATOR: Why was it that you wanted to erect this fence?

NEIGHBOR A: I wanted some privacy so that they were not staring into my patio every time they walked onto their deck.

MEDIATOR: Why did you decide you needed it to be at that height? [*The height was a big concern for Neighbor B.*]

NEIGHBOR A: That just seemed like the right height to me.

MEDIATOR: [*Pauses.*] Can you tell me more about that?

NEIGHBOR A: Well their new house is so tall that I thought it would be OK for me to build a tall fence.

MEDIATOR: The new house is a problem?

NEIGHBOR A: They just moved in here and built this house out to the setback, and they made it so tall it looms over us. They never talked to us about this or considered what it would be like for us—and now they complain when we build a fence for privacy.

Perhaps we have now reached the depth at which this conflict really exists, but maybe not. We only can tell by how people react when we try to investigate this level.

MEDIATOR: As you see it, is there an issue about the new house that they built that we need to talk about?

NEIGHBOR A: What good will that do? It's already built.

This is the point at which we have at least identified the relationship issue that these neighbors appear to be avoiding, one that could have long-term implications for them.

The mediator now has the choice of probing the relationship issue further or retreating to the issue of the fence. Or perhaps the issue is not the way the new house came to be built but the attitudes or values about community relations that it represents. We are often faced with the decision of how deep to go in trying to understand and frame the conflict. We can stay too shallow (just the fence) or go too deep asking, for example, how this decision triggers feelings about the use of power in each of their families of origin. When we arrive at the right level at which to work, important discussions about enduring issues can take place. Of course, sometimes the operative level for one party is the wrong level for another party, and then a negotiation about how to work between the two levels is needed.

Breadth

Conflicts can be defined too broadly or too narrowly for productive engagement. A workplace dispute between a manager and an employee can be viewed as a single instance of a tense interaction around a specific issue, one of many such interactions between the two, or as an example of a more general workplace conflict that exists among all employees and managers in the organization. (It can also be defined at various levels of depth—depending on whether it is about how overtime is allocated, how decisions are made, how communications occur, or how trust and respect function or fail to function, for example.) Often, because of the structure of grievance mechanisms, conflicts about broad issues become grievances about specific incidents, but if those broad concerns are left out of the process, then resolving the particular grievance may accomplish little. However, it is also possible to define an issue far too broadly, as a means of avoiding the most poignant conflict, as I observed when facilitating a discussion about workplace relations:

"Communication here is awful," I was told. "No one tells you what is going on, nobody cares about what employees think, and managers treat us like servants." In other words, relations between managers and employees were really bad, and that is why I was asked to facilitate a discussion about morale and communication for this team of financial specialists. Upon further investigation, however, I found that all the conflicts seemed to revolve around one supervisor and a long-term employee. And their relationship, which had once been quite good, seemed to have gone sour a couple of years earlier. The employee was experiencing a personal crisis, and the supervisor, in an effort to be supportive had, perhaps inadvertently, let the rest of the department know about the crisis. The supervisor and the employee had never talked about this interaction. When they finally did, they seemed to be in a much better place with each other, and so were all the others in the department.

The question faced in this situation was how broadly to define the conflict. Was the focus on the broader issue of communication essentially an avoidance of the tension between two strong personalities, or was the focus on their particular dispute a way of avoiding looking at widespread problems in the organization (or both)? Was this in fact an enduring conflict masquerading as a transient one, or as sometimes occurs, a transient conflict masquerading as enduring one? We can help people hone in on the most poignant aspect of a conflict, the one that they most need to confront over time, by exploring the problem or conflict from several angles and in different sizes and then ascertaining the reactions we get. When we run into resistance, we ought to at least take note of it, even if we decide to "go with the resistance." It may be that the resistance represents an attempt to avoid the most important but anxiety-provoking formulation, or it may be that we are simply barking up the wrong tree. Conversely, we may get a response that indicates we have arrived at a formulation that reflects the core issues that people are facing.

Length

Of particular concern when looking at enduring conflict are the time frames that people put around a conflict. Is it all part of the past? Is it a one-time occurrence? Has it gone on forever? Is it endless?

I am often impressed by how readily people dismiss the possibility of progress occurring in the Middle East by arguing that the conflict has been going on for 2,000 years and more—the implication being that not much can be done about conflict that is that rooted in ancient history. As discussed in Chapter Two, the historical roots of this conflict are extremely significant. They can readily be traced back to around 1900, with the most essential history beginning in 1948. That in itself is a long time, but it is modern history not ancient history. Framing the conflict in terms of thousands of years may underscore its drama but does not guide us to a productive framework for thinking about it nor a practical approach to staying with it.

Our task is to help people establish a productive time frame so that effective work can be done. We have to consider whether to point to the potential for a definitive conclusion to a conflict or to maintain a focus on its ongoing elements. Our tendency, as I have discussed, is to gravitate toward a linear narrative with the goal of resolution. Instead, when dealing with enduring conflict we need to help people frame the conflict in terms of both the ongoing process and the more immediate tasks or problems to be addressed.

Dimension

People generally characterize conflict in behavioral terms because that is the most tangible dimension and the one most amenable to problem solving. But, as I discussed earlier in this chapter, conflict has two other critical dimensions as well—cognitive and emotional (Mayer, 2000). Often we can help people look at the enduring elements of conflict by suggesting they look at a different dimension of the conflict (or a different combination of dimensions). We naturally and unconsciously do this all the time. When people seem stuck because they don't trust someone, we suggest looking at behaviors, guarantees, monitoring provisions, and consequences—that is we substitute behavioral considerations for attitudinal or cognitive framing around trust. Similarly, we may substitute cognitive framing for a focus on behavior. When we are dealing with divorced parents who are arguing about every minor alteration in the visiting plan (behavioral), we might ask them to talk about how they think (cognitive) they ought to relate to each other. Every time we change the language we use, moving from what people are doing to how they are thinking or to how they are feeling, we are refocusing on a different dimension of the conflict.

These variables can guide us to a more thoughtful and intentional approach to helping people frame their conflicts. With this approach we can guide people to a more operational and useful awareness of the enduring aspects of conflict. This is not a one-time effort. Intentional and thoughtful framing is a challenge throughout the life of a conflict.

TECHNIQUES FOR LONG-TERM FRAMING

When people operate from a narrative of conflict that incorporates long-term elements along with short-term tasks, that is not simply outcome focused but includes process considerations, that is hopeful and realistic, that is flexible enough to allow space for other people's narratives, and that incorporates both the distributive and integrative approaches to conflict, they are best poised to stay with conflict. By working with people on the depth, breadth, and length with which the conflict is framed and by considering the interplay of the behavioral, emotional, and cognitive dimensions of conflict, we can help people develop a constructive and powerful narrative.

But it is easier to say this than do it. Working with people on their narratives and their fundamental framing of a conflict requires more than simply reframing statements or suggesting a new way of looking at conflict. Our efforts require repeated engagement with the people involved, working from within their original narratives, and using the system of conflict interaction to build altered or new narrative frames. Six approaches can be helpful here: naming, deconstructing, reconstructing, substituting, seizing new frames, and working with metaphors.

Naming

Naming the frame that disputants are using and discussing its implications are often the first steps and sometimes the only steps needed in reconstructing a narrative. By helping people to articulate an operative frame, we can encourage them to consider for themselves how to move to a different narrative.

In the dispute between the neighbors about the fence, the mediator could have said: "As I hear it, you are saying this is a dispute about the location, size, and design of the fence, and that if we settle that, your conflict will be resolved." The mediator could also have commented that this view implied that the dispute was not about how the parties communicate, the impact of the construction of the new house, or the history of the parties' relationship, although such elaboration might have been unnecessary. Simply by naming the frame and discussing what it implies for approaching a conflict, we give people an opportunity to embrace the offered frame, distance themselves from it, question it, express uncertainty, or offer a new framing.

The act and art of naming is not a solitary one. It involves careful listening, enlisting parties to a dispute in articulating the nature of the frame, and inviting them to discuss it. Naming often also involves pointing out the difference between parties' frames. In divorce mediation, frequently one party describes the conflict as being about logistics, finances, schedules, and decision-making procedures whereas the other describes it as about communication, trust, security, or retribution. Finding a simple way of naming each party's framing of the conflict—the nature of each person's story—can open a discussion about how to develop a more inclusive narrative and frame the conflict in a more fruitful way.

Deconstructing

A step beyond identifying or naming the narrative is deconstructing it—working with parties to understand its essential elements and in particular its structure. For example, it is often helpful to people to identify the nature of the story in terms of the characteristics and variables discussed earlier. Discussing, for example, who the key players in a story are, what roles they are playing, who is being excluded from consideration, and what the essential nature of the story line is (tragic, comic, long term, linear, and so forth), may assist people in reworking their understanding of a conflict.

We can also ask about or suggest the values and cultural norms embedded in a story as well. I often find it useful in listening to discussions of conflicts between workers and managers to identify the values of loyalty, independence, consistency, transparency, and hard work that are implied but often not articulated in a story. In a mediation between a Native American group and a corporation, for example, I found it useful to point out the differences between the identity-based narrative embedded in the long history that the Native American leaders were presenting and the short-term, instrumental, business-focused narrative that was the basis of the business group's approach (this example is discussed in more detail later in the chapter).

Reconstructing

Deconstructing may be enough. When the structure of a narrative is brought to the surface, the disputants, either separately or in interaction, are often well able to start the process of constructing a new narrative. But our help is sometimes also needed in reconstructing a narrative, in helping people consider new elements around which a new narrative can be developed or an old narrative significantly altered.

This does not require the creation of an entirely new way of looking at a conflict, rather it means building on the existing story while offering some new elements that in some significant way change the overall picture. Often this means adding a player or changing the role assigned to a player in a dispute. For example, consider two parents arguing over parenting arrangements for an adolescent. Each might frame this as a situation in which the child is the victim of the parents' conflict. Each could see himself or herself as the hero trying to rise above the conflict, while the other parent is portrayed as the villain who escalates and perpetuates it. Although it is important to be aware of the effects that parental conflicts have on adolescents, sometimes the effect of adolescent behavior on conflicting parents is equally important in understanding the nature of the conflict. A change in the narrative frame can sometimes be accomplished by suggesting that each parent is a victim in his or her own way. In other words, we might suggest that the question the parents need to struggle with is not simply, "How do we stop putting our child in the middle of our fights?" (which often really means, "How can I get you to stop interfering with my parenting?" or, "Why can't you stop fighting with me all the time?"). A different question the parents might want to ask is, "How do we help each other deal with our child's acting out behavior?" The difference may seem slight, but it represents a significant change in the framing and can in fact lead to an important alteration in how people see the conflict and their ongoing challenge.

Substituting

Sometimes we need to help people consider an entirely new and different story line because the approach they are currently using cannot be easily reconstructed in a useful way. We can offer this help by suggesting a new way of thinking about things, telling a parallel story to see if people can own it, or asking people to try telling a different story themselves. These new frames do not necessarily crowd out the old ways of looking at things, and they may retain some features of them, but they present an essentially new approach that can allow a discussion to move forward in a different way.

Recently, I was asked to cofacilitate a dialogue among researchers in family violence, victim advocates, mediators, judges, and others. The goal was to find some common ground between people associated with the conflict resolution field and those identified with the victim advocate community concerning the issue of family violence and divorce. This is a classic case of an enduring conflict. It has been going on for at least twenty-five years, and each community sees this issue through very different lenses and has framed the problem accordingly. The mediation community has emphasized the importance of client autonomy in decision making, so long as there are safeguards in place to ensure that victims of violence aren't coerced or endangered in mediation (Ellis and Stuckless, 2006). The victim advocate community has focused on issues of power disparities and the danger involved in consensual decision making (Garrity, 2000; Grillo, 1991).

Both of these framings have merit, and for many years efforts have been made to combine these approaches by talking about how to protect people, recognize the danger of violence, create adequate screening mechanisms, and train interveners appropriately. This has led to some progress, but working together has continued to be difficult, and discussions have often been tense and not particularly productive.

In this new effort, convened by the Association of Family Conciliation Courts and the National Council of Juvenile and Family Court Judges, a new frame was put forward. The issue was discussed in terms of differentiation. This way of thinking about the issue emphasized recognizing that there is a range of types of family violence and that to work effectively with this problem requires learning the characteristics of that range, identifying ways of assessing what type of violence is occurring, and recognizing the implications of this information for decision making, parenting plans, communication, and research. One aspect of this framing that made this discussion constructive was that the issue was no longer simply divorce decision making. It was expanded to apply to the whole system of interaction, including parenting arrangements, among people who have experienced different degrees of violence.

This new framing will not end disputes over this issue. It is truly an enduring conflict because of its roots in values, systems, power, identity, and safety. But at least for the moment, this formulation has opened the door to a considerably more constructive set of interactions. This can be seen in operation in the special July 2008 issue of the *Family Court Review*, which brought together leaders on different sides of this issue as coauthors (Olson and Ver Steegh, 2008).

Seizing New Frames

The easiest way to significantly alter narrative frames or to substitute new ones is to seize the new frames implied or suggested by disputants themselves. Disputants often offer a new way of looking at a conflict, even though they may not know they are doing this, and we can work with these new frames by recognizing them, highlighting them, inquiring about them, asking people to develop them further, or simply going with them.

I have mediated a number of child protection cases where parents have faced the prospect of the termination of parental rights and as a result have had to consider whether to agree to a voluntary relinquishment and if so under what circumstances. In one case the interaction among a parent, the foster-adopt family, and the various professionals involved changed completely when the parent said:

> I have been thinking until now about how unfair this whole situation is for me, and how badly I have been treated. I am not allowed to see my girl hardly ever, and everyone treats me like I am a bad person. I have felt that I had no rights or power at all.

> But I realized last night that I do still have some power here. I have the power to do what is best for my baby. We need to talk about what has happened to her and what should happen to her, not what has happened to me.

This was remarkable, and of course it did not come out of thin air. It was the result of a long process of coming to terms with the reality of the situation and beginning to do some of the grieving work involved in facing termination of parental rights. The clarity and courage of the parent in facing the issue was strongly expressed in the new frame she was suggesting, and my job was to seize this frame and go with it, shifting the focus of the discussion from what she was going to do to how she could arrive at clarity about what was best for her child.

Working with Metaphors

The key to a more effective framing is often found in the metaphors people use in conflict. Conflict communication, like all communication, is laced with metaphors (Gadlin, Schneider, and Honeyman, 2006, argue that people think in metaphors). We can use metaphors to help people begin to look at conflict somewhat differently and in particular to begin to think about staying with conflict rather than ending it. Consider, for example, the following statements:

"If you up the ante, I will up the ante, and then we can have a real brouhaha." (Contract negotiation)

"We don't want Big Brother to come in here and tell us how to lead our lives." (Community resisting new zoning regulations on fences, wells, and septic systems)

"It's time to grow up and stop acting like a spoiled teenager. I have a job to do and so do you." (Financial controller to project manager who objected to "the flood of paper that is swamping this project")

All of them contain metaphors that offer both tools and options for ways to proceed. Upping the ante is a metaphor from poker, the quintessential distributional game and the source of many conflict metaphors ("put your cards on the table," "call your bluff," "show your cards," "keep your cards close to your vest," and so on). This metaphor promotes a distributional narrative and one implying an either-or choice: keep the stakes low and the interactions mellow or a real explosion is going to follow. Working from within the upping the ante metaphor ("let's show some cards before we increase the size of the pot") or shifting it ("maybe you have each raised a red flag [or 'bared your teeth'] to let each other know just how serious this situation is to you—why don't you say some more about that?") are two initial approaches we can take to using metaphors to begin to alter the narrative frame.

We can look at each metaphor used by the people we are working with and ask four questions (of ourselves or the disputants) in order to unpack it: (1) What is the literal meaning of the metaphor? (2) What is the message it is communicating in this context? (3) What does it reveal about the way the person is thinking about and framing the conflict? (4) What does the speaker intend to communicate? We can then decide to use the metaphor, explore it, change it, or ignore it.

SPECIAL CHALLENGES IN FRAMING ENDURING CONFLICT

All of our efforts to reframe a narrative will be effective only to the extent that we form a partnership with our clients in searching for an effective framing. Seldom can we do this in one neat intervention. Usually, we have to work with the disputants' system—the context of the interaction—and we have to do so in an interactive, iterative, tentative, and ongoing way. Often we will use a combination of the approaches described previously, and our efforts at achieving an effective framing for enduring conflict are seldom final—as long as conflict endures the effort to develop and maintain an effective framework will have to continue.

No matter how skillful we are and how much rapport we have built with our clients, we always face some significant obstacles in developing effective frames for enduring conflict. These obstacles are related to the very reasons that conflicts endure. Three of the most troublesome obstacles are

- The roots of narratives in the identity of the disputants

- The systemic and cultural sources of distributive, exclusive, fatalistic, or internalized narratives

- The difficulty of changing a narrative frame without losing significant meaning

Narratives and Identity

Powerful narratives are powerful for a reason. Conflict narratives arise not only from concerns about a particular set of issues or reactions to a particular set of events but from people's sense of who they are, the culture they are part of, and the values that they deeply hold. If that identity is wrapped up in a particular approach to conflict, changing the narrative that gives voice to that identity is not only very hard, it may be impossible.

I once did some work organizing a discussion among abortion supporters and opponents about ground rules for picketing outside an abortion clinic. My colleague and I faced an enormous challenge in getting people to agree to sit down together at all, and finding any mutually acceptable framing of the issue (for example, "how to allow freedom of expression without interfering with legal access to the clinic") was almost impossible because every possible framing attacked some element of someone's narrative ("We do want to interfere with people committing murder"; "Our clinic clients' freedom of expression and choice is what is really at stake"). People could not even agree on how to refer to each other. *Pro-choice* groups felt they were the ones most genuinely supporting "life" and *pro-life* groups felt they were the ones offering real "choice." The narratives reflected the basic identity each group had adopted, and the ability to create a less closed, distributional, or fatalistic narrative seemed to be nonexistent, at least with this group. In a way the identities were mirror images of each other, which was one of the reasons they were so rigidly adhered to—each group found meaning in the struggle to protect the vulnerable against dangerous and sinister forces.

There were stark and rigid characterizations of victims, villains, and heroes, and the only thing that everyone could agree on was that the women seeking to terminate a pregnancy were victims, although there was no agreement about how they were victims and who was victimizing them. What we finally did was to focus on an extremely narrow framing of the immediate issues ("How close can people come to the clinic and to people approaching the clinic?"), but of course this led to equally narrow discussions and did not allow for a conversation about the atmosphere of fear, intimidation, hostility, and anger that surrounded these daily interactions.

When we face problematic narratives (problematic at least for constructive engagement) that are rooted in identity issues and deeply held values, we usually have to focus on the following goals: to help people present their narratives in as constructive a way possible; to find a way to describe and validate each narrative; to help the various parties understand the differences in their characterizations of the situation, and to pose the challenge of learning to engage despite these differences (this in fact becomes a new meta-narrative, or meta-framing—a framing about framings). So the challenge that might have been put to those involved in the abortion debate, and was put to the Native American and corporate representatives I worked with, would be to talk despite these differences. The mediator could ask that they face their profoundly different descriptions of the nature of the problem, and the mediator would have had to be clear that he or she was not advocating that they change their values, and then the mediator could challenge them to accept the importance of working together or at least communicating despite this difference.

Systemic and Cultural Sources of Narrative Frames

The conflict narratives that people develop have external as well as internal sources. They are grounded in the social system and the culture within which the conflict is taking place, and these sources can both reinforce the strength of narratives and make them more resistant to change. The poker metaphor discussed earlier is more than simply a convenient way of symbolizing a distributive take on a conflict. It is also deeply embedded in cultural norms about how people should behave in negotiations and conflict (particularly men). The message of this metaphor (reinforced in many ways in popular culture—for example, by movies like *Casino Royale* and TV offerings like the *World Series of Poker*) is that to be effective in conflict, one has to be tough, mysterious, misleading, and intimidating.

To change from a poker metaphor and the narrative it expresses to a more integrative and inclusive narrative, expressed perhaps by a musical metaphor (point and counterpoint, discord and harmony—ingredients in exciting music), requires more than capturing the imagination and concerns of a particular disputant. It requires in a sense taking on a whole culture.

The power to define a conflict, to enforce a narrative, or to put parameters around a discourse is one of the strongest forms of social control, and sometimes one of the most destructive. Racism and racist policies were historically reinforced by defining the issue in very limited terms. In the early years of U.S. history the issue was where to allow slavery, and for some how to abolish it, not how to give all people the same economic, social, and cultural opportunities. To this day the problem is still defined as equal access to opportunity created by our economic system. Whether instead it is the economic system that has to change so that extreme levels of inequality are not built into its very structure is a question that most people would not even think to ask. In similar ways, cultural and social systems exert extremely powerful control over everyone's narratives, and for the most part, we don't even realize the cognitive limits that every one of us lives under. It takes major change in a system or culture before people can break through these limits (the true meaning of that much overused term, *paradigm shift*).

Sometimes we simply have to accept that a narrative frame is not easily open to change. But we can usually lengthen the frame somewhat, complicate it a little, and encourage people to add different elements to the narrative as well. We can lengthen the narrative (as discussed earlier) by asking people to apply their way of thinking to a longer time frame. I have suggested to people who were using the language or metaphor of poker that good poker players know that they won't win every hand nor will they come out ahead every evening and that the key to success is to keep people at the table. We can complicate narratives by encouraging people to add different players to their stories or to look at system dynamics. For example, asking the parents in a divorce negotiation to think about the people in their children's lives whom they want to make sure stay in their children's lives, and to consider how they can ensure this, implicitly suggests a more systemic look at the situation.

I believe it is essential to help people open up their narratives so that elements of others' narratives can be included. This often means looking for any opportunity to create flexibility in the story or to ask people whether there is any part of another narrative they can accept. To return to the issues of the Middle East, the different stories, histories, and takes on Jerusalem have made constructive engagement on this subject difficult. But whenever people have been able to accept any part of another side's narrative, the prospects for dialogue have opened up—and one thing that has helped to make this happen is to loosen the definition of what Jerusalem is. After all, it is a city whose boundaries have changed repeatedly. An interesting project that seeks to amalgamate extremely different narratives by creating a *super narrative* is the Abraham Path Initiative. This project seeks to create a common story for Christianity, Islam, and Judaism by focusing on the potential cultural and commercial value of encouraging people to retrace the historic journey of Abraham. As described on the initiative Web site: "The Abraham Path is a route of cultural tourism that retraces the journey made by Abraham (Ibrahim) through the heart of the Middle East some four thousand years ago. Three and a half billion people—over half the human family—trace their history or faith back to Abraham, considered the father of monotheism. The Abraham Path honors this shared cultural heritage by linking together into a single itinerary of outstanding interest and beauty the ancient sites associated with Abraham and his family" (Abraham Path Initiative, 2008).

The Abraham Path Initiative at its heart is a challenge—a challenge to build on the common history and heritage of these three major religious and cultural traditions. In so doing it has created a meta-narrative of the common story that includes each individual narrative.

Losing Meaning Through Changing the Frame

The fundamental challenge we face whenever we try to alter a narrative frame is that we will lose meaning that is essential to the disputants and that reflects a basic element of the conflict. We might achieve a short-term success if we do this, but over time we will not have contributed to constructive engagement. We have to be committed to helping people give voice to their beliefs, values, feelings, and concerns, even when these are not particularly appealing, constructive, or "nice."

I have been very concerned that the use of reframing in mediation has focused too much on how to detoxify language and find middle ground rather than on how to help people say what they really mean in an effective way. It's better to work with a highly unpleasant frame than to suppress real meaning that will continue to motivate the conflict. Consider this interchange (which I think I mishandled) from a discussion between animal rights activists and trappers and hunters:

TRAPPER: I think if you really understood how we do our work, you would see that it is not so inhumane, and reflects practices that Native Americans, frontiersmen, and our ancestors have been doing for centuries. [*Starts to take a trapping device out of a satchel.*]

ANIMAL RIGHTS ACTIVIST A: We don't want to see your weapons of death.

TRAPPER: Wild animals are killed all the time—almost always by other animals. Most of the animals we trap are ones who live by killing others, and killing them in brutal, painful, and ugly ways.

ANIMAL RIGHTS ACTIVIST B: You are murderers, and we won't tolerate murder.

FACILITATOR: Let's see if we can't tone down our language here. It doesn't help to call each other names. The point is you have very different values about this and you are not going to agree with each other or convince each other that you are right. But that does not mean that you can't talk with each other. People should say what they think, but do it respectfully.

I thought that this acknowledgment of their differences would help and also that I had to interfere with what was an increasingly acrimonious interchange. But of course I came across as somewhat patronizing and as trying to "shush" (the word she later used) Activist B. I wonder what would have happened if instead I had said something like this: "You have very different beliefs and values about this, and it's important that everyone be able to give voice to these, even if they are hard to hear. When you say that these are weapons of death and those using them are murderers, you are telling us about what you believe and what is underneath your position on this issue. It may be a difficult conversation, but let's see if we can have it. And let's also hear what you [*the trapper*] think and believe when you hear your actions labeled in this way."

I am not sure it would have made any difference in the long run, but I think this approach would have had the advantage of encouraging people to share their most complicated meaning, rather than suppressing it. Part of the meaning that was so important to the activists was that trapping was a form of murder and that the fact that it was animals who suffered did not alter the fact that they saw trapping as murder. That meaning needed to be part of the conversation, painful though it may have been.

The challenge of framing a conflict for the long term is essentially that this involves changing consciousness. Our goal is to help people to understand their conflicts in a different way, one that allows them to see a conflict's enduring aspects and to realize that this ongoing nature does not equate to hopelessness or futility. Engaging in an enduring conflict is not the same as being deadlocked or at an impasse. Constructive work can be done. The conflict can be handled well or poorly. Some of the most important growth that people experience comes through learning to deal with enduring conflict.

Framing the conflict in a way that expresses this challenge is an important part of helping people stay with conflict. It's an important step in creating a context within which constructive communication among the participants in a long-term conflict can occur. In the next chapter I will discuss how to help people communicate effectively and to sustain that communication in long-term conflict.

5

Communicating in Enduring Conflict

Bill and Art were partners in an artistic enterprise for over twenty-five years. Their work was extremely popular, commercially successful, and influential and continues to be popular today, many years after their deaths. An entire facility was built to accommodate their work, and many people's livelihoods derived from it. Yet the two of them did not get along. They were essentially chained to each other by their success, but they fought frequently and furiously and repeatedly needed third-party assistance to mediate their relationship. Bill was confrontational, thin-skinned, and emotional. He was also kindhearted. Art was a conflict avoider, more formal, and somewhat rigid. Art felt he was forced to compromise his work to ensure that it fit into Bill's framework, and Bill felt the same about his own work. On several occasions Art and Bill could not agree on the subject matter for their next endeavor, and their work ground to a halt, despite contractual obligations. On another occasion, Bill accused the owner of the facility of cheating them. Art sided with the manager, and it looked as though their cooperative ventures might be finished. Only mediation efforts by the publisher of their work allowed them to go forward. Each occasionally collaborated with others but never with the same success. Yet despite all of this, they persevered—they stayed with conflict—and today we hail the works of William Gilbert and Arthur Sullivan as cultural treasures.

Staying with conflict is hard work, and no one always does it elegantly. But the rewards can be great.

Gilbert and Sullivan's well-known conflict is emblematic of both the challenges and rewards of staying in communication to stay with conflict. Over time, Gilbert and Sullivan neither avoided their conflict nor sacrificed their most important values, but there were times when they wished they had never met one other. What it took for them to continue their tempestuous but creative partnership is a model for communicating through an enduring conflict—not a perfect model by any means but an instructive one. Some of the elements that characterized their efforts were

- Perseverance
- Maintaining communication in some form, even when direct communication was ineffective
- Using multiple channels of communication
- Speaking their truth (if not always clearly or respectfully)
- Attending to what the partnership required to continue
- Using third parties, coaches, and advocates
- Taking time out
- Responding to conciliatory gestures
- Affirming each other (albeit only occasionally)
- Choosing their battles

Gilbert and Sullivan's relationship would not have endured without the support of numerous *third siders*. They needed help with communicating, and fortunately they were willing to use the assistance that was offered. Perhaps the biggest of all challenges in enduring conflict is finding meaningful ways to communicate and to keep on communicating, even when the communication is painful and unpleasant. In overcoming their differences, Gilbert and Sullivan were no doubt partly motivated by financial incentives, but they were also aware of the artistic rewards (even though they questioned these at times too).

Staying with conflict requires finding a path that allows communication over time with people who may not want to communicate, whose approach to communication may be ineffective or destructive, and with whom one would often prefer to have nothing to do. The set of communication skills that we focus on in short-term interventions, such as listening, framing, reframing, raising conflict productively, and attending to nonverbal cues, are important in all human relations, including staying with enduring conflict. But additional communication skills are needed for long-term conflict.

Finding the determination and means to stay in communication in the face of a tremendous urge to avoid conflict is one of the foremost challenges for disputants to face. Staying with conflict also requires a strategy for communicating in the face of anger, resistance, hostility, silence, and even dishonesty. Over the course of a long conflict, time-outs are sometimes necessary, as is reengaging after a breach has occurred. We need to be prepared to help disputants respond to the ebb and flow in communication that is a central feature of enduring conflict. Maintaining optimal communication over time may be a great goal but it is not a realistic one, so we need to be ready to help people face their own communication lapses and accept responsibility for them. This chapter looks at these challenges, particularly as they relate to the natural rhythm of long-term disputes. Let's start with looking at maintaining communication, which sometimes simply means staying in contact.

STAYING IN CONTACT INTENTIONALLY

For many people in conflict the last thing they want to do is stay in contact with those they consider to be adversaries. They see no benefit from communication and therefore no reason to endure the negativity, tension, or anxiety of dealing with a conflictual relationship. Furthermore, they have no idea of how to stay in contact in a useful way. Although we as conflict specialists need to address the tactical question of how disputants can stay in contact when emotions are high and communication seems destructive, we ought to begin by addressing the prior question of whether people should stay in contact.

As we explore this with disputants, I believe the conversation needs to migrate to a consideration of what kind of interaction makes sense, because in conflict, there is always communication. However, staying with conflict requires an *intentional* approach to communication. Rather than leave communication to chance, it is better for disputants to make an affirmative decision about the kind of contact they want to maintain with each other and the kind of messages they want to be sending.

There are times when all communication seems to make things worse, when people are just not in a good place to raise their concerns or listen to others, when no matter what one person says it will be heard as negative or angry by the other, and when a time-out is necessary. At other times communication can be dangerous—that is why courts impose restraining orders, for example. I discuss the rhythm of communication later in this chapter, but we should be clear that it is not always appropriate to encourage direct communication among people in conflict.

Moreover a false assumption lurks underneath the question of whether communication is always important, because the alternative to direct communication is not the absence communication. When people are engaged in a conflict, there is communication of some sort transpiring through court actions, silence, public actions, coded signals, surrogates, third parties, and the like.

We should therefore be raising a series of questions that foster intentionality in communication and the awareness that no matter what disputants do, they are sending some kind of message to each other. For example, we should be asking our clients to consider whether direct communication should occur. Should disputants take a time-out from communicating? Should any intentional messages be sent? Should third parties be used? Should a direct message about not having direct communication be trans-mitted? Should a safe and constructive channel of communication be established?

We should always consider the message that is being sent by whatever approach to communication people are taking, includ-ing ceasing contact. All communication occurs on at least two levels. In addition to the direct message, how people commu-nicate (or avoid communicating) also sends a message, and it is important to pay attention to both layers (Tannen, 1986). When working with disputants, it's often helpful to ask them to put into words the message they are trying to send by the manner in which they are communicating or, alternatively, how they are avoid-ing direct communication. This was the challenge facing Joe and Jane:

Joe and Jane were managers of two units in a large technical con-sulting firm and had been part of the same general division for years. They had also not spoken to each other for years. Because their units had different responsibilities and areas of expertise, they both acted as if they had no need to communicate. They sat in the same managerial meetings, reported to the same area director, and were both affected by the company's overall performance, but they did not talk. On the rare occasion when some information had to be passed from one to the other, they used e-mails or memos. They studiously avoided eye contact or informal interaction. But of course there was communication occurring, and it was mostly damaging to the company. Furthermore, everyone was keenly aware of the nature of their relationship, even though neither ever talked about it.

Whenever one of them made a suggestion (from the trivial, such as where to hold a Christmas party, to critical, such as how to han-dle layoffs), the other was sure to criticize or belittle it, but usually not directly and never by mentioning the other person. If they did find themselves in a small-group conversation, they would never directly address each other, but one of them might make a comment to another person that was in fact a response, usually with an edge to it, to what the other manager had said.

Joe and Jane may have been able to carry out most of their responsibilities without direct communication, but they were conveying a message to their colleagues (and to themselves) that their relationship was dysfunctional, and this had an ongoing negative effect on the organization.

Finding a means to gain control of the meta-message and developing an approach to staying in contact that not only allowed Joe and Jane to conduct their business but enabled the organization to function with less tension was essential for the long-term health of their division. This did not mean that their conflict had to end but rather that they needed to find a way of communicating constructively despite the ongoing nature of their differences (whatever they may have been).

When we work to help people stay with conflict, we are often confronted with the question, sometimes the challenge, of why disputants should communicate at all. As a general rule I do not find it particularly useful to argue for the benefits of direct communication, at least not initially, so instead I work with people on identifying what they are communicating by their current stance, what kind of message they would like to communicate, and how they can best convey that message. In addition I ask people to think not only about what they want to say but also about the avenues of communication that seem appropriate given the nature of their relationship.

AVENUES OF CONTACT

When we work with people on how they communicate, we usually talk about the message and how best to frame it. But often the more productive focus, especially for enduring conflict, is on the avenue of communication. By this I mean the mechanism, medium, or arena that is used to communicate among disputants—the press, e-mail, letters, phone, intermediaries, regular face-to-face meetings, press releases, or court filings, for example.

Over the life of an enduring conflict, many messages will be communicated. The content and framing will vary tremendously, as will the responses. When we work with disputants, we often focus on the micro-interaction—how a particular message is transmitted or framed or responded to, but in enduring conflict the more important and useful work is to look at the long-term patterns of interaction and communication and to consider which is the most conducive to constructive engagement. Although avenues of communication can also change over time, they are often the more durable element in a long-term communication, and therefore one that we should pay particular attention to.

The hotline established between Washington, DC, and Moscow after the Cuban missile crisis reflects the awareness that leaders of the United States and the Soviet Union had about the importance of maintaining a robust emergency system of communication with regard to the most critical issue of that time (and perhaps still today). What would be said or how it would be framed could not be anticipated. What could be anticipated was that the conflict between the United States and the Soviet Union, the so-called Cold War, was not about to end (it went on for about thirty more years), that there would be crises in the future, that some forum or avenue of emergency communication would continue to be necessary, and that it had to be readily available and very direct.

Using Intentional Avenues

Labor officials and management representatives, leaders of opposing political parties, corporate competitors, and diplomats are often well aware of the need for regular contact of some kind (and are usually also aware of the significance of breaking off such contact), but they often let such structures slide. When conflict intensifies, an escalating event occurs, or a key player leaves, the viability of these avenues of communication is put to the test and often determines how destructive an interaction will become. The same can be said for interpersonal conflicts between parents and children, husbands and wives, neighbors, or coworkers. Although formalized channels of communication are not as common in these interpersonal conflicts, given the informal nature of the parties' relationships, avenues of contact are still important, especially in the face of enduring conflict. For example, in many conflicted family systems, one member may act as the channel for communication (sometimes to his or her great disadvantage).

People in a long-term conflict may dread the idea of setting up or maintaining a channel of communication with those they are in conflict with, and if they do establish such a system, it may quickly fall into disuse. But establishing an intentional avenue for ongoing communication and maintaining it is critical for staying with conflict. This avenue may be an only occasionally used channel, available when necessary but dormant otherwise, like the hotline; an occasional face-to-face meeting; a third party, an avenue commonly used in high-conflict divorce (Baris and others, 2001); an exchange of e-mail addresses or phone numbers; or a set of ground rules and expectations about how communication will take place. There are many possible avenues that can be established, and a robust approach to enduring communication requires the establishment of perhaps overlapping approaches that are designed with a sensitivity to the context and culture within which they are located. For example, consider the following structures for communication between disputing parties:

- Alan and Jonathan, developer and contractor, fight all the time, but are obligated to work together. They agree to call each other first thing every morning to let each other know of any unexpected delays or concerns that either might have. They always do this by phone, even if they will be on site together thirty minutes later.

- Pat and Margaret meet once a month with their supervisor, more often if necessary, to talk over issues of mutual concern. Pat and Margaret have a poor relationship but have to work together.

- Joel and Joan are divorced and relations have been tense. They agree to e-mail each other by the fifth of each month to report what they have spent on children's clothing, medical expenses, and other items that are their joint responsibility, and at the same time to let each other know of any unusual expenses anticipated in the next month.

- Carol and Paul have a history of intense conflict and don't believe they can communicate at all about child-care issues. They agree to take all disputes about parenting to Christina, a child development expert, and to abide by her recommendations.

There is nothing magical or complicated about these avenues. In each case, an alternative approach could probably work as well. However, each is an example of an intentional structure that allows disputants to stay in contact over time. They are important both as practical mechanisms to communicate throughout enduring conflict and as statements that the disputants recognize that they need to communicate even though that is sometimes difficult.

Identifying Effective Avenues

People involved in enduring conflict often try to find some mechanism for maintaining contact, but not all avenues are effective, durable, or productive. Some in fact may be destructive. For example, many divorced parents (often unintentionally) use their children to communicate, sometimes putting them in the middle of stressful interactions in the process. E-mail is often used as the major avenue to carry on a tense exchange, and although it sometimes can be useful, it is often counterproductive. E-mail does not allow the transmission of tone and nuance that face-to-face or even phone communication does. Furthermore, people can and do save e-mails forever and occasionally use these saved messages as weapons.

In working to help people to stay with conflict, we need to consider the following criteria for effective communication avenues:

- *Safety (psychological and physical)*. Will this avenue put anyone at risk?
- *Durability*. Can the avenue survive the inevitable flare-ups or withdrawals that are part of enduring conflict?
- *Predictability*. Is the mechanism regular, understandable, stable, and reliable?
- *Mutuality*. Will this avenue work for all the key players in the conflict? Do they all buy into this avenue?
- *Efficiency*. How resource intensive or time consuming is this approach?
- *Timeliness*. Can this avenue be readily accessed when needed?
- *Depth*. Does this sufficiently allow for the depth and breadth of communication that the conflict may call for?
- *Flexibility*. Can this avenue be adapted to changing circumstances or changing needs?
- *Accessibility*. How simple, user friendly and clear is this approach?
- *Culturally appropriate*. Will this avenue work within the cultural norms and practices of all the participants?

Finding the Right Fit

Finding one avenue that fits all these criteria can be difficult, so sometimes multiple avenues are necessary. For example, a durable and efficient approach may not allow the depth and flexibility of communication that is also important. That's why the hotline was never intended as the sole or major avenue for U.S. and Soviet leaders to use to communicate. As conflict specialists we often have to discuss what structures will work and to assist in creating monitoring mechanisms to test them. These negotiations about how to communicate are sometimes at the center of our conflict intervention efforts.

Francine was the hospital administrator, Jo Anne the president of the nurses union local. They did not do well with each other, and the tension between them contributed to abysmal labor relations. It seemed that the only times Francine and Jo Anne communicated were in contract negotiations, grievance hearings, or public forums. Each claimed it was pointless to talk to the other because "you can't trust her to tell the truth,""she distorts everything I say," and "we never end up accomplishing or agreeing about anything."

My comediator and I facilitated several joint conversations, which began with a difficult but fairly straightforward exchange about their issues with each other, and a commitment to engage in a process to address overall organizational concerns. We suggested that Francine and Jo Anne needed to establish a regular forum for communicating. What good would that do, they both wondered? We basically turned the question back to them, asking that they consider what they were communicating to their "people" by not having some regular communication mechanism.

In the end they agreed to have regular Wednesday morning breakfasts in Francine's office (food seemed important—even if it were hospital food), limiting the meeting to thirty minutes. They also agreed to maintain a norm of confidentiality and insularity, meaning that no one else would attend. If they needed to have a discussion that involved others, they would set up additional meetings.

This contact, although tense at times, seemed to open up communication more generally by sending a message that nurses and their supervisors needed to talk, even if they did not like each other. What seemed particularly important was that these contacts were regular, brief, informal, and off the record. Francine and Jo Anne did not become best friends, but this change, taken in conjunction with other changes made in the hospital, seemed to make the overall tension less debilitating.

In addition to the avenues already mentioned such as face-to-face meetings, phone calls, e-mail, intermediaries, reports, public meetings, video conferences, and logs (written or on-line), we might find that new technologies offer interesting communication channels. I have never mediated an agreement that specified using My Space or Facebook as an avenue of communication, but I can well imagine that this and other Web-based approaches will become increasingly prevalent. Disputants can be very inventive about this, but they often need encouragement to establish such avenues and help in thinking through whether, why, and how they want to set up a communication channel as well as what they want to create.

STAYING IN CONTACT IN THE FACE OF AVOIDANCE

If everyone who is party to an enduring conflict were to understand the need to stay in contact, our job would be a lot easier. But the situation is almost always more complicated. Maybe one party is avoiding the conflict, maybe both are, or maybe they have very different ideas about what staying in contact means. We may have access only to one side of a dispute, or if we are in a third-party role, we may still be dealing with a situation in which not everyone sees the need for ongoing communication. Of course we should never assume that ongoing direct contact is in all parties' interest, but we can usually assume that it should at least be considered, and we should help people think it through and imagine what staying in contact might look like. In addition we often need a strategy for times when some of the disputants want to stay in contact but others do not.

In Chapter Three I discussed four broad approaches to avoidance (denial or minimization, misdirection, escalation, and premature problem solving). It is useful to consider the nature of the avoidance when developing an approach to dealing with it. For example, I often hear disputants say such things as, "there is no real conflict between us, so we don't really need to talk," or, "if we communicated regularly, then we would really have a fight on our hands." They may be telling the truth, but it is important to note the combination of minimization with a threat to escalate. This suggests a significant level of fear about being in conflict, and that fear is worth exploring.

In general, while always respecting the disputants' autonomy and wisdom about their own needs, I think it is useful to ask three questions.

- What are the disputants specifically avoiding (for example, communicating, meeting in person, dealing with a particular issue, the unknown), and why?

- What are the immediate and long-term consequences of staying in direct contact, and also of avoiding direct contact?

- Is there an approach to staying in conflict—a channel, an intermediary, a structure, a set of ground rules, or a particular focus—that can encourage a step in the direction of constructive communication?

We should ask parties to think through these questions for themselves and also to consider them from the vantage point of those they are in conflict with. In other words, what do they think their adversaries are avoiding, and why might it be in those adversaries' interest to stay in contact or to avoid contact? By asking these questions, we can help people think more strategically about communication and move away from an either-or position on whether or not to reach out to others.

One advantage of a long-term conflict process is that it offers multiple opportunities to open up communication, and part of our role is to encourage people to keep trying, to consider when others might be ready, to accept it when they are not, and to become attuned to the rhythm of communication. It is natural for interactions to ebb and flow, and people need to approach different points in this process in different ways.

WORKING WITH THE COMMUNICATION EBB AND FLOW

In long-term conflicts, communication goes through many phases. Intensive interaction, which often accompanies intense conflict, is sometimes followed by extensive periods of minimal direct communication. Avenues of communication change. Relatively friendly or open communication gives way to more hostile and threatening interchanges and vice versa. Communication is sometimes one sided, sometimes more mutual. Occasionally, we can discover a rhythm in this, but often it can appear random and chaotic. Each phase of interaction challenges disputants in a different way, but our overall challenge is to help people develop a long-term communication strategy that can handle the ebbs and flows of communication over time. Parenting adolescents, for example, requires ongoing learning about teenagers' rapidly changing desire for and approach to communication.

Finding an Effective Voice

Communicating effectively over time requires being both consistent in one's values and approach to communication and flexible in reacting to others' responses. On the one hand consistency is important because it allows trust to develop and because predictable responses can influence others to behave in a reciprocal fashion. On the other hand not all circumstances call for exactly the same approach nor do all disputants respond to a particular approach to communication in the same way. Also, what works at one moment in a conflict interaction will not necessarily work at the next. Finding an effective, realistic, and authentic consistency in one's approach and yet being flexible and adaptable to different circumstances is an elusive but important goal for staying with conflict.

Communication is at the heart of our field, and principles of effective communication are our stock in trade. Working with people on honing each message to what is really essential, using I-messages, speaking in a culturally appropriate manner, listening and listening some more, using effective questioning techniques, framing artfully, reframing, and raising difficult issues are always at the core of our work, whether we are dealing with enduring or transient conflicts.

But we also have to respect the individual styles of communication that people find comfortable and natural. As important as this is when considering specific interchanges, it is even more critical when helping people deal with long-term conflict. In our devotion to principles of sound communication, we may at times promote an approach that is more rule-bound than natural. But principles that are not integrated into people's natural communication styles will not be followed over time, especially in the face of attacks, emotional charged interactions, or high-stake confrontations.

Helping people identify their natural style of communication, particularly in conflict, is often a good place to start. There are many tools to assist us with this—for example, the Strength Deployment Inventory (www.personalstrengths.com), LIFO (www.bcon-lifo.com), and the Meyers-Briggs Type Indicator (www.myersbrigg.org)—but even though these tools can provide interesting insights and points of departure for discussing communication with disputants, individuals' own self-assessments are usually the most powerful platforms from which to work. It's helpful for disputants to think about what they find to be the most effective way to get their message heard and what their attitudes are about listening to others. It's also helpful for them to think about what their natural inclination is when faced with negative communication or no communication from others. From this baseline, we can begin to work with people on what to do when their approach is not producing the results they want.

Of course it can still be valuable to teach and reinforce certain key principles of communication. The point is to build from an individual's own style rather than from a set of external guidelines promoted by communication gurus. Often it is useful to find an anchor by way of a metaphor or aphorism that people can use to remind themselves of an effective approach to communication. This too is most effective if it comes from their own experience or sense of themselves. For example, I have found Stephen Covey's fifth *habit*, or principle—"seek first to understand, then to be understood" (Covey, 1989)—a helpful point of departure for many disputants, but only after they in some way arrive at it themselves.

Another important principle, which may seem obvious but is often overlooked, is that we should promote constructive communication. In discussing how to do this with disputants, I often think of the lessons described by Robert Axelrod in *The Evolution of Cooperation* (1984) and derived from an experiment based on the Prisoner's Dilemma exercise. This experiment pitted different strategies of cooperation and competition against each other in a highly formal and abstract context. Axelrod concluded that four principles were key to achieving successful results:

- *Niceness.* Always start out with a cooperative or conciliatory gesture.

- *Provocability.* Be willing to respond with consequences to competitive or confrontational moves (but keep these responses in proportion).

- *Forgiveness.* If someone changes from a competitive to a cooperative strategy, respond to the change, don't continue to base one's actions on a desire to impose consequences for past behavior.

- *Simplicity.* People should be able to understand the strategy you are using or they will respond defensively.

These are not golden keys to constructive communication, but they are helpful anchors for people to consider as they develop a long-term approach to communication. And they help people begin to understand how they can be both consistent and flexible at the same time.

Adopting a Flexible Approach

Flexibility is a critical component of constructive communication. A consistent voice is essential to effective long-term communication, but without flexibility, consistency becomes rigidity and is not constructive. Albert Einstein reputedly said that insanity is doing the same thing over and over while expecting different results. If so, we are all insane at times, because a very natural response to poor results from a particular approach or action is to try to employ the same approach more intensely and diligently. If kindness does not work, be more kind. If listening does not work, listen better. If an apology does not work, apologize more. If getting angry does not work, get angrier. Getting people to recognize their dysfunctional patterns of interaction can encourage them to develop more flexible approaches. I look for ways of making patterns of interactions obvious or tangible to make it easier for disputants to begin to think of alternatives. I also sometimes ask people to come up with two or three things they could do differently in communicating—any two or three things, even if they are minor. This can break through a defensive response and also open the door to creative discussions.

The following case example describes how adult children and their elderly parent had gotten locked into a cycle of unproductive communication. The conflict intervener, in this case a conflict coach, helped by pointing out the pattern. The children could then figure out alternatives themselves.

Charles was an eighty-six-year-old widower with two children and several grandchildren. He lived on his own and was very proud of his continued self-sufficiency, but his driving was causing great concern to his family. He had been in several minor accidents, his vision was fading, his hearing was poor, and his reactions were slow. His children had tried to prevail upon him to give up driving, but he adamantly refused. A typical conversation went like this:

"Pop, we are worried about your driving. We are worried for you and worried for others."

"My driving is fine. I don't drive in bad weather, rarely at night, and I have been driving these roads for seventy years. I know what I am doing."

"We know you are careful in your own way, but you just don't see very well anymore. You have got to stop."

"I do not. You can't tell me what to do."

"It's not safe—someone has got to tell you."

"Not you."

And so it went—over and over again. The children consulted a specialist in elder-care conflict, who discussed with them the issues involved for their father—autonomy, power, long-term family dynamics, fear of being isolated, and cognitive deterioration. They felt they had tried everything they could think of short of legal action. The specialist then asked whether there was anything they might do differently in how they talked about this issue. They were at a loss at first. She pointed out the circular nature of the conversations they had had with their father. They raise a concern, he resists. They raise their concern more intensely, he resists more intensely. In the end it becomes a power play. Finally, one of the children said, "Well—maybe we should offer to help him more with those times he has chosen not to drive."

The next time they met with him they began discussing who could help him get to places at night or in bad weather or to unfamiliar places. He responded: "I won't let someone [other than family] drive me unless they use my car—I want to keep driving in my car."

Now a whole new conversation evolved—not an easy one, but a less circular one.

DEALING WITH PERSISTENTLY DYSFUNCTIONAL COMMUNICATION

When someone's natural style is highly confrontational, positional, and threatening, finding a constructive and natural approach can be extremely difficult. When we encounter an individual who is consistently employing a dysfunctional style of communication, the chances are that this is part of a larger, self-defeating pattern of behavior. This could well require a comprehensive intervention, which may involve psychotherapy as well as some imposition of authority or limit setting.

What can we do when we are called in to help a disputant figure out how to respond to another disputant's dysfunctional communication style? This challenge requires that we address both the use of power (which is discussed in the next chapter) and approaches to communication (which I discuss here). Some of the most important work we can do to help people through enduring conflict is to assist them in developing a strategy for dealing with consistently negative or destructive communication patterns. Four questions are central to this effort.

What Is Really Going On?

Are disputants actually dealing with a persistently negative pattern of communication? If so, is it generalized or specific to that conflict or that relationship? Why is it happening? What is the message of this pattern of communication? What are the power relations informing it? As discussed in Chapter Three, people may avoid conflict by ascribing it to the evil, crazy, or stupid behavior of others, a tactic that releases them from the responsibility to engage constructively with the conflict. However, what is destructive behavior from one point of view may be justifiable or at least comprehensible from another. Putting words to the message behind the behavior (for example, "I don't trust you, don't want to deal with you, and don't have to deal with you") can help people begin to consider how to respond.

Does This Communication Style Have Any Constructive Aspect?

There are very few purely negative or purely constructive communications in the world of conflict. Most messages are a mixed bag, and people usually can choose the element they will respond to. When an employee threatens to quit unless her contribution is recognized, an employer can respond to her threat to quit, the tone of her communication, or her desire to be recognized for her contributions. Maybe all elements need to be dealt with eventually, but the employer has a choice about where to start. Building on the constructive elements in order to establish a platform from which the more toxic elements can be dealt with constructively is sometimes the best alternative for dealing with destructive approaches. Highly hostile communication often has at least this to say for it—it is communication, which is easier in some respects to deal with than no direct communication at all.

Is It Advisable to Limit Communication, and If So How?

At times, putting a limit on or withdrawing from all direct communication is the only way to prevent a negative or threatening pattern of communication from continuing or escalating. People may resort to this approach too quickly or they may use it to avoid dealing with important issues. But the fact that this approach is often misused does not mean it is never appropriate. A victim of domestic violence often has no safe alternative but to cease all direct communication and obtain legal support to enforce this move (and this alternative is not always safe either). More generally, if someone uses all direct communications to intimidate, to bully, or to escalate a conflict, putting limits on communication may be essential to the long-term prospects for constructive engagement.

But we should also remember that there is a world of difference between saying, in essence, "Go away and leave me alone," and saying, "This is not working; until we figure out a better way we need some space." When dealing with persistently destructive communication, people often have to decide whether to discontinue all direct communication or to focus instead on establishing clear limits on communication. Sometimes it's better to have a complete cessation, but often it is more productive—and even safer—to set up a limited but ongoing avenue for direct contact. Divorced parents, for example, might schedule a ten-minute, once-a-week phone call to coordinate plans and limit all other contact. Employees may feel they have no choice but to continue to interact with a colleague but may chose to only do so with other people present or during formally scheduled meetings. Similarly, even though groups or nations involved in hot conflict may need to limit direct communication, breaking all off all direct communication usually does more to escalate the dispute or close off opportunities for improving the relationship than it does to leverage more productive behavior.

Conflict specialists can help disputants to limit communication when necessary, assisting them to think through how to do this, facilitating the decision-making process, serving as intermediaries, providing a forum for limited contact, and occasionally acting as limit setters where we are in a position to do that—as, for example, when we ask people involved in a difficult grievance not to communicate with each other between mediation sessions.

How Can Direct Communication Be Reestablished?

Over the life of a protracted dispute, there may be times when communication diminishes or ceases and times when communication can be revived. We can help disputants think through whether, when, and how to reestablish or reinvigorate direct communication. Whether we are dealing with avoidance patterns or with reasonable fears about the feasibility or advisability of resuming direct contact we can suggest ways in which disputants might reestablish communication if they choose to do so. We can encourage them to periodically probe for whether it is possible to reopen communication, to identify potential openings and conciliatory messages that others may be sending (even if well disguised), to think about how to send a message that encourages more contact, and to consider avenues for restarting direct communication.

Sometimes we are in a position to encourage or facilitate renewed interactions focused directly on the conflict itself, but at other times it is wiser to restart direct interaction by dealing with less controversial issues. The so-called Ping-Pong diplomacy of the early 1970s (exchanging table tennis teams during a time when overt diplomatic contact between the United States and China was nonexistent) was critical to moving the conflict between China and the United States in a more positive direction. Cultural exchanges, social interactions, citizen-to-citizen contacts, or ice-breaking conversations are often critical precursors to reestablishing direct communication about controversial or conflictual topics.

SPEAKING TRUTH THROUGH CONFLICT

As conflict professionals we pay a lot of attention to—and give a lot of advice about—culturally appropriate ways to listen, frame, reframe, and respond. But in the end, what moves a conflict forward and what builds trust over time is honesty, authenticity, and forthrightness in the disputants. Even if the message is painful or contentious, what best promotes effective communication is truthfulness.

Truthfulness is not, of course, a straightforward concept. As Oscar Wilde (1919) said, "the pure and simple truth is rarely pure and never simple." We are not talking about objective or factual truth here, but about the intention to say what one thinks, to share one's key concerns, and to reveal one's intentions. The problem is that no one can always do this, and maybe it can never be done completely, especially in conflict. It is not always wise to share all of one's truth or beliefs. And even when one's truth is told with great sincerity, it won't necessarily be perceived as truth by the other side.

For truth telling to have any useful meaning in conflict, it has to be seen as a reciprocal and evolving process that builds on a developing relationship and a process of interaction. When people are operating from very different frames of references and incompatible conflict narratives, then the truth of one side can easily be seen as a manipulation or attack by the other. One side of a debate about a war calls for peace; the other side hears this as surrender. One party asks for fairness; the other side hears this as special privilege. So we cannot simply advise people to go out and speak their truth and all will be well. Instead we have to work with people to engage in an often long-term process of truth telling. If people can do this over time, then over time even the most difficult conflicts can be approached constructively. But this is no easy task.

The Truth-Telling Process

People tend to think of truth, honesty, sincerity, and trustworthiness as innate traits that lie within the individual and are under his control. Certainly, anyone can be committed to being honest

and truthful. But the work of actually revealing one's most important meaning to others is not solitary work. It requires the engagement and support of those with whom one is communicating.
This support can take the form of active questioning, reflection
on what they have understood, and devotion of the time and
attention it takes to understand complicated or emotionally laden
messages.

In conflict the safety, mutuality, and reciprocity that allow for
truth-telling communication to occur is often missing, and therefore, even with the best of intentions, people often can't effectively say what they are thinking or make their meaning clear to
others. And even when the most concrete meaning can be conveyed, the spirit or tone that the sender wishes to convey (for
example, funny, sardonic, hopeful, or tentative) is often lost. In
other words, even if the message gets through, the meta-message,
which is a key part of the meaning, does not. That is one of the
main reasons people need help in conflict.

The process of truth telling involves several components:

- *Clarity*: accurately understanding one's own meaning or
  truth
- *Framing*: finding an effective way of presenting the
  message
- *Selecting an arena*: finding the right medium, time,
  place, or mechanism for communicating
- *Reciprocity*: developing the two-way process that allows
  for the reception as well as the transmission of the
  meaning and for the adjustment of the communication
  to account for the messages, questions, or feedback that
  are being returned
- *Iteration*: engaging in an ongoing effort to refine, clarify,
  correct, or amend the meaning in interaction with the
  recipients

The process of speaking one's truth is seldom easy or straight-forward. Because of the complexities involved in doing it effec-tively over time in conflict, people often do it only sporadically or give it up. Even when people are committed to speaking their truth, they often do not know how to do so in a wise, effective, or even recognizable manner. Long-term disputants often become discouraged about the possibility of others ever really listening to, much less understanding, what they are trying to convey.

Conflict specialists are often called on to help disputants gain clarity, frame their message, identify the appropriate arena, develop a reciprocal process, and keep at it. Often we are also called on to encourage and assist people to keep speaking their truth in the face of ongoing conflict and discouraging responses. It is sometimes hard to maintain one's faith in the value of this, but without it, constructive engagement is not ultimately possible. Speaking one's truth in conflict, hard as it sometimes is, is at the core of conflict engagement. It is this effort that breaks through destructive avoidance patterns, inaccurate framings, exclusive nar-ratives, and power tactics aimed at suppressing important issues. Throughout the life of an enduring conflict, effective moments of truth telling provide the key impetus for constructive engagement.

Strategies for Speaking Truth Through Conflict

Part of the challenge here is motivational. Unless people believe in the value of speaking their truth in a constructive way and understand that part of the purpose is to encourage reciprocity, it is unlikely they will devote the energy needed to do so or take the risks involved. We can help to motivate people to do this by asking them to articulate their own values about truth telling, providing them with a vision (and some practice) for what the truth-telling process might look like, and finding ways of helping them take small steps in that direction so they can develop their own approach, allay some of their fears or anxieties, and experi-ence some constructive results.

But in the end motivation has to come from within—we can't force someone to be motivated. I have often found that after discussing the importance of revealing significant concerns and raising difficult questions and after also discussing how that might best be accomplished, the best I can do is to leave people with the question and the means to make whatever choice about engaging, communicating, and speaking their truth that they think makes the most sense. By doing so, I put the motivational question exactly where it belongs—with the disputants themselves.

Even when disputants are motivated, the question of how to speak the truth remains. What guidelines can conflict specialists offer to assist people in speaking their truth through conflict? Four strategies or approaches are central to effective truth telling.

Effective Framing

I have already discussed constructing an effective narrative frame (in Chapter Four). Ultimately, developing and refining a constructive, powerful, and durable narrative is the key to being able to speak with authenticity and power over time. In the truth-telling context, an effective frame is one that conveys the important core meaning in a clear and unambiguous way and that takes into account how the message is likely to be heard by the intended recipients.

Timing and Pacing

Speaking one's truth does not mean speaking all one's truth with all one's energy on every possible occasion. Nor does it mean immediately and consistently countering every statement of others with which one disagrees. Quite the opposite. People's essential messages are lost if they are constantly thrust at others in a conflict. Truth telling requires a great deal of listening and dealing with the reactions that others have, and it requires repeated, often interrupted efforts, to deliver what is often a very difficult message.

The keys here are patience and taking an incremental approach. It may take time to convey a message effectively, but rushing to say everything that is on one's mind often means that the opportunity for genuine communication is lost. We need to work with disputants so they can engage in genuine listening, time their statements effectively, frame them well, and deliver them with confidence.

Positive Assertion

Disputants need to consider whether they wish to focus their communication as a response to what others are saying or as an independent assertion of their own point of view. Important communications are often lost in the reactive, argumentative style of much conflict discourse. People have to find ways of asserting their own needs and viewpoints in a positive manner, focusing on what they want or are in favor of as opposed to what they don't want or are opposed to. They also need to project a nonreactive manner, so it is clear they are saying what they think, not just reacting to what the other person thinks. As we work with people on identifying what they really have to say, how to frame it, when to deliver it, and how to promote a reciprocal system of communication, we will often find it helpful to ask people to articulate their beliefs or needs independently of their responses to what others have said. Sometimes this means simply asking people to focus on what they are for, rather than on what they are against.

A focus on positive assertion does not mean that disputants should never dispute or respond to what others say or point out specific areas of understanding, agreement, or disagreement. This too is important and at times essential. But what sustains long-term communication is not the point and counterpoint of a typical debate but ensuring that the essence of the message is rooted in one's own beliefs, values, and needs and one's willingness to stand up for these. Conversely, a commitment to oppose the values and interests of others (even when one profoundly disagrees with those values) is seldom effective as the primary focus of communication in the context of an enduring conflict.

Sometimes this may seem merely a matter of how something is framed, but positive framing accesses the deeper concerns that motivate enduring conflict. So, for example, even though a fight for equal rights and opportunity may seem the same as a struggle against discrimination and oppression, the search for justice and equality is basically an affirmative quest. Rights and opportunity are what people want; discrimination and oppression are what get in the way of attaining them.

Considering the Recipient

People often spend a great deal of time figuring out how to articulate their views but almost no time on how their views will be understood or interpreted. But considering the recipient is important and should not be overlooked. I often ask two simple, even obvious, questions of disputants who are considering what to say to someone with whom they are in conflict:

- How would you react to that statement if someone made it to you?
- If someone wanted to convey this to you, what would be the best way of doing so?

This exercise asks people to think about the interactive nature of communication, and not just their own message. Once they have thought about how they would respond to their own statements, we can proceed to help them think about how others, who may be different in background, culture, gender, age, race, or just personality, might respond. People often expect others to react as they would to something they say, and when the reaction is very different, people can easily feel mistreated, misunderstood, or manipulated.

We can help people to sort this through by discussing this dynamic and anticipating these differences. But we can only go so far with this because we can never be sure how others will react, and we don't want people to become so concerned about reactions that they lose sight of their essential message and fall into an avoidant pattern. This is another reason why our attention often has to be on the system of reciprocal communication rather than the specific message to be delivered at any given time.

RECOVERING FROM A DESTRUCTIVE INTERACTION

Over the course of an enduring conflict, everyone will have plenty of opportunities to learn how to recover from poor or even destructive communication interactions. We can assist in the recovery process by providing an outlet for people to express their emotions and thoughts and by helping them understand or deconstruct what happened, decide whether the negative experience needs to be dealt with directly and if so how, and plan how to move forward. If we are in a third-party role, we may be asked or we may offer to provide a forum and facilitate the renewed communication.

Perhaps the trickiest challenge here is to help people face up to their own contribution to the poor interchange. Often the most healing and constructive thing people can do after a negative interaction is to look at their own behavior and take responsibility for it. Conflict specialists can play a very helpful role by encouraging people to accept responsibility, even limited responsibility, for what happened. We can also work with people so they can hear the apologies given or ownership of responsibility taken by others, even though these may be buried in excuses or accusations and even though it is difficult to hear an apology when one is hurt or afraid. And sometimes we have to help disputants face the likelihood that they will receive no apology whatsoever because those on the other side may not feel they have anything to apologize for or may not be able to accept responsibility for their behavior. In that case it is important to help people consider how to proceed in the absence of an apology.

Of course receiving or delivering an apology is not all that disputants want following a destructive interaction. They also want some reassurance about the future, about not having to experience the same behavior or interaction again and sometimes they may want restitution of some sort for the damage that might have occurred. Unfortunately, in long-term conflicts it is seldom possible to guarantee this and people know it. At the very least people need to be able to give voice to their concerns and desires about the future, and they need help with facing the limits on what can be done to ensure that things will be different. They may also need support in taking whatever reasonable steps are available to prevent the recurrence of the most seriously negative aspects of an interchange. Recovery or healing usually requires some space, some nurturing, and some time. This may not always be easily achieved, but often, even in the midst of very high levels of involvement, providing some psychological or physical space is possible and desirable. Maintaining communication throughout the life of an enduring conflict sometimes requires a time-out from communication as well.

THE GUERRILLA COMMUNICATOR

Communicating through conflict over time requires energy, persistence, creativity, and courage. No one can always be at the top of his or her communication game, and sometimes the forces militating against constructive communication seem enormous. The anger, structural impediments, cultural barriers, power games, and personality challenges that may be present can make it seem impossible to turn a negative communication pattern around. In order to do so, disputants must sometimes mount a concerted effort against seemingly insurmountable obstacles—in a sense they must become guerrilla warriors for good communication. This warlike metaphor may be a paradoxical and perhaps overused one for constructive conflict engagement, but it is useful to play it out. Consider the circumstances of guerrilla warriors. They are trying to engage in a change effort against superior forces, and in doing so they have to figure out a strategic way to bring their strengths to bear.

The classic modern formulation of guerrilla tactics, written by Mao Zedong in his predictator period, derives from Sun Tzu's *The Art of War* (2005), written many centuries earlier. A guerilla war is essentially a war of attrition. The guerillas wear down the opposition until the power dynamics can change. Mao's summarizing aphorism was, "The enemy advances, we retreat. The enemy camps, we harass. The enemy tires, we attack. The enemy retreats, we pursue" (Mao Zedong, 1937/2000).

So let's reframe this in terms of dealing with communication in conflict. If adversaries in a conflict speak, listen. If they become hostile or threatening, limit communication or look for alternative safer channels. When communication is not occurring, probe, offer openings, seize communication opportunities. When adversaries let down their defenses, enter into more direct communication, consider opening multiple channels of communication. When the resistance to constructive engagement breaks down, be prepared to participate fully, don't let the past history of negativity or hostility prevent seizing new opportunities to communicate. Perhaps the overall message of this metaphor is persevere, be creative, be flexible, and be principled when dealing with the ebb and flow, or rhythm, of communication over the course of an enduring conflict. (For two other interesting takes on guerrilla approaches to conflict see Adler, 2008; Benjamin, 1998.)

Our role in establishing, conducting, and maintaining constructive communication systems over time is at the center of our work in enduring conflict. We are constantly faced with the temptation to focus exclusively on immediate interactions and thereby neglect the challenge of promoting an enduring approach to communication. As important as it may be to deal with the interaction before us, we need also to attend to the long-term patterns and means of communication if we are going to help people stay with conflict.

Even so, good communication is not enough. To stay with conflict people also need to know how to develop their power, use it responsibly, respond to the power of others, and do all this in a manner consistent with the goal of a long-term, effective, and constructive engagement in conflict. Sometimes this means knowing when and how to escalate conflict. In the next chapter we turn our attention to power and escalation.

6

Using Power and Escalation

It seems to me that whereas power usually means power-over, the power of some person or group over some other person or group, it is possible to develop the conception of power-with, a jointly developed power, a co-active, not a coercive power.

Mary Parker Follett (1940)

As much as we conflict professionals might like to think that rational problem solving, effective communication, and good process can resolve or at least ameliorate most conflicts, we cannot escape the role of power in conflict. Unless people have a reason to change their approach to conflict, they are likely to continue what they have been doing, even if it is destructive, unfair, or insensitive. Furthermore, destructive or harmful approaches may escalate or become entrenched if they seem to be achieving the goals of the person employing them. In the face of destructive or injurious actions, disputants often have to consider how to change the dynamic so that it is no longer in a perpetrator's interest to behave negatively. This means finding a constructive but powerful way to respond to the destructive use of power.

Power is always present in conflict, and to be effective in handling conflict disputants have to know both how to use power and how to respond to it. But power can be a dangerous tool. When disputants employ power, particularly coercive power, conflict can easily escalate, relations can rupture, and people can get hurt. So a central challenge we face in working with people in conflict is finding a way to help them develop and use power wisely.

Enduring conflict poses additional challenges. How can disputants nurture their power, sustain it, and use it to encourage long-term constructive engagement? How can they respond to the power tactics, in multiple variations, that they are likely to face over time? How can they encourage an enduring and reciprocal use of constructive power—that is, how can disputants use their own power so as to encourage others to promote their own interests in a productive, nondestructive way over time? Over the course of an enduring conflict, there will be times when escalating a conflict may be necessary. How can we help disputants recognize those times and escalate in a powerful and yet responsible and constructive way?

When working with enduring conflict, our goal is not to prevent, suppress, or counteract the use of power but to guide it into productive channels. What makes the use of power productive depends greatly on the circumstance, but our overriding goals ought always to be to promote integrative, normative, sustainable, and nonviolent approaches. We should do this, however, with an understanding that power is not a one-way process but a reciprocal set of interactions. In the pursuit of a constructive pattern of interactions, sometimes less "nice" approaches have to be used along the way.

Inevitably, when we discuss power we run up against some fairly confusing terminology, which conflates power with aggression, coercion, or force. We often talk about power-based approaches as opposed to interest-based or rights-based approaches (Mayer, 2000; Ury, Brett, and Goldberg, 1988). But even when pursuing interest-based or rights-based approaches to conflict, power is always part of the picture. So we need to start with a useful approach to understanding power.

POWER AND CONFLICT

Power has been variously defined as the ability to promote one's interests, to further a goal in the face of opposition, to cause something to happen, or to maximize one's freedom of choice and action. For our purposes, we can think of power in enduring conflict as the ability to accomplish one's goals and have an impact on the actions and thinking of others over time. In other words, power is interactional (we can understand it only with regard to the responses it calls forth from others) and longitudinal (the amount and effectiveness of one's power is related to its sustainability and consequences over time). Power is an elusive but important concept in enduring conflict, and in order to understand it, we have to look at its many aspects. In particular, we need to consider its nature, how it is applied, its reciprocal dynamics, and how it is sustained (or not) over time.

The Nature of Power

In enduring conflict, as in all conflict, every party has some power or there would be no conflict. However, the type of power disputants can muster varies tremendously (Coleman, 2000; Gamson, 1968; Etzioni, 1975; Mayer, 1987). For example, the formal authority of an employer is significant but by no means absolute. The legal rights of employees, their power to resist or enable a decision, and the skills they have on which the employer depends are powerful barriers to the untrammeled exercise of power by the employer. Employers who rely too heavily on formal authority or economic leverage, even when they have an enormous advantage in these areas, can easily find their ability to promote their goals over time severely limited.

One way to help disputants develop a sustainable approach to conflict is to work with them to develop multiple sources of power, focusing on power that they can sustain and that is consistent with their long-term goals. In this context it is useful to look at seven overlapping variables concerning how power can be brought to bear on a conflict. In most circumstances disputants have some degree of each type of power. However, the type they gravitate to or that is most accessible to them is critical to how they approach conflict and the consequences that will result from their application of power.

- *Formal and informal.* Formal power derives from a legal right, a contractual prerogative, or an organizational role that gives an individual or group the authority to take action or make decisions. Informal power derives from custom, social status, personal characteristics, or group affiliation. The president of the United States has considerable formal power, but his or her greatest power may be the ability to influence perceptions, attitudes and public opinion—to use what Theodore Roosevelt called the *bully pulpit*. (The ancient Roman distinction between *imperium* ("power") and *auctoritas* ("influence") is a version of this; Everitt, 2006.)

- *Structural and personal.* Structural power derives from the nature of a situation, the resources available to people, people's formal authority, and their genuine alternatives. Personal power derives from a person's personal conviction, motivation, intelligence, emotional resources, or other personal attributes. For example, think of the power a teacher has over a class of students. Much of it derives from the structure of the school— the ability to grade, reward, punish, with the backup of the school administration and the community. But some teachers, because of experience, force of character, wisdom, or self-assurance, are much better able than others to maintain control of their classrooms.

- *Integrative and distributive.* Integrative power can be thought of as *power with*, distributive power as *power against*. Integrative power comes from one's ability to add to the overall power of all the parties to a conflict. Distributive power is the ability to pursue one's goals in the face of resistance from others. The power of both management and workers to cooperate to increase productivity and creativity is integrative, whereas each side's ability to force the other side to do something (for example, raise pay or give up benefits) is distributive.

- *Reward and sanction.* Reward power is the power to provide a benefit or a positive incentive, whereas sanction power is the power to impose a punishment or a negative consequence.

- *Individual and social.* Sometimes power resides primarily within an individual but it is usually dependent on association with others. Groups, communities, peers, and the general public have power that is largely social in nature. The power of leaders, arbiters, or executives is more individually based. Some people are best able to exert or experience their power in a group context. Others are comfortable with the individual or autonomous expression of power.

- *Legitimate and illegitimate.* Some types of power, such as persuasion and judicial authority, are considered legitimate. Other types, such as violence, and extortion, are not. However, these variables are dependent on context, gender, and culture—what is acceptable in one context, one gender, or one particular culture may not be in another. For example, in some contexts, offering financial incentives is an acceptable positive reward; in others it is considered bribery.

- *Time limited and ongoing.* Sometimes power is dependent on a short-term set of circumstances whereas other types of power are more enduring. The ability to negotiate a settlement to a claim may quickly change once a court has ruled on a particular legal question. If I have something you need, I have a certain amount of power over you—until you no longer need it, find another place to obtain it, or I no longer have it. The power that derives from social standing, financial resources, or personal charisma is usually more durable.

- *Implied and applied.* Implied power is the power that people have and that others are aware they have but that is not overtly brought to bear. Applied power is power that people directly, overtly, and intentionally use (Mayer, 2000). Theodore Roosevelt (who had a lot to say about the use of power) famously said, "Speak softly but carry a big stick." He certainly brandished the potential of the U.S. government to exercise coercive power—for example, sending a U.S. Navy fleet (the Great White Fleet) around the world. He may not have spoken as softly as he suggested, but his point was that it's more important to develop one's capacity to use power than to actually use it (Morris, 2001). A more modern formulation is suggested by Fisher and Ury (1981) when they advocate that people increase their power by developing their BATNA (best alternative to a negotiated agreement). The more alternatives people have to a voluntary agreement, the better the agreement they are likely to get—even when they do not threaten to resort to those alternatives.

These variables cannot only help us to understand the nature of power that is being applied but can also point to ways disputants can increase the constructive power available to them in long-term conflict. Generally, disputants are more aware of some elements of their potential power than others, and these are not always the most useful aspects of power available to them. For example, disputants often fail to realize the importance of informal, integrative, social, reward, or implied power. In helping people to stay with conflict, one of our most important challenges is to help disputants recognize the potential of other types of power and develop the ability to use them constructively over time.

Using Power

In an enduring conflictual relationship, disputes are exacerbated by the type of power disputants choose to use. For example, people may play to an immediate weakness of an opponent (using time-limited approaches to power), but the long-term result is a destructive power struggle (for example, an arms race). Or disputants may focus on how to obtain the most of a limited resource for themselves (distributive power) rather than how to increase the size of the available resources for all (integrative).

Often it is useful to ask people to focus specifically on how they choose to use the power they do have. In general, power can be applied in a normative, utilitarian, or coercive manner (Etzioni, 1975; Gamson, 1968). That is, one can choose to persuade others to act in a certain way because it is "the right thing to do" or "makes the most sense" (for example, accords with a set of shared norms), to induce others to act by offering incentives or rewards or displaying a cost-benefit analysis, or to force others to do something by threatening unpleasant consequences, such as punishment, dismissal, or legal sanctions.

All three approaches are occasionally necessary, but in general a reliance on coercive or utilitarian approaches is less easy to sustain over time. Coercive approaches require an ongoing maintenance of power over others, which often provokes retaliation, resistance, and a coercive response. A coercive approach is sustainable only if the party employing it can maintain enough coercive power to dominate a relationship and force compliance. This seldom leads to constructive engagement over time and makes it extremely difficult to elicit the full cooperation of others. The short-term application of coercive power is sometimes necessary, in part to counteract the coercive tactics of others, but it is normally best if disputants can switch to other approaches as quickly as possible.

Utilitarian approaches may be more sustainable but require an ongoing application of adequate resources and encourage a what's-in-it-for-me approach to decision making. Enduring conflict requires participants to consider not just immediate benefits but the need to find a wise and sustainable approach to a long-term problem. This need is usually best met by maximizing the normative use of power, which appeals to the values, judgment, and wisdom of all parties. Furthermore, the normative application of power, if reciprocated, is most likely to encourage parties to take an integrative (power with) approach rather than a distributive (power against) approach.

For example, in the long-term struggle between environmentalists and the energy industry, coercive tactics may sometimes be necessary (lawsuits, direct action, injunctions), and utilitarian approaches (settlement negotiations over environmental damage or taxes on pollution) also have their place, but over time the normative approach to exerting influence is probably the most sustainable (consider, for example, the impact of the 2006 documentary *An Inconvenient Truth* on the debate about climate change and energy policy).

Power often diminishes the moment it is employed. Developing the capacity to take legal action may be more powerful than either threatening to take it or taking it. Employers will often work very hard to keep a valuable employee from leaving, but when that person threatens to quit, especially if she makes this threat repeatedly, the power of that possibility can begin to diminish. What disputants do not often think about is which approach to the use of power is sustainable and which plays to their strengths over time. They also do not pay sufficient attention to what kind of power they would like to encourage others to use, and instead concentrate exclusively on how to counteract others' use of power, assuage them, or force them to accede to their demands.

In general the broader and more balanced the range of power that disputants can access and the more strategic they are in using it, the more effective they will be at staying with conflict. In enduring conflict, in particular, it is important to help people to diversify their approach to power and to move beyond a rigid reliance on one approach to exerting influence. The narrower disputants are in their approach to power, the more likely they are to perpetuate destructive or ineffective patterns of power exchange. When power is used ineffectively, conflicts can become impasses, as was the situation with a divorced couple, Kendra and Bart.

Kendra was always rational and soft-spoken when negotiating child-care arrangements with Bart. Bart was volatile (not violent, but quick to anger) and would readily threaten legal action if he did not get his way. But Kendra seldom gave way on anything, not even in response to Bart's most reasonable requests. She calmly repeated her point of view, referred to their divorce agreement, and remained adamant. Bart would become loud and emotional and threaten to get "the meanest lawyer in town," but would then give in and sulk. As a result they had almost no ability to resolve any problems between them or arrive at mutual agreements about vacations, school, schedule changes, or extracurricular activities.

The problem was not that Bart was trying to exercise power, but that he was doing it in an ineffective and nonsustainable way. His reliance on threats, anger, and emotionality were actually disempowering to him and caused negotiations to deadlock. To change this Bart needed to focus on his genuine source of power and consider what he had to offer Kendra that might motivate her to act differently or how he could apply the power he had in a less coercive, more normative manner.

The Reciprocity of Power

Critical to our work with enduring conflict is an appreciation for the interactional nature of power and the reciprocal patterns in which power is used over time. To fully understand power, we need to look at how one person's approach affects the approach that others take. If I threaten to leave my job if I am not treated differently, what will you as my boss do? Will you accede to my demands? Will you react to my threat? Will you ignore me? What will I do in turn, and where will this lead us?

Staying with conflict requires that disputants achieve a stable and constructive approach to the reciprocal application of power. Let's consider six reciprocal patterns:

- *Escalation.* One party increases the use of distributive, coercive, or sanction-based power, and the other party responds in kind. Each party responds to the other party's escalation with an escalation of his or her own until some crisis point is reached—often with destructive consequences. A period of relative calm ensues, and then the pattern reasserts itself. A volatile, divorcing couple and gang warfare are often examples of this pattern. (I will consider the appropriate use of escalation later in this chapter.)

- *Dominance (submission).* One party exerts coercive power while a second party submits or avoids. This then encourages the first party to exert more coercive power, resulting in more submission on the other side, until a pattern of dominance (sometimes with passive resistance) is entrenched. This pattern can often be seen in domestic violence and tyrannical workplaces.

- *Stalemate.* One party matches the other party's use of power until no further escalation occurs (or is possible). Parties are then stuck in a power dynamic that they cannot walk away from and that does not produce constructive results for anyone—although one party's needs may be better met by the status quo than the other party's are. This pattern is frequently found in dysfunctional academic departments, in divided legislative bodies, and in communities in conflict about issues of development and preservation.

- *Mirroring*. Each party matches whatever power approach is used by the other. When one party threatens the other threatens, when one escalates the other escalates, and when one de-escalates the other follows suit. This can sometimes be functional but often leads to stalemate or to a rigid and nonstrategic approach. Reverse mirroring occurs when one party takes the opposite approach (to the extent that there is one) to what the other party is doing. If one escalates the other de-escalates. If one offers rewards the other threatens sanctions. Both mirroring and reverse mirroring can often be seen in couples' relationships, among school-children, or between parents and children.

- *Cycling*. Parties engage in a repeating pattern of power moves. Consider two business partners who often disagree about whom to hire. One offers an incentive ("if you agree to hire her, I will agree to let you choose the next hire"). In response the other threatens consequences ("if you try to blackmail me into hiring her, I won't help you on any of your projects"). This leads the first partner to announce a withdrawal from communication ("if that is the way you are going to be, we don't have to work together") and then to clam up. The second partner then appeals for forgiveness ("I'm sorry, I shouldn't have gotten so angry"). The first then reverts to the offer of a reward ("well, if we hire this person, I will make sure that you get the first opportunity to get her assistance when you need it"), and the pattern repeats.

- *Mutuality*. Parties respond to each other's power with the goal of withdrawing from destructive patterns of power exchange and moving toward compatible, mutually reinforcing, and constructive approaches. For example, one party may escalate, and the other may escalate a bit in return but ties this to an incentive to de-escalate. The other tentatively responds with a counterincentive, and both gradually move away from a coercive mode and toward a utilitarian mode.

Many variations on each of these reciprocal patterns exist. Some patterns are more constructive or functional than others. In particular, a pattern that gravitates toward mutuality and away from escalation, dominance, or stalemate is more constructive and sustainable. Often we can help people identify the reciprocal pattern of power exchange that they are using and help them think through alternative approaches that lead to a more constructive, mutual approach to power. This was the challenge faced in working with Kendra and Bart. By pointing out to them the cycling nature of their power interchange and helping them consider other approaches to how they might influence each other, they could begin to develop a more mutual pattern of power exchange. Working on developing constructive patterns of power interchanges is critical to staying with conflict. When effective reciprocal patterns of mutual power have been developed, it is as if the parties to a conflict have learned to dance with each other in a graceful way, as when two aikido or tai chi masters work with each other.

Sustainable Power

Some approaches to the use of power are more sustainable over time than others. Sustainability is dependent on the reciprocal pattern of power that has been established and the types of power available to other parties. If one party has an overwhelming edge in physical or financial resources, that party may be able to sustain the use of coercion or financial rewards and sanctions for quite a while. In general, however, unless this pattern changes to a more mutual one, it is probably not sustainable over the long haul and certainly not in a constructive way. Therefore one of the most important goals of working with people to stay with conflict is to consider what approaches to the use of power are sustainable—for all involved.

One source of escalation is the fear that if power is not used it will fade. After the election of probusiness public officials, corporations involved in extractive industries may feel that they have no reason to try to work out accommodations with environmental groups. In fact they may feel that an aggressive approach to extraction, an attempt to bypass or overturn existing regulations, and an effort to marginalize antidevelopment groups is their best policy. They may reason that if they do not use their advantage in the current political climate, it will soon disappear or diminish. Yet it is precisely because that advantage will disappear, that it may be in their interests to use their temporarily stronger position to encourage a more mutual approach to the use of power.

To complicate things further, one objective that conflict participants might have is to make the approach to power used by others unsustainable. Terrorist groups and guerrilla fighters are not often able to gain their end objectives directly, but they can often make others' application of power extremely costly. Or consider, in an entirely different context and with much less destructive impact, an employee who constantly files grievances, perhaps never winning, but discouraging an employer from giving negative performance reviews.

The social setting in which power is exercised also affects sustainability. For example, in settings such as prisons or the military the use of threats and coercion is supported and therefore more sustainable, but in settings such as businesses, partnerships, and neighborhoods such an approach violates important norms and is harder to sustain.

Acceptable and sustainable approaches to power are broadly affected by gender and cultural dynamics. Whether fair or not, applications of power that are acceptable when used by men may violate important social norms when used by women. Or power that is acceptable for men to apply to men or women to women may not be acceptable or sustainable across gender lines. Gender norms about power are one way in which glass ceilings are created and enforced. If the norm in an organization, for example, is that a leader has to be blunt, direct, and willing to employ coercive power, but at the same time women who employ power in that way are seen as harsh, shrill, or emasculating, then women are at a considerable disadvantage in exercising leadership.

Similarly, African Americans have faced many unspoken but extremely powerful normative limits on how they exercise power or influence in workplaces, where they are often too easily labeled as threatening, overbearing, or presumptuous. Although these discriminatory norms ought not to be condoned, they continue to have a significant impact on sustainable approaches to the exercise of power.

We have to be careful not to make overly broad generalizations about which approaches to power are more sustainable because of the reciprocal and contextual issues discussed previously. Sometimes coercive approaches may be sustainable. But we should also be aware that in enduring conflicts, when disputants' reliance on coercive, formal, distributive, or sanction-based approaches to power overwhelms their use of normative, integrative, informal, or reward-based methods, the chances of achieving a constructive, mutual, and sustainable pattern of power use diminishes considerably.

HELPING DISPUTANTS USE POWER WISELY

As conflict specialists we are constantly dealing with the ways disputants access and use the power they have. We work to help people recognize the potential power they can bring to bear on a situation, connect their use of power to their goals and interests, employ power in a way that is consonant with their values, and anticipate the response they might get from others. In general we work to encourage a constructive exchange among disputants, helping them use power wisely.

Effective Uses of Power

Often we may think our goal is to encourage people to avoid using power at all. But as I have discussed, this is based on a false understanding of the nature of power. Our mission should be to help people use power effectively and wisely over time. Here are some of the hallmarks of an effective and strategic use of power:

- *Intentionality*. It is important that power be used toward an intentional end and in an intentional manner. We can help disputants become aware of the power they are (or are not) using and make a decision about whether they want to continue or alter their approach. Unless people are aware of the power they are bringing to bear, it's hard for them to approach their use of power in a strategic manner.

- *Realism*. People use power better when they are realistic about the power they have or do not have, the effectiveness and limits of using that power, the potential power of others, and others' likely responses to the use of power.

- *Focus*. It is wise to focus one's use of power toward specific purposes and particular people. One of the main ways in which we see disputants using power ineffectively is that they take an unfocused or scattershot approach or to direct their power toward inappropriate people or ends (for example, becoming directive, assertive, or angry at one's family or at a coworker when the real issue is a conflict with a boss).

- *Proportionality.* Disputants are most effective when they respond to a circumstance or ongoing conflict with enough power to accomplish their goals, but not so much as to squander power or unnecessarily escalate a conflict.

- *Incrementalism.* It generally makes sense to start with a normative, integrative, informal, and personal approach and move in small steps and only as needed to other approaches. Massive retaliation and sudden and dramatic escalation are rarely effective in an enduring conflict.

- *Congruence.* A disputant is almost always more effective when acting in accordance with her own values and in a manner that is congruent with who she is, with her personal style, strengths, and sense of self.

- *Reciprocity.* As discussed previously, it is essential to use power with an understanding of the reciprocal pattern of power that is being developed or encouraged.

- *Nonviolence.* For our purposes the principles of nonviolence are almost always appropriate (regardless of one's personal beliefs about violence). We should encourage people to approach the use of power with respect for others and with a determination to avoid violent coercion or force, because this almost never leads to a constructive reciprocal process.

- *Sustainability.* It is critical to use power in a way that is sustainable over the long haul. This often involves developing specific personal resources and support systems. For example, in order to stay involved and effective over time, a community leader may need advisers, coaches, emotional support, and someone to share the burden of addressing the media or local officials. (See Chapter Eight for a fuller discussion of sustainability.)

- *Flexibility.* It is also essential to adapt one's use of power to particular circumstances and to be willing to change one's approach as circumstances change or in accordance with an assessment of the effectiveness of a particular approach.

- *Predictability and transparency.* Disputants sometimes think that being unpredictable gives them more power, but in fact this usually just encourages defensiveness and rigidity. The more predictable and transparent people are in their use of power, the more likely it is that they will engender a constructive response.

When disputants use power in an intentional, realistic, focused, incremental, proportional, congruent, nonviolent, flexible, sustainable, and transparent way, they are most likely taking a constructive stance toward conflict. Of course there are values built into some of these hallmarks (such as transparence, nonviolence, and reciprocity), and we need to be aware that not all disputants share these values. People may not feel reciprocity is a value they wish to embrace yet still be able to understand that it is nonetheless critical to sustaining themselves through conflict. Whatever our conflict practitioner role or approach, these characteristics of the constructive use of power can help us to frame our work with disputants.

Discussing Power Dynamics

When we work with disputants, we are generally dealing with the ways power is used to promote a particular end. In this effort we need to consider people's sources of power, how to use power in a sustainable way, and in particular how to encourage a constructive, reciprocal approach to the application of power. Sometimes we can rehearse with disputants how they will use power, sometimes we can *game it out* (play out a series of moves and countermoves that might occur or play out alternative approaches), and often we need to debrief what happened in a previous power exchange to help disputants learn to use power more effectively in the future. When using this techniques, it is usually best to focus on specific interactions (asking, What did you do? What did they do? and What did you do in response? kinds of questions) rather than to engage in general or abstract discussion. Bringing to bear the hallmarks of constructive power exchanges described previously can also be useful.

We may often do this as coaches or in individual meetings with disputants, but it can be particularly instructive and worthwhile to discuss power dynamics with all parties present. This turned out to be the turning point in a child protection mediation involving a very quiet mother and aunt:

When Carrie was two, she was removed from the care of her mother (Karenna) and placed with her mother's aunt (Selena) due to her mother's addiction problems (neighbors had called in the police when they observed Carrie in the backyard with Karenna—who had passed out). Carrie had been with Selena for six months while Karenna was supposed to be attending a variety of programs (AA, parenting classes, therapy, and job training). But Karenna was missing many of her meetings, and the division of youth services (the child protection agency) did not feel she was making progress. They were recommending that serious consideration be given to placing Carrie with Selena permanently. Karenna said her treatment plans were impossible to maintain and claimed that she was being set up. Furthermore, what had started as a constructive relationship between Selena and Karenna was deteriorating as Karenna began to feel that her aunt was conspiring with the agency to "steal my baby." The case was then referred to a child protection mediation program.

Selena remained quiet through much of the meeting, saying only that she wanted to do the right thing for Carrie but she also did not want to upset Karenna. Karenna was sullen and quiet during most of the meeting, letting her lawyer speak for her. What she did say, repeatedly, was that there were too many meetings, too much traveling by bus, and that she could not keep to the schedule. The social worker and the agency lawyer asserted that their obligation was to find a permanent home for Carrie and that unless Karenna proved she could be a fit parent they had no choice but to terminate parental rights. Karenna's lawyer argued that her client was being set up, that the agency had to come up with a reasonable and feasible treatment plan for Karenna, and that she was quite happy to take this case to the judge. The more the lawyers and the social workers argued, the quieter Karenna and Selena became. Finally the mediator said:

"Everybody's trying to pressure each other about what should happen. The agency is trying to get Karenna to agree to follow through on a treatment plan or face losing her child. Karenna's lawyer is trying to get the agency to alter the plan by invoking the power of the judge. But the two most powerful people in room, powerful in that they can make any decision here work or not work, are Karenna and Selena, and they are not saying anything. By withdrawing from this conversation, the two of you can make sure that no agreement is reached that you don't like, but you won't be able to get people to agree to what you do want either."

As tempting as it was to try to suggest some alternatives or to frame some questions about what Karenna might be willing to do, what Selena might contribute, or to work with people in caucus, the mediator felt that the most important thing was to alter the power dynamic—and that meant putting the power issues on the table and suggesting that the way people were using power with each other was ineffective. This was a one-time intervention, but it was about an interaction that in one form or another had gone on for years and was likely to continue for the foreseeable future, even after a permanent arrangement for Carrie had been worked out.

RESPONDING TO OTHERS' USE OF POWER

If disputants are to remain strategic and constructive in the use of power in enduring conflict, they need to learn how to respond to overt and aggressive power moves on the part of others. Disputants often face the challenge of responding both to the substance of what they are being asked to do or not do and to the use of power itself. We all can relate to the dilemma posed when we are told that we must do something "or else." We can easily lose sight of how we feel about what we are being asked to do and focus instead on the "or else." This is natural, and it raises the question of how one should respond to an approach to power that seems illegitimate or coercive.

Disputants involved in enduring conflicts need to find a steady and strategic response that coaxes others into a steady and constructive approach to the use of power, one that is not impulsive or focused simply on immediate advantage. This does not mean lying down in the face of destructive or bullying tactics, but it does mean taking a longer view on how to induce different behavior.

It may be necessary to set consequences when someone employs destructive or manipulative tactics, but these consequences ought to lead people out of a pattern of escalation, dominance, stalemate, or mirroring rather than locking them into it. Consider three situations:

- A suicide bomber kills a number of innocent people. The government reacts by bombing targets in the community from which the suicide bomber comes. More people want revenge and more bombings occur.

- A worker refuses to accede to the request of a manager to take on a work assignment that feels punitive. The manager threatens to discipline the worker. The worker acts out by talking back to the manager in front of other workers and acting defiant whenever possible. The manager finds a pretext for suspending the worker for a week, and the worker organizes his or her associates to file a series of grievances against the manager.

- A faculty member refuses to vote in support of the hiring, promotion, or tenure of anyone supported by another faculty member with whom he or she has a long-standing conflict. The second faculty member responds in kind and starts a campaign to discredit the first faculty member, who responds by refusing to talk with the second faculty member at all.

Each of these situations involves exchanges in which a power struggle has overtaken a conflict about potentially important issues. In each a powerful response may be called for, but the challenge is to find a response that turns people away from power games rather than locking them into a perpetual, destructive power struggle.

In general, conflict specialists have three goals when helping disputants respond to someone else's use of destructive or coercive power:

1. We have to help disputants separate their power struggle from concerns about policy, substantive issues, relationships, or communication. That means making sure that the desire to counter what is perceived as an illegitimate use of power does not preclude entering into a separate or parallel process to address people's legitimate concerns. In other words, the fact that someone is taking a coercive or unacceptable approach to furthering his or her interests does not mean the interests themselves should be ignored or discounted.

2. We need to help disputants respond to destructive or aggressive power moves in a measured, effective, and ethical way, so that the continued use of destructive power is discouraged without resorting to countermeasures that are also destructive.

3. We need to help disputants encourage a gradual move away from destructive power to more positive, integrative, and normative approaches to the imposition of power. And we need to do all this as transparently as we possibly can.

Let's consider these goals in reference to the three situations presented previously. In the first situation, analysis suggests that the government should always be looking for a forum in which to address the concerns behind the bombing, even if these are extremely hard to address. A government is unlikely to want (or be able) to address the goal that the bombers might have of destroying the entire state, but they can address concerns about human rights, economic issues, and national identity. Whether or not it is appropriate to deal directly with the perpetrators of the bombing, it seems clear that to fail to address the underlying concerns in the long run is likely to play into the hands of the extremists.

In the second situation the manager can work with the worker on his or her concerns about job assignment practices even as the manager develops appropriate consequences for inappropriate behavior. To refuse to deal with the worker's concerns until the behavior changes may be tempting but is probably ineffective. The faculty member in the third situation needs to find some mechanism for exerting power (formal complaints; opposing the other's candidacy for department leadership; private, perhaps mediated, conversation with the other faculty member) that does not make other department members or prospective faculty victims of the struggle. The common thread here is that the destructive application of power encourages a coercive and potentially destructive response. Moreover, this is not generally a sustainable approach and in fact can be disempowering in the long run.

Our three goals do not, however, mean that people should always turn the other cheek, be coolly reasonable, or pour oil on troubled waters. Sometimes the only way to deal with the illegitimate use of power or with the suppression of disagreement is to escalate.

CONSTRUCTIVE ESCALATION

In enduring conflicts, constructive escalation is sometimes essential. When a serious concern is being ignored, unacceptable behavior continues, conditions are oppressive, or coercion is increasing, disputants sometimes have no alternative but to escalate a conflict or accept the unacceptable. Constructive escalation is an essential tool for staying with conflict. The problem with it is that escalation can take on a life of its own and even when used with care and discipline can lead to unpredictable and sometimes destructive results. Working with disputants to recognize when some form of escalation might be useful, to develop a wise and constructive approach to escalation, and to open the door to de-escalation when circumstances allow is an essential part of our role.

Escalation takes many forms. Whenever someone seeks to bring a conflict to a higher level of intensity and increase the amount of pressure on others to act differently, some form of escalation has occurred. When suits are filed, court action is threatened, public accusations or demands are made, additional people are brought into the conflict, or more powerful consequences are imposed, a conflict is being escalated.

Whether a particular behavior is an escalation is to some extent a matter of perception. If I tell children that they cannot watch TV until they finish their homework, they might see that as a threat or punishment (an escalation), but I might see it as a simple and reasonable limit. Mediators often handle escalating behavior by normalizing it and trying to define it in less toxic terms. For example, when a party to mediation threatens to go to court if he does not get a concession, a mediator may respond by pointing out that one interesting characteristic of mediation is that it is voluntary and does not prevent anyone from exercising other alternatives if the mediation fails. Has an escalation occurred? It depends on how one looks at the situation.

The conscious use of escalation remains an essential tool in conflict; without it constructive engagement is often impossible. The problem is that once disputants use escalation, they often lose sight of its strategic and limited purpose. Rather than trying to change behavior, they try to change people. Rather than seeking a more productive reciprocal power relationship, they want revenge. Rather than constructive engagement, they seek victory. When we work with disputants on how to escalate, we have to help them maintain fairly limited goals and leave themselves a graceful way out of continued escalation.

We generally help disputants arrive at a constructive approach to escalation by the questions we ask and the advice we provide, but we can also provide a structure for escalation (for instance, a facilitated interchange in which parties can raise the ante in a conflict). When we work with disputants on escalation, we are generally trying to help them achieve these ends:

Clarity about goals. The best guard against excessive escalation is clarity about why one is choosing to escalate, not just the immediate objectives but also the fit with long-term goals.

Built-in limits. Whenever possible, it's best to have structural or built-in limits to escalation so that it does not take on a life of its own. This is the genius of a commitment to nonviolence. At the same time as a conflict is escalated through direct action, a promise is made to limit the escalation and to respect the adversary. Similarly, the laws that govern labor relations allow for power to be exercised and escalation to occur but define strict parameters for those actions. We can help disputants to define limits (limiting court action or public statements, maintaining communication, keeping others informed about planned actions) or to choose approaches with built-in limits.

Proportionality. When people start to escalate or to focus specifically on the exchange of power (as discussed earlier), they often put aside internalized constraints and act as though any power they bring to bear is justified by the action of others. In addition to ensuring that built-in constraints are in place, we need to help people escalate incrementally and in proportion to the problem they are addressing or the behavior they are responding to.

A values-based approach. Like any other constructive use of power, value congruence is a source of power as well as a limit on its use. In essence, we need to ask people to consider whether there is something more important to them than the conflict or the concerns that it represents. What would they not be willing to do to pursue their goals? What principles guide their view of what behavior is acceptable? If there are no limits on what an individual or group is willing to do, then escalation is very dangerous and will be very hard to contain.

Attention to safety. Although sometimes necessary, escalation is almost always unpredictable, and it's important for disputants to face this. It's particularly important to know that escalation can be dangerous—sometimes fatal. As important as it is for victims of domestic abuse to gain the legal, programmatic, and personal support necessary to put an end to the violence or to leave the relationship, there is not always a safe way of doing this. Standing up against oppression, coercion, or intimidation may be of vital importance, and the alternative to standing up against oppression may also be dangerous or even fatal. But we should never be naïve about the danger that is involved in engaging in conflict. This is especially true when disputants escalate the level of conflict or intensify the power that they chose to bring to bear.

Even in disputes where violence and oppression are not directly involved, safety may be at stake. For example, there may be a danger of losing or harming a relationship, of provoking retaliation, or of losing an opportunity to work with another person. Sometimes these are risks worth taking, but we should help disputants do so with open eyes.

Consideration for adversaries. Disputants sometimes devalue each other in order to justify their actions or beliefs. Respecting one's adversary, valuing her right to promote her interests, and preserving her self-esteem are not only good values—they are smart moves when escalating a conflict. Such consideration helps encapsulate an escalation, makes it easier for an adversary to respond constructively, and guides a power exchange in a more productive direction.

Tactical sophistication. Specifically, we need to continually reinforce the interactive and reciprocal nature of power exchanges.

Disputants need to consider the variety of responses they may receive when they escalate a conflict and what their next move might be. In other words, we want to help disputants think through several moves at a time but also to beware of the unpredictability of what is in essence a complex system of interaction.

An exit strategy. Escalation should never occur without first considering how de-escalation can take place. Sometimes the only way out of an escalated conflict that disputants can envision is surrender or victory. That's not adequate for promoting constructive engagement over time. The goal of escalation generally ought to be a better pattern of power exchange and a more constructive approach to engagement—not a final and absolute outcome, particularly in enduring conflict. The goal of ending a conflict once and for all through a decisive act of escalation is almost always elusive, usually unrealistic, and often dangerous.

We need to help disputants recognize when to de-escalate their use of power and how. This means developing a gradual and reciprocal approach to decreasing the use of distributive or coercive power. It also requires helping disputants recognize when the purposes of escalation have been served, when it is no longer useful, and to seize on any signs that others are willing to modify their approach in a more constructive direction.

Our natural instinct as conflict professionals is often to resist or end escalation as quickly as possible, but as hard as it may be to escalate in proportional and tactically sophisticated ways, that is sometimes the key to moving a conflict situation forward. This was the case in a divorce mediation I conducted that was referred to me by collaborative lawyers (see Macfarlane, 2008, or Tesler and Thompson, 2006, for a description of collaborative practice).

Perry and Melissa had been trying for two years to negotiate their divorce. Although they had made a great deal of progress, they could not close the deal, and they were furious at each other. So much emphasis had been put on settling out of court, that the threat of going to court was seen as a serious escalation. Shortly after entering these negotiations, I emphasized with each of them that going to court, particularly after they had tried so hard, was a legitimate alternative. I encouraged them to talk about why they might do that and to discuss what they would have to do to continue their co-parenting as effectively as possible as they entered a litigation process. I felt that Perry and Melissa needed to be able to use the alternative of going to court as a legitimate means of trying to influence each other. I hoped that by legitimizing this option, they might be able to consider the use of court (even to threaten it if they chose) but also to leave themselves considerable room to back off from the threat as well. One effect of this discussion was to diminish the emotional tension associated with considering the court alternative. Although it remained a real possibility, it seemed to be less of a toxic threat looming over the process.

This was by no means a perfect escalation, but it was more respectful, proportional, limited, and tactical than the interactions Perry and Melissa were having before we started, and it moved their conflict forward after a long period of stalemate.

The unspoken assumption that the values and structure of many conflict resolution procedures imply is that escalation is bad. That norm is one reason why people are sometimes reluctant to use our services. We have to be very careful that we do not operate with this assumption. We need to be clear with disputants that we understand escalation is sometimes necessary, but we also need to emphasize the importance of doing it strategically. We need to help disputants think through how they can be both powerful and humane, effective and considerate; how they can both protect their interests and preserve their relationships with the people they are in conflict with; and how they can do all this in a way that accords with their fundamental values.

We ought to emphasize constructive approaches to power—integrative, personal, normative, nonviolent, reward-based approaches. But we need to do this in a way that helps all disputants be genuinely powerful, and that sometimes means helping people to make strategic use of the less sunny approaches to power, approaches involving sanctions, threats, distributive efforts, and even coercion. In short, we need to assist people to take a strategic and wise approach to the occasional use of escalation.

THE POWER LENS

Power is an important lens for making sense of conflict and developing a constructive approach for dealing with enduring disputes. But it is only one lens among many. We can also understand conflict as a system of interaction, an attempt to achieve important goals or further basic needs, a narrative, a communication process, or an emotional exchange.

The power lens helps us understand the conflict process and in particular the ways in which disputants try to achieve their goals, protect themselves, and enhance their options. It also provides some important clues about ways in which we can help people productively stay with conflict. Furthermore, an awareness of power dynamics can quell our tendency to view conflict resolution as essentially a rational, problem-solving process, and in particular it can help us approach some of the worst problems that conflicts pose, such as oppression, violence, intimidation, coercion, and bullying. Without a proper understanding of power dynamics, for example, we can easily fall into dangerous practices when dealing with domestic violence, sexual harassment, racism, bullying in the workplace, or government-sponsored violence.

It's not that understanding power necessarily opens the door to solving these issues or moving these conflicts in a constructive direction. Powerful forces reinforce enduring conflict dynamics, and we have only a limited capacity in our role to change these dynamics. But without a clear view of how power plays out over time in enduring conflict, we cannot offer disputants the necessary perspective for making sound decisions or developing effective approaches to serious conflict. With an understanding of power, we are better able to help people develop a wise approach to intense conflict where power is a major currency.

So a power lens is essential, but as with all frameworks, people may rely on it too much and overlook other important dynamics. For example, disputants often define a conflict in power terms and then fail to understand the real needs, concerns, emotions, or stress that other disputants may be under. A genuine offer is then viewed as a manipulation. An emotional appeal with tears is viewed as an attempt to force a guilt trip. A proposal to put together a financial package that benefits everyone in a divorce is seen as an effort by one party to maintain control over the other. There may be some truth to these perceptions, but the power lens can also be a constricting framework that limits creativity and discourages people from taking the risks necessary to move a conflict forward.

Sometimes we ought to encourage people to disregard the power game and focus instead on how to achieve progress. Sometimes the best way we can assist disputants is by suggesting that they take some chances—take an offer or a communication at face value, offer a concession, risk entering into an agreement or opening up a communication in a way that might make them feel vulnerable. There is power in these moves as well. The paradox here is that the more people focus on power and worry about power, the less powerful they may be. So as important as the power lens is, there are times when we need to put it aside, encourage people to take risks, and search for whatever progress or immediate agreements may be possible. I turn in the next chapter to a consideration of negotiation in the midst of enduring conflict and the use of agreements as a platform for staying with conflict.

7

Agreements in Ongoing Conflict

Diplomacy is a continuation of war by other means.
Zhou Enlai, *as quoted in* Saturday Evening Post,
March 27, 1954

*Take the diplomacy out of war and the thing would fall flat
in a week.*

Will Rogers *(attributed)*

Staying with conflict does not require abandoning the goal of resolving conflict or ending the search for constructive outcomes to difficult disputes. Rather it requires that we put these goals in perspective. They are not the end all and be all of dealing with enduring conflict. We need to rethink how we understand the process of negotiation and decision making when working with enduring conflicts and make sure that the search for immediate agreement opportunities does not overwhelm our focus on the long-term challenges. At the same time, we do not need to abandon that search altogether. Instead we need to learn to view potential agreements and our work in helping parties achieve these agreements as single steps in a long journey, periodic platforms from which constructive engagement can proceed, and short-term goals in service of a long-term effort.

OPPORTUNITIES AND PITFALLS OF AGREEMENTS

The landscape of enduring conflict is dotted with agreements—some beneficial, some irrelevant, some controversial, some disastrous.

Clearly, the goal in enduring conflicts is not agreements per se but agreements that move the overall conflict process in a constructive direction. Consider three historic agreements that have had very different impacts on the course of the struggles out of which they came: the Munich agreement of 1938 in which France, Britain, and Germany agreed that Germany could annex Sudetenland, which had been part of Czechoslovakia; the Kyoto Protocol of 1997, which set targets for reduction of greenhouse gases; and the Good Friday Agreement (or Belfast Agreement) of 1998, which established a power-sharing agreement in Northern Ireland and committed the signers to renounce the use of violence.

The Munich agreement is widely viewed as a disaster, an effort at appeasing the imperialist ambitions of Germany that only spurred Hitler on in his aggressive intentions. The Kyoto Protocol is controversial. Key parties have not ratified the agreement (most notably the United States), and others (such as Japan), despite ratifying the accord, have stated that they are unable to meet its targets for the reduction of carbon emissions. Critics say this agreement is unrealistic, lacks teeth, and lets major emitters like China and India off the hook. Proponents argue that it has set important targets and established the framework for further dialogue and that the alternative to this approach is to do nothing in the face of climate change, which would be a horrendous mistake (Victor, 2001). The Good Friday Agreement is widely hailed as a breakthrough that was both a cause and a reflection of the transition of the Northern Ireland conflict from an armed struggle to a political process. Major paramilitary organizations have disarmed and some disbanded. Violence has diminished considerably and Catholics and Protestants have committed to sharing power in the government of Northern Ireland. But at the time of the agreement, many were skeptical. Some felt it was a sellout and others that it would simply not work. For some, the jury is still out on whether the fundamental issues of nationality, discrimination, and political structure have been successfully addressed.

Clearly, agreements per se are not necessarily helpful or positive, and it behooves the conflict practitioner to consider what makes for constructive agreements and what signals counterproductive efforts. Let's consider the potential benefits and pitfalls of agreements in enduring conflict.

Constructive Uses of Agreement

Aside from the obvious benefit of arriving at a potential solution to a genuine problem or issue, agreements play a critical role in setting the stage for a productive approach to ongoing disputes. Agreements can stabilize the nature of a conflict and allow disputants to engage in the conflict in a new and often more constructive way. Consider the potential of agreements to produce the following benefits:

- *Contain the conflict.* Agreements can create behavioral guidelines for disputants and thereby help to prevent destructive conflict escalation. When divorcing parents agree not to fight in front of their children, to make derogatory comments to their children, or to interfere with each other's parenting time, they are taking steps that can contain a conflict, even if they have not resolved the conflict itself. The Geneva Conventions have also served this purpose.

- *Focus the conflict.* By agreeing to end one part of an enduring conflict, disputants can focus their energies on the remaining areas, which may be more significant. When a series of grievances about overtime or job allocations can be settled, for example, the energy of workers and managers may be freed to focus on more essential struggles over job security and productivity concerns.

- *Create new platforms or processes for conflict.* Sometimes the most important element of an agreement is the creation of a more productive conflict process or arena. Agreements to create police-community task forces or councils to deal with ongoing tensions or specific incidents, for example, can direct an ongoing conflict to a more productive arena.

- *Establish relationships and promote dialogue.* Sometimes the process of interacting to work out an agreement is more important than the agreement itself because of the relationships created and the communication set in motion. When dealing with tensions between ethnic communities, finding some topic for them to work on, for example a common concern about a deteriorating local school or community center, can sometimes forge important personal connections that will promote more constructive approaches to enduring tensions.

- *Create a new conflict frame.* Agreements can have an often unintended side effect of promoting a new conflict frame or narrative. In the work on an agreement for a particular manifestation of a long-term conflict, the fundamental conflict may be redefined. Arms control agreements, for example, may not end the threat of war or deadly destruction, but they can redefine a conflict. Prior to an arms race the focus is likely to be on who is going to prevail and who is going to be vanquished. Afterward, the focus is on containing the damage of the arms control agreement and preventing conflict from spinning out of control. A divorce agreement too can change the nature of a conflict, perhaps from who gets what to how parents who do not get along can raise their children and lead their lives.

- *Protect rights.* Agreements may not achieve disputants' most significant goals, but they can often prevent the worst alternatives or outcomes and protect the rights of those who are less powerful. The laws prohibiting segregation and discrimination that grew out of the civil rights era have not put an end to racial tensions, disparate opportunities, or even discrimination. But they have protected the rights of some historically vulnerable groups and prevented the worst forms of discrimination.

- *Deal with immediate problems that demand attention.* Many enduring conflicts express themselves through specific issues that require immediate attention. Disputants and others affected often cannot wait for the long-term conflict to progress to address these issues. Collective bargaining contracts have to be negotiated, grievances resolved, and strategic business decisions made and executed even though the underlying conflict remains.

- *Reflect and memorialize progress.* Sometimes agreements are a means of moving an enduring conflict forward, sometimes they deal with immediate necessities, and sometimes they reflect and solidify progress that has been made. It is not always obvious how these different elements come together in a particular agreement. The degree to which the Kyoto Protocol reflects a growing consensus about the nature of the climate change challenge rather than being a means of pushing that consensus further along is not clear, nor does it necessarily have to be. When enduring conflicts do evolve, agreements often serve to capture that change in concrete and tangible ways.

The Pitfalls of Focusing on Agreements

Although negotiating an agreement can provide a context for constructive engagement, it can also be a distraction from doing the work of staying with conflict. In focusing on the immediate task of sealing a deal or forging a compromise, disputants can lose sight of the ongoing effort to create a constructive environment for conflict. In their eagerness to conclude divorce negotiations, parents often set themselves up for long-term conflict by creating overly rigid structures or failing to develop approaches for handling the ongoing struggles they are likely to have. Social movements frequently face the dilemma of whether to compromise to achieve concrete results or whether to deepen a struggle and build toward a long-term engagement.

As conflict professionals, we are frequently so focused on how to help people resolve their disputes that we may not understand the downside of this for those focusing on building a long-term movement for change. When an agreement solidifies gains and gives people a sense of their power and capacity to. make a difference, they may become more motivated to commit energy to a longer-term effort. But at other times the agreement, or at least the energy devoted to obtaining it, is a diversion from that larger goal. For example, consider this dilemma faced by a group of community activists concerned about public transportation.

The Alliance for Responsible Transportation (ART) was dedicated to promoting the expansion of affordable public transportation. The state legislature had recently authorized a study to investigate the possibility of constructing a light rail service from a downtown area to several adjacent suburbs. This was both good and bad news for ART. If approved and funded, light rail would be an important step forward, and ART was invited to participate in a public input process about feasibility and routing. But this also seemed like a very small step to take in the face of a very major problem, and while this study was being conducted, even more funds were being devoted to the expansion of the freeway network.

The (entirely voluntary) leadership of ART needed to decide whether to focus on promoting the proposed light rail service, opposing the highway expansion, or advocating for a much broader, more aggressive approach to regional mass transit. This posed a genuine dilemma for ART's leaders. They had limited resources and did not want to appear reflexively obstructionist, but they also felt the best way to leverage their resources was to take an opposi-tional stance. They ended up taking part, if somewhat sullenly, in the public process, but they felt that their overall position was undercut every time they agreed to any particular recommendation.

As conflict professionals we may believe that parties can par-ticipate in negotiating processes and still hold on to larger, long-term objectives. But for political, logistical, financial, or emotional reasons, the parties may in fact find this hard to do. A focus on agreements in the middle of an enduring conflict can present several dangers. Such a focus can

- *Sap energy.* Agreement efforts are often energy inten-sive. An environmentalist involved in an intensive negotiation about a major water project once said to me: "I am one of two paid environmental organizers we have in this entire region. This effort is taking up all my time. No matter how good the outcome, I can't afford to let it dominate my work."

- *Disempower disputants.* A focus on agreements in the midst of long-term conflicts can take away the power of disputants by isolating them, focusing them on a lesser issue, and undercutting the source of their power. Some environmentalists, for example, argue that they are much more effective in opposition, by raising issues and organizing protests, and that whenever they take part in consensus-building processes their most effec-tive source of power is neutralized.

- *Cloud the essential issue.* Agreements can crystallize an issue, but sometimes they obfuscate it. Concentrating

on the resolution of specific grievances and on individual actions of managers and employees might
underscore more fundamental problems in workplace
relationships, but it might also obscure those systemic
problems.

- *Damage relationships.* Interestingly, some agreements
  can actually make relationships worse—particularly
  when one side feels coerced into an agreement by
  another without having been able to address important
  concerns. Agreements can also set up long-term problems by raising unrealistic expectations, which when
  unfulfilled are seen as evidence of bad faith behavior.
  Failed efforts to achieve agreements can also harm relationships. For example, the Camp David talks between
  Palestinian and Israeli leaders in 2000 and the subsequent peace efforts made during the final months of
  the Clinton administration seem to have undercut the
  more moderate forces on both sides and to have contributed to a significant deterioration in the relationships among the main players.

- *Encourage destructive behavior.* As conflict professionals
  we often have to contend with the argument that negotiations reward bad behavior and should therefore not
  be allowed. This is often a counterproductive stance.
  As Yitzhak Rabin said when criticized for negotiating
  with terrorists: "You don't make peace with friends. You
  make it with very unsavory enemies." But agreeing at
  the wrong time, on the wrong terms, and in response
  to coercion (as happened with the Munich agreement)
  can encourage further destructive behavior.

Of course agreements seldom offer only positive or only negative consequences. And in the midst of conflict it can be very

hard to tell whether seizing the opportunity to agree on something is a wise move to contain a conflict, solve a problem, and move a conflict process forward or a mistaken effort that will isolate, disempower, misdirect, or even escalate a conflict. Agreements usually display a little bit of all these outcomes, and only over time can their full impact be measured.

Furthermore, serious conflicts can seldom be constructively addressed without taking some significant risks. If on the one hand, the stance of disputants is always governed by a desire to protect themselves from being taken advantage of and they therefore resist communicating with each other, sharing important information, or considering even partial or interim agreements, then the conflict will surely escalate. On the other hand, if disputants naïvely assume that it is always in their interest to pursue agreements, they may make themselves unnecessarily and unproductively vulnerable. Conflict specialists must help disputants walk their way through this dilemma.

USING AGREEMENTS TO STAY WITH CONFLICT

Conflict professionals need ways to help disputants think through their approaches to negotiations or settlement processes and the ramifications of those approaches for the long-term course of a conflict. We are often adept at helping disputants think through the long-term implications of an agreement. However, we are less practiced in helping them understand how a process that generates agreement can also create a more constructive platform for staying with conflict.

I believe there are four especially important ways that agreements and the agreement-making process can enhance the capacity of disputants to stay with conflict. Agreements can be used for bridge building, boundary creation, process formation, and conflict framing.

Bridge Building

Every time people engage about a specific issue they are also engaging about their relationship, even when they are working through surrogates. So the process of working toward an agreement offers the opportunity to build bridges among disputants. Sometimes the substance of the proposed agreement is better suited to this purpose than at other times. For example, if disputants are working on an agreement that will require ongoing contact (grievance procedures or parental decision making), it's natural to focus on how to relate, how to communicate, and how to make decisions. But if the agreement is about a one-time allocation of resources, the settlement of a financial claim, or the termination of a contractual relationship, it may be less natural to focus on relationship building. Even in these latter circumstances, however, relationships are occurring and an opportunity exists to build new or better bridges where none existed.

For this reason it is often useful to look for an opportunity to work out agreements—about anything—with the potential to build some relational bridges. Of course it's important to be sincere about the negotiating process and attentive to the substantive issues involved, while also keeping an eye on the development of relationships. I once heard a police hostage negotiator explain that he and his colleagues were always looking for something that they could negotiate with hostage takers about—coffee, food, heat or air conditioning, water—in order to establish the habit of negotiating, to build some rapport, and to begin to condition the hostage takers to making reciprocal concessions ("OK, you got your coffee; how about letting me talk to one of the hostages?").

To some this may sound like the approach advocated by Robert Bush and Joseph Folger in *The Promise of Mediation* (1994). Bush and Folger argue for the transformative potential of mediation, which can be realized if mediators focus on empowerment and recognition rather than on need satisfaction through agreement. Their insights offer an important perspective, particularly in their analysis of the way a focus on outcome can actually shut down or interfere with genuine engagement.

My point here, however, is not that mediators or other conflict professionals should focus mainly on relationships, empowerment, or recognition. Instead, conflict specialists have to be aligned with the parties in their goals to reach agreements on specific issues and should also help them find opportunities that support the development of relationships that can provide a context for constructive engagement in enduring conflicts. This was an important element in the work we did to help two departments of a public agency deal with a long-standing conflict:

Two departments of a federal agency, accounting and information technology, had been at odds for a long time. One was oriented toward obtaining the best and most up-to-date equipment, the other toward controlling costs and ensuring federal acquisition regulations had been scrupulously followed. Furthermore, the leaders of these departments had a long history of a rocky relationship.

While working with the two departments on how they could operate together more effectively, my colleague and I came across an immediate and specific issue. The accounting department's accounts payable software was badly in need of an upgrade, and the IT department was in no hurry to help. As a side activity to the larger efforts, one manager from accounting and another from IT were detailed to come up with an upgrade plan. They were also asked to use this side process as a model to show how workflow between the groups might ideally occur. Although this did not lead to an immediate change in how the two departments did business, the upgrade was worked out and the process built some goodwill and engendered a positive connection between the two up-and-coming midlevel managers.

In this situation, as is often the case, the agreement itself may have been less important than the relationship built by working together on it. The importance of encouraging better rapport between important participants in long-term conflicts is obvious, and when we see opportunities to promote this, we should take advantage of them. Of course working on agreements is not the only way of accomplishing this. Meeting in dialogue groups, working on common projects, sharing social activities, connecting on issues unrelated to the long-term conflict, finding common interests, and discovering (or developing) family ties are examples of other ways in which this can happen. But the agreement generation process is a very important way in which we can assist people to build relationship bridges that can make a difference in how an enduring conflict is conducted.

Boundary Creation

Although they may seem contrary to the goal of constructive engagement, good boundaries are in fact essential. For constructive engagement to occur, disputants have to feel safe; to have a picture of how, when, and about what to interact; and they need to know the limits on the extent to which a conflict can invade their whole experience. Divorced parents, for example, must respect each other's homes, personal space, privacy, decision-making prerogatives, and independent relationship with their children if they are to have successful engagement. For feuding business partners to engage on the issues on which they need to collaborate, they need boundaries, spheres of decision making and control, and ground rules about when and how to interact.

In a sense all agreements are about boundaries of some kind, because their subtext almost always involves power, communication, and rights. A number of years ago I conducted a mediation between business partners who were also siblings. It concerned serious differences about workload, compensation, decision making, and work-life boundaries. The creation of a few simple agreements about when they could make business calls to each other (no calls after 8 P.M.), and how they could keep other family members from getting caught up in business issues were essential to allowing them to continue to work together at all.

Agreements can establish boundaries in two ways—through explicit negotiation or through implicitly demonstrating them and thereby creating a set of norms. Many negotiated agreements are essentially about boundary creation. For example, when a divorcing couple negotiates agreements about when communication can occur, areas of decision-making authority, parenting prerogatives, and what to do if conflict escalates, they are essentially negotiating norms or rules of engagement that will act as a new set of boundaries for their relationship. Negotiations often result in agreements that establish boundaries or ground rules for how a conflict can be expressed or pursued.

Alternatively, agreements can create an understanding or model about boundaries. Divorce mediators often find that they are implicitly guiding parents to a new model of communication by the language they are encouraging the parents to use, one that has less of the rhetoric of intimacy and more of the vocabulary of business partners. Discussing a structured approach to communication, for example, with scheduled meeting times, agenda items, and written summaries of agreements helps to establish a new format for communication and is modeled by the negotiation process itself (see, for example, Ricci, 1997). The point is not to prevent the parents from contending when they need to, but to put some boundaries around how they do this and the way in which they express and use their emotions.

Process Formation

Working on agreements can also promote constructive engagement through the creation of conflict processes. One way agreements do this is through the design of dispute systems (Ury,

Brett, and Goldberg, 1988; Constantino and Merchant, 1995). Although most dispute system design work emphasizes prevention and resolution, systems for helping people engage in conflict are also valuable.

Some conflict systems, such as those created for handling grievances, tend to require that conflicts be reduced to specific complaints and actionable items. An employee or group of employees that is unhappy about circumstances at work has to focus on a specific complaint in order to make use of the grievance system. But not all conflicts can or should be reduced to specific grievances or actionable items. Creating forums that promote dialogue, allow for the airing of concerns, encourage the discussion of differences, and help keep all sides of a conflict informed can be essential for a healthy conflict engagement process.

Systems for resolving future disputes are often created during the course of negotiations about more time-limited issues. For example, a couple might negotiate an agreement that specifies that they will use the services of a child development expert if they have disagreements about child rearing in the future. Sometimes, people build into mediated agreements a provision for returning to mediation in the future should a dispute arise.

Many if not most formal disputing processes are created with the idea of preventing or resolving conflicts, and success is often measured by settlement rates. But the more important function may be providing a legitimate and constructive arena for conflicts to be addressed and continued. Whether the systems created are regular or periodic processes for police and community interactions, ongoing meetings between leaders of management and labor, or regularized contact between divorcing parents, the point is to allow people to continue to express their concerns, hear what others have to say, and promote their points of view.

Perhaps the most significant example of this dispute process is the United Nations, which is often criticized for its inability to take decisive action about important conflicts. However, that criticism often misses the point. The United Nations has provided a legitimate forum in which international conflicts can be expressed and pursued in a relatively constructive way, and not having that kind of outlet would be a significant step backward. But we do not have to look on such a grand scale. Wherever we see enduring conflicts, we can see the need for the creation of processes through which people can interact, communicate, and occasionally fulminate. Sometimes participants in such processes feel the need to generate tangible agreements about specific issues so they don't feel they are just spinning their wheels. But the process of communication and relationship building is often far more important than the agreements reached.

Conflict Framing

The evolution of an enduring conflict can be tracked by the various ways the conflict has been framed over time. Deeply rooted conflicts are not transformed simply by how they are framed. Framing reflects the way a conflict is understood by a disputant and the system or structure out of which it arises. Nevertheless, how a conflict is framed does influence how it is understood and engaged in and ineffective framing can interfere with a constructive and sustainable approach to enduring conflict (as discussed in Chapter Four).

Struggles over framing are often central to the way a conflict is enacted. Abortion rights supporters have long framed the conflict over abortion as a matter of choice, women's rights, and safety. Abortion foes have framed it as a matter of life and the rights of the unborn. Others have tried to refocus the debate toward the issue of preventing unwanted pregnancies. Environmental disputes are variously framed in terms of protection of the planet, biodiversity, individual rights, government intrusion, economic development, and sustainability (to name a few). Each of these framings both reflects the nature of the conflict and promotes a particular set of interests and approaches to engagement. One of the most profound impacts of agreements in enduring conflict is their potential for developing, promoting, and solidifying a new framing of a conflict. To the extent that these new narrative frames are rooted in the fundamental needs of the disputants and the structure of the conflict they can have a permanent impact on how people engage a conflict.

The process of arriving at an agreement often requires that disputants modify their current narrative frames. To find common ground on the issues involved, each disputant's frame must often become less distributive and exclusive (allowing some aspect of the other parties' narratives into it). Furthermore, as the focus of the conflict is shifted away from the immediate issue to the broader ongoing dispute, the nature of the conflict frame naturally changes.

For example, in contested divorces the dispute is often cast in very distributive terms. Each parent tries to minimize the rights and role of the other parent, as if the issue were which parent will be able to become the dominant and therefore "real" parent. The issue is framed around who gets custody, where the children are going to live, and who gets to make which decision. But after the divorce is finalized, there is often (but by no means always) a migration to a focus on how to minimize interference, create effective boundaries, and cooperate when necessary. The issues now involve how flexible, rigid, consistent, interfering, supportive, or communicative the other parent is. This new framing reflects how the conflict has evolved, and it now supports a different kind of engagement, one that is focused on the long-term issues parents might face.

THE AGREEMENT PROCESS IN ENDURING CONFLICT

I have used *agreement process* as a generic term for the method of arriving at an agreement, rather than *negotiation*, *consensus building,* or *problem solving,* because agreements are generated in a multiplicity of ways in enduring conflict. Sometimes agreements are arrived at through a deliberate, face-to-face, consensus-building process such as mediation or negotiation. But agreements may also be imposed, arrived at implicitly, spun off from other processes (for example, a fight in which people agree about what they are not fighting about or a planning process on an issue different from the conflict issue), or achieved by preexisting automatic or formulaic procedures ("You got to decide last time; I get to decide this time"). The following sections address three of the most common processes for arriving at agreements in enduring conflict: implicit agreements, derivative agreements, and negotiations.

Implicit Agreements

Groucho Marx famously declined membership in a club with the remark, "I refuse to join any club that would have me as a member." The Groucho syndrome—an agreement with an adversary has to be a bad agreement simply because it is an agreement with an adversary—is common in polarized disputes. In enduring conflict the very idea of making an agreement with someone who is perceived as "the enemy" can seem intolerable to a disputant. Any explicit agreement (or recognized negotiating process) can appear to legitimize the opponent or the opponent's cause. Such deep distrust and alienation is of course one of the reasons enduring conflicts persist. Conflict scholars have labeled this phenomenon "reactive devaluation" (Ross, 1995).

Despite the power of this tendency, participants in long-term conflict develop implicit but nonetheless quite powerful agreements all the time. They have to if for no other reason than that their involvement in each other's lives requires it. These can be agreements about rules of engagement, appropriate tactics, containing a conflict, protecting mutual interests, timing, confidentiality, and often, substantive decisions that must be made. Consider this example:

Several years ago a law firm hired me to help the partners deal with a number of internal problems. The first issue, which almost everyone I talked with raised, was a long-standing dispute between two senior partners who refused to talk to each other—about anything. They did not acknowledge each other when they passed in the hall, and they studiously avoided any meeting attended by the other. They had gradually separated almost all their functioning—using separate secretaries, clerks, associates, and consultants. None of this could have occurred if they had not in some way arrived at a quiet understanding that this was how they were to go forward. Occasionally something occurred in which their rules of disengagement did not hold, and without ever agreeing to this, they almost always took the matter to a third senior partner for a decision.

This was a remarkably effective disengagement, as far as their need to avoid each other went. Unfortunately, because they were such powerful players in the firm, it made planning, staff development, or strategic decision making extremely difficult. My task was in part to make the implicit agreements explicit and to see if some modifications in the rules of disengagement could be arrived at that would allow the firm to move forward. For example, we discussed when, for the firm's sake, it might be important for both partners to take part in the same meetings or processes. We discussed how they would do this, and what they would do if they found themselves at odds about the issues involved.

Implicit is not the same as unconscious or unintentional, and so implicit agreements can be used in a strategic way. Sometimes both sides can acknowledge that an agreement exists, but sometimes that acknowledgment can actually set a process back. The law firm partners were agreeing to stay off each other's turf, but to try to codify that in any way could have created many more conflicts. They could identify that they had found a way of disengaging, but they could not go further in making the agreement explicit without creating problems that they were unable to deal with. That is why they needed outside help.

Conflict specialists can help disputants make constructive use of implicit agreements by

- Making implicit agreements explicit
- Encouraging a discussion about implicit agreements
- Helping disputants expand on those agreements
- Looking for areas in which implicit agreements might be possible, and testing these areas out
- Encouraging disputants to consider when and how to make agreements explicit
- Suggesting how to proceed *as if* an agreement existed (for example, assuming an agreement has been made not to speak publicly about a dispute and proceeding accordingly to see what happens)
- Helping parties consider whether implicit agreements might be dysfunctional (for example, not talking with others about a dispute)
- Recognizing when it is best to leave an implicit agreement implicit

Categorizing agreements as explicit or implicit (and the line is not always so clear) is not what is important here. What is significant is to recognize the ubiquitous nature of implicit agreements and to work with them when appropriate to move a conflict process forward.

Derivative Agreements

Derivative agreements occur as outgrowths of other processes, some directly related to the conflict, some not. In many conflicts, even in the course of a dramatic escalation like a lawsuit or an armed conflict, agreements are made along the way. For example, when people agree about what they are not fighting over or when they stipulate areas of factual agreement, they are making agreements that will frame the future course of a conflict. These agreements are often essential for limiting the damage done in conflict and pointing to areas where constructive engagement may be possible.

Sometimes agreements emerge out of seemingly unrelated issues. These derivative agreements can be made intentionally, but they often seem to be an unplanned and often unnoticed side effect. I was once asked to help set up a strategic planning process for a nonprofit organization in which there was a great deal of tension between the board president and the executive director. The plan arrived at called for a three-person steering committee consisting of the director, the president, and the chief financial officer. This committee structure then became the framework within which the director and president communicated not just on strategic planning but on a wide range of issues.

Sometimes significant new approaches to deeply entrenched problems arise in unanticipated ways from seemingly unrelated issues. Consider the following example from an enduring conflict in Bulgaria that my colleague Susan Wildau and I worked on with our Bulgarian partners (The Bulgarian Foundation on Negotiation and Conflict Resolution) in the mid-1990s.

> CDR Associates was involved in a multiyear project to deal with ethnic conflict in Bulgaria, Our Bulgarian partners made it clear that we could never frame what we were doing in terms of ethnic disputes, which in that part of the world meant extreme violence and ethnic cleansing. Instead we focused on multicultural understanding.
>
> In one municipality where there was extreme tension between the police, the social welfare agency, and the Roma minority, we were invited to visit a particularly poor Roma neighborhood and participate in a meeting between local government officials and community

leaders. As it happened, the night before, a youth from the neighbor-hood had been shot by a police officer. When we arrived the neigh-borhood was up in arms, and neighborhood leaders were debating whether this visit should go forward. Susan and I decided we could not offer useful advice to this debate and said we would do what-ever the leaders wished. They decided that a quick walk through the neighborhood and then a brief cup of coffee with a small group would be OK.

The walk was an intense experience. As we worked our way through the neighborhood (accompanied by municipal officials but no police), the crowd of people joining us grew and grew and became more angry and vocal. People were determined that we should know just how bad their situation was. Our interpreter trans-lated as much as she could of the streams of angry and loud state-ments hurled our way. We asked questions where we could but mostly just listened and walked.

At the end of the visit, a smaller group of residents ended up in a classroom in the local school, where a discussion ensued. Again Susan and I were mostly listeners. As a result of this discussion, municipal officials and neighborhood leaders made a decision to appoint a few neighborhood liaisons to the welfare department to facilitate commu-nication between neighborhood members and the agency. These liai-sons played a significant role over the next few years in easing tensions and helping neighborhood residents obtain services.

As with many derivative agreements, no one even realized that an agreement was being made. The intention of the meeting organizers was simply to conclude the visit with no one getting hurt and with-out exacerbating the situation. The level of anger remained high, and of course the fundamental conflict continued. But out of this inter-change a system of communication and interaction was set up that stayed in place for several years and that went a long way to allowing the neighborhood and the municipality to engage more effectively.

Susan's and my roles were hard to define. We were mostly cata-lysts for a conversation to occur. Through translators we were able to assist in changing the tone—a little—from defensiveness and recrimination to listening. When we heard someone suggest that a liaison would be helpful, we pushed to make this outcome as concrete as possible. The agreement that emerged seemed like a sidebar to the essential problem that we had been hearing about, and had almost nothing to do with the police shooting. Nonetheless it enabled the community and municipality to engage in a new way.

As conflict specialists we are often involved in working on issues that appear to be tangential or even unrelated to the enduring conflicts central to people's lives, but our work in these areas often produces derivative agreements that can significantly alter the course of long-term disputes. Our role is to do the job we are asked to do, to attend to the concerns that people have, but also to remain alert to the opportunities that arise for derivative agreements to emerge and to make sure that these opportunities are not ignored.

Negotiation

Negotiation is at the center of most dispute resolution, consensus-building, and agreement-generating approaches. It is a core skill that conflict specialists need to master. The literature of the conflict field is rich in books that promote, analyze, and teach different approaches to conflict resolution (for example, Raiffa, 1982; Honeyman and Schneider, 2006; Lax and Sebenius, 1986; Fisher and Ury, 1981). The capacity to assist disputants in being effective negotiators is at the center of much that we are called on to do as conflict professionals, whether we are acting as mediators, advocates, system designers, facilitators, or coaches.

Staying with conflict requires all the negotiation skills that time-limited conflicts require:

- Understanding the underlying motives (interests, needs, driving forces) of all involved

- Being able to deal with the integrative (joint gains) and distributive (dividing up limited resources) aspects of conflict

- Communicating effectively, particularly across cultural boundaries

- Tracking the multiple layers of negotiation, and dealing with multiple parties

- Creative problem solving

- Using power wisely and effectively

- Responding to cooperative, competitive, and mixed messages

- Seeing where potential agreements may be found

- Attending to implementation and review concerns

- Making creative use of ambiguity to allow a negotiation to go forward—this involves knowing when to nail down specifics and when to recognize that a certain amount of ambiguity about specifics is what allows parties to reach more general agreement (Honeyman, 2006)

- Drafting effective agreements and closing the deal

However, negotiating in the context of enduring conflict adds another dimension. It requires skills at simultaneously attending to the long-term ramifications and to the immediate requirements of both the negotiation process and outcome.

Much of the negotiation literature wrestles in one form or another with the negotiator's dilemma (for example, Mnookin, Peppet, and Tulumello, 2004; Schneider, 2002; Lax and Sebenius, 1986). Related to the Prisoner's Dilemma (Axelrod, 1984), the problem all negotiators face is how to preserve relationships and protect interests, to create value and claim value, to pursue joint gains but obtain a reasonable amount of limited resources, to prepare for competition and promote cooperation, or as I have sometimes thought of it, to avoid being either a sucker or a jerk.

Dealing with enduring conflict adds another dimension to the negotiator's dilemma. How can negotiating parties be fully attentive to the costs and opportunities inherent in the present negotiation interaction while maintaining a focus on the long-term requirements of staying with conflict? How can they be fully present—prepared to seize the moment, as it were—and sufficiently objective or removed to take the long view? Mostly they can't. That's one of the reason conflict specialists are essential for helping people to stay with conflict.

Our job, in addition to all the other ways we might assist negotiations, is to help with the enduring conflict dimension of the negotiator's dilemma. To do this we sometimes have to

- Slow down a negotiation process including progress toward an agreement to allow consideration of long-term ramifications.

- Bring in other people or groups who can represent the long-term challenge (often the role of nongovernmental organizations (NGOs) in environmental negotiations).

- Encourage disputants to negotiate—even when they believe their most important issues are nonnegotiable.

- Prepare disputants to negotiate in the face of bad faith negotiation (figure out how to use negotiation either to promote good faith behavior or to protect disputants from bad faith tactics).

- Frame the negotiation so that the long-term dimension is included ("We need to focus on how you want to raise your children, given that you will be living in separate households").

- Build in ongoing communication or negotiation processes.

- Guard against *agreement fever*—when the eagerness of parties to reach a settlement overtakes their ability to consider the wisdom or fairness of the agreement.

- Pay attention to the relationship development process and potential of negotiation.

- Consider when the immediate problem is significant enough to require forging an agreement whose long-term consequences are unknown or potentially dangerous.

That said, our concern about staying with conflict should not act as an inhibitor to negotiating agreements. If we let the uncertainties of the future intimidate us and prevent us from seizing the opportunities of the moment, we will find ourselves on the road to conflict stagnation and deterioration. No progress in serious conflict can occur without taking risks. The safest immediate course is often the most dangerous long-term course. And we can never know the long-term ramifications of the immediate actions that we take. Our goal, however, remains to try to use the opportunities presented by negotiations to further the long-term goal of constructive engagement. We want the enduring challenge of conflict to inform disputants' negotiation and agreement-making process, not paralyze it.

The choice we face in most conflict is not between reaching an agreement and continuing the conflict, although that is how it is often posed. The true challenge is to see the resolution process as an ongoing part of the conflict process. Wise agreements solve problems, but in the case of enduring conflict, their more important function is often that they allow conflict to proceed as constructively as possible. We see this in every arena of conflict. Cease-fires attempt to guide conflict to less violent and more diplomatic or political channels. Collective bargaining agreements set up dispute procedures. Agreements to create habitat for endangered species solve a specific problem even as the underlying conflict about sustainable development continues.

Very little of this is news to us in the conflict field. We know that all conflicts and all agreements take place in the context of larger conflicts and have ramifications for those larger conflicts. Often, however, we fail to see that agreements are not the end goal, and we do not help our clients to put them in a proper perspective or approach them with that understanding. Being conscious and intentional about the role of agreements in the ongoing process of conflict is essential to our ability to sustain disputants through a long-term conflict. Another way to support this ability is to focus on sustainability itself, which I turn to in the next chapter.

8

Taking a Sustainable Approach to Enduring Conflict

If I can't dance, I don't want to be in your revolution.
Emma Goldman (attributed)

Staying with conflict requires that people maintain the energy to engage productively over time. Conflicts deteriorate when disputants' energy flags to the point that they feel they must either escalate to try to end a conflict or avoid the conflict, allowing it to fester and get worse. Although there is a time for neglect and a time for escalation, if these are the dominant modes of approaching a significant conflict over an extended time (and the conflict has not genuinely ended or transformed), a constructive engagement process becomes impossible.

In enduring conflict, finding a sustainable approach to engagement is critical. Far from trying to help people withdraw from battle, our job as conflict specialists is to help them engage in it. But our view has to be far-sighted. We have to consider how to help people engage over time. Or put differently, we have to consider how to help disputants take a balanced approach to conflict, one that allows them to conserve their energy and resources so that they can expend these as and when needed.

To carry out these tasks conflict specialists need to pay attention to the rhythm of engagement, emotional management, resources and support systems, and achieving a balanced approach to engaging and encapsulating a conflict. We should always remember that there is no one right approach to conflict. What constitutes an effective strategy for engagement depends on the disputant, the conflict system, the cultural context, and the stage of the conflict. In some circumstances, intense periods of high engagement separated by long periods of low involvement work best. In others, a low-key, steady, and consistent approach to involvement is more effective. Let's turn first to a consideration of engagement rhythms.

RHYTHMS OF ENGAGEMENT

Different conflicts exhibit different patterns of interaction intensity, and different disputants gravitate to and exhibit different rhythms of engagement. By *rhythm of engagement*, I mean the pace and pattern of active emotional and behavioral involvement in dealing with a conflict and also the ebbs and flows in conflict communication. For example, consider the rhythm of engagement in a conflict between the Boomers and Weiners.

> The Boomers and the Weiners are neighbors who have had a long-standing dispute about the noise emanating from the Boomers' house from parties, dogs, children, fights, and in general a more boisterous style of living and communicating. The Weiners from time to time have raised direct complaints. When complaining they can get quite agitated and sometimes loud themselves. At other times they have called the police, or shown their displeasure by playing loud music in an open window facing their neighbor's house late at night. But often they do nothing except complain among themselves and to other neighbors. The Boomers sometimes get agitated in response, sometimes modify their behavior, and occasionally apologize. Over the years, long periods of no contact between the two families have been interspersed with intense periods of arguing, fighting, and acting out. There have even been some times when the two families have appeared to get along reasonably well, but these always end with the next noisy outburst from dogs or teenagers late at night.

In some respects the Boomers and Weiners seem to have found a sustainable rhythm of interaction, but it is one dependent on never really engaging with the issue and using a variety of avoidance mechanisms. To genuinely engage in this conflict that is likely to be ongoing, they all would need to look at how they could alter their patterns of communication and their rhythm of interaction and they would need to do this in a sustainable way.

Finding a natural rhythm that fits one's life circumstances and personal style and allows for replenishing one's energy is essential for sustaining constructive engagement in conflict. This is true for groups as well as individuals. If the rhythm of engagement is too intense, burnout, exhaustion, and poor judgment are likely. If the rhythm is too slow or sporadic, then focus and motivation can suffer.

For example, contract length is often a contentious point in union and management conflicts. Each side sees various benefits from locking in a contract for its preferred length of time, and one consideration in setting this time is each side's evaluation of how frequently it can handle the intensity and demands of the contract bargaining and the high levels of interaction and conflict entailed. Public advocacy groups need to keep enough action going to keep their forces mobilized, their issues alive, and funds flowing into the organization. But they also need time to recover, regroup, and take care of the more mundane aspects of keeping the organization growing. Similarly, most intense interpersonal conflicts are characterized by periods of high interaction and emotional intensity interspersed with periods of relative calm and distance.

This raises several questions for conflict specialists. We have to consider how to help disputants become aware of their natural rhythm of interaction, and consider whether the rhythm of the conflict they are engaged in is working for them. If the rhythm is not constructive or sustainable, we need to help them think about how to change it. We also have to consider the impact our interventions have on these natural rhythms.

Entering into the Rhythm of Conflict

We conflict specialists don't always have a choice about the point at which we enter a conflict system. That depends on our role, when we are contacted, and when parties are open to our intervention. Conflict anticipation and prevention are valuable and underused conflict intervention skills (Honeyman and others, 2007), but they require that we have access to the system or the players involved before conflict has taken root. And sometimes our most important work occurs after a conflict has been going on for many years, and the parties are feeling pain.

It is not always clear whether our intervention changes the dynamic or just plays into the natural rhythm of a conflict. This was a question I had when I worked with a dysfunctional team held hostage to a long-term interpersonal dispute.

Karen, a manager, and Dennis, an employee who reports to her in a government agency's accounting department, had been involved in a periodically intense conflict for several years. As a result the whole accounting department was becoming increasingly dysfunctional. When I was first asked to intervene, the problem was presented to me in terms of overall bad feelings within the team about hiring, job assignments, and promotions. After a series of interviews it became clear that most of the conflicts revolved around these two employees, who had been working together for about fifteen years. For the first five years or so, they had been coworkers and were friendly, but then Karen was appointed team manager, and afterward their relations deteriorated quickly and severely. Mostly they tried to avoid each other, but about once every six months they had flare-ups in which one would accuse the other of doing something malicious, vindictive, or insubordinate. There would be a flurry of intense conflict, and then everyone would retreat to avoidance.

This pattern seemed to work well for both; they were at least in sync about the rhythm of conflict. But there were two problems: they never actually worked through any of their issues, and the rest of the team members were caught in a conflict they wanted no part of.

I facilitated a discussion between Karen and Dennis that cleared the air about some past issues, established some boundaries around involving others, and created some ongoing procedures for interaction, but I was never clear whether we had made progress on the core conflict.

Karen, Dennis, and the rest of the department seemed to feel this was a real step forward, and although progress had certainly been made, I also wondered if part of what happened was that my efforts were subsumed into their natural rhythm of interaction. After a period of intense conflict that had led to my being brought in and after the intensity of interaction our work together had involved, they were ready to enter a period of less intense interaction. Would these new rules of engagement serve them when an intense interaction period reoccurred?

We should never hold or encourage the expectation that an intervention we make in one time frame will help disputants through all the future circumstances they will face. It would be hubris for us to believe a single intervention in a long-term conflict will change the nature of the whole conflict. Although we can pay attention to the rhythm of engagement, we should not expect that the effect of what is essentially a short-term intervention will endure through the course of a complex and unpredictable system of interactions. However, we should take the pattern of engagement into account as we enter into a conflict interaction.

Working with the Conflict Rhythm

Sometimes the rhythm of engagement is outside the control of disputants because of systemic and structural factors. For example, therapists and family mediators have observed that conflictual interactions are likely to increase around the end of the school year, during the Christmas holidays, and at the beginning of a new year, especially in divorced families. Contractual or statutory factors often govern collective bargaining or annual budgetary processes. The National Environmental Policy Act governs patterns of public input in association with environmental impact statements. To the extent that these structures for interaction interface with enduring conflicts, they can impose a rhythm of engagement that can be anticipated and prepared for but not easily altered.

Understanding, facing, and preparing for these rhythms is important and helps disputants sustain themselves through a protracted conflict. Furthermore, even if the structures of interaction are firm, the nature of the emotional investment or engagement can usually be worked with. If divorced parents understand that they will likely have some kind of struggle as summer vacation approaches each year, they can anticipate it and consider how to handle their own emotional investment in the interaction. They can also think of ways to minimize the intensity of the anticipated interaction. I have mediated many agreements that set up procedures for decision making around vacation or holiday plans, well in advance of the time that such interactions were expected to heat up. These procedures did not necessarily prevent the intense phase from taking place, but they did allow parents to take a certain degree of control over the rhythm and to put some parameters around the engagement.

At other times the rhythm of a conflict derives less from external factors and more from the internal forces within and among the disputants. For example, parents often recognize that there is a pattern and rhythm to children's conflictual behavior. On the one hand, children may have more difficulty at bedtime, as the school week starts, or after a transition from one home to another. On the other hand, parents may notice that every third or fourth day (or week) a child seems to have a "melt down," almost as if on a schedule.

When we work on a conflict, we can speculate about what drives the interaction rhythm, and sometimes we can figure it out. For the most part, however, our role as conflict specialists does not allow us to make this analysis (which belongs more to the realm of psychotherapy), and even if it did, focusing on this analysis might distract us from what we are better able to do, which is to help disputants identify the pattern itself so that they gain some control of the rhythm or at least their response to it.

Conflict specialists can use the following strategies to help disputants begin to take charge of or change the conflict rhythm.

- *Identify the pattern and plan accordingly.* We can work with disputants to recognize the pattern of engagement and disengagement. Sometimes the very concept that a pattern or rhythm exists can help people to understand the nature of the enduring challenge. Furthermore, once a pattern is identified, people can anticipate and prepare for it, for example, by clearing their schedule or creating channels of communication that can be used when the most intense periods occur.

- *Match the rhythm or counteract the rhythm.* On the one hand, when a disputant is upset, wired, and excitable, it is sometimes helpful to counteract this state by being calm, even, and slow paced. On the other hand, it is sometimes necessary to match the rhythm first, to join the energy and intensity level, and then to begin to change it.

- *Go with the rhythm.* Taking matching one step further, sometimes it is best to go with the rhythm or even to push disputants to go further into an unsustainable rhythm than they are initially inclined to go themselves, so that they then want to slow down, space out, or deintensify the pattern themselves. I have on several occasions suggested to disputants who seemed to want to quarrel with each other that they did not seem to be fighting often enough, given the level of their conflict and its importance to them, and I have suggested that they find an arena in which to interact much more often and more directly. In a sense this is applying the principles of aikido (a Japanese marital art that encourages defenders to join with the energy of an attacker rather than resist it) to the rhythm of conflict (Crum, 1987).

- *Develop an incremental approach.* Usually it is easiest to change the rhythm of interaction in small steps—to gradually slow it down or speed it up, to slowly increase the level of intensity or gradually reduce it. Dramatic changes are occasionally necessary, in response perhaps to an extended and highly unproductive pattern, but usually a wisely chosen incremental change is more likely to succeed.

- *Change timing.* Working more specifically on timing and intensity can also change the pattern of conflict. We can sometimes encourage disputants to slow down their pattern of engagement (to delay reengaging) or to speed it up. For example, sometimes it is helpful to encourage people not to respond immediately to a new provocation, and at other times it is more helpful to encourage them to raise issues earlier and more frequently. We can also look at how intense their engagement becomes. Sometimes the degree of intensity can be moderated, so that when people pull back, they don't become quite as disengaged and when they reengage in a conflictual interaction, they don't become as all consumed by it.

These mechanisms for influencing the pattern or rhythm of engagement can help disputants confront their avoidance and develop more constructive approaches to communication, and they play an especially important role in helping parties develop a sustainable approach to conflict.

Direct and Indirect Approaches to Rhythm

We help disputants address the rhythm of engagement with conflict either by coaching them and helping them plan for themselves how to work with the rhythm, or if we are directly involved in the interaction—as mediators or advocates, for example—by working directly to match or counteract, take incremental steps, attend to the aikido of rhythm, or change the timing, intensity, or direction of particular engagement efforts. In a sense, every move we make, from when we enter a conflict to when we leave it, is about influencing the rhythm of interaction. We are usually not thinking in those terms, but this is a critical way in which we can influence both individual interactions and patterns of interaction.

A story attributed variously to King Solomon, Abraham Lincoln, and Sufi tradition tells of a search for a magic ring (or text) that has the capacity to make a happy person sad and a sad person happy. After much searching, this magical ring is found to be a simple band of metal on which are inscribed four words, "this too shall pass." In Jewish tradition, when one is offering condolences or solace to someone in pain, it is common to say these words in Hebrew (*gam zeh ya'avor*). Truly, the wisdom of this saying lies not in any sense that everything will be better but in the idea that there is a rhythm to the easier and the harder times in life and that all people need to appreciate the rhythm itself.

MANAGING EMOTIONS OVER TIME

How emotions are managed over time can be a source of sustainability or an impediment to it. As conflict specialists we are usually well aware of the emotional dimension of conflict. However, we have tremendously different ways of approaching it. Some mediators see emotions as something to control and keep off the table, believing that they get in the way of focusing on settlement. Mediators taking this stance might ask disputants to approach the mediation process as if it were a business transaction and to keep personal issues or feelings out of the discussion. Others believe we cannot and should not avoid emotions. Rather, emotions should be brought to the surface and expressed. But most mediators (and other conflict specialists) probably agree that emotions play a role in conflict and that the mediator needs an approach to dealing with them. We may believe that emotions require considerable attention, acknowledgment, and expression or that they should be referred to some other process. But even in seemingly impersonal contexts, it seems clear that the emotional dimension cannot just be willed away.

In my own practice I have come to view the emotional content of conflict as a helpful component, an aid to effective conflict work, not a problem. Our challenge as conflict specialists is to help disputants give expression to the emotional side of conflict in a way that is culturally appropriate and in balance with the other components of conflict. Of course this does not mean that emotions should be gratuitously stirred up either.

The question of how directly we should deal with disputants' emotions is tricky, as is finding the culturally and gender-appropriate ways to do this. The art of most conflict work requires that we find a way of dealing with the behavioral, emotional, and cognitive aspects of conflict, but not necessarily with a straight on, explicit approach. We don't have to use the F-word (feelings), but we do have to recognize the role of emotions and develop an approach for their appropriate expression.

And there are additional challenges in dealing with emotions in order to help disputants develop a sustainable approach to conflict. How emotions are handled can be either a source of enduring strength or a drain. We need to work with people on how they will express and manage their emotions over time. This means helping disputants accept the emotional impact of a conflict, think about how and when to directly express their emotions, and consider where they can find an outlet for emotional expression and sustenance.

These are not easy tasks. In fact for almost everyone these are lifelong challenges and struggles. Any attempt to provide a simple formula for doing this should be treated with skepticism. But the fact that it is a large task does not mean that it should be avoided. Let's consider five questions about emotional sustenance that we might want to ask ourselves and also discuss with disputants.

What Are the Disputants' Emotions?

Unlike their stereotypes in popular culture, psychotherapists, mediators, and facilitators do not go around asking constantly, irritatingly, and out of the blue, "How are you feeling?" I have been told by a number of people entering into mediation, "Please don't ask me about my feelings; let's just get this thing settled." Fair enough, but I have yet to see a conflict interaction, even an apparently very substantive or data-oriented one, where emotions were not a subtext of some sort. Even the statement "Please don't ask about my feelings" is itself heavily laden with emotions.

Often it is helpful to ask disputants what the emotional cost of a conflict has been for them. Even if people do not want to discuss their own emotional reactions, they are often able to think about other party's emotions and how those feelings might be affecting the conflict. And if we can't talk about emotions, we can talk about reactions, perceptions, energy, and endurance. Furthermore, most people find it easier to talk about some emotions than others.

The more people are aware of their own emotional reactions, the higher their emotional intelligence (Goleman, 1995) and the better able they are to sustain themselves through conflict. Finding a way of identifying just what the emotional dimension is, what the emotional demands of a conflict are, and what triggers or invokes different disputants' emotions is extremely useful in helping people endure through conflict.

How Can Emotions Be Expressed?

Over the course of an enduring conflict the parties' ability to find an appropriate means of experiencing, expressing, and living with their emotions is a core element of sustainability for them. Knowing that many disputants are not comfortable even with owning their emotions, much less expressing them, we still have to recognize that emotions can both sustain people through conflict and drain their energies, sometimes at the same time.

Emotional work is done in many ways. Emotions get expressed directly, vicariously, indirectly, toward the wrong people, on seemingly unrelated issues, in constructive or destructive (sometimes self-destructive) ways, and with both good and awful timing. Emotions are labeled as good or bad or acceptable and nonacceptable when of course people don't really choose which emotions to experience, although many emotions are suppressed. We are not psychotherapists (at least not in our role as conflict specialists). Our job is not to help people work through all their feelings, understand the origins of these feelings, and discover the various conflicts that have been repressed. But we do have to recognize that emotions will influence conflict and will be expressed in one way or another over time.

Sometimes we can simply ask people what they want to say (either to us or to other parties to a dispute) about how they are feeling, thinking, or reacting to what is going on. Sometimes we have to supply disputants with a vocabulary to use in expressing their feelings because they often lack effective words for expressing feelings like anger, sadness, or fear. Sometimes we have to help them develop and use an effective emotional arena, a context in which they can safely express their feelings. Sometimes we have to respect the desire of disputants to act as if there is no emotional content in a dispute, but we have to find a way for them to express the emotional side of the conflict anyway.

When we can help people, directly or indirectly, to find a venue and vocabulary for understanding and expressing the emotional dimension of their conflict, we are working on one of the core elements of sustainability. This is true when we are dealing with groups as well. The collective anger, frustration, and unhappiness or the excitement, hopefulness, and joy that groups may feel in conflict will one way or another be expressed. If we can help groups find an appropriate means of doing so, their ability to stay with conflict will be greatly enhanced.

How Can Emotions Be Contained?

As important as it is to express emotions, containing them at times is also important. Emotion dumps (the uncontrolled expression of high levels of emotion directed at other disputants) are seldom helpful, often harmful, and almost always exhausting. Containing emotions involves the ability to control the timing, direction, manner, and expression of emotions. Sometimes it requires withholding their expression until the time and circumstances are more appropriate. This does not mean suppressing feelings but managing when and how they are released. As discussed in Chapter Three, people often avoid conflict and therefore exacerbate it because of a fear that they will open and let loose a Pandora's box of emotions. Timing is also crucial, as there are times when it is not appropriate or even possible to express emotions.

Of course no one is always able to achieve the balance between expression and containment that is neither repression of nor fixation on one's emotional life. Everyone "loses it" occasionally or becomes emotionally disconnected or aloof. We need to cut disputants (and ourselves) some slack here. But developing some skills in emotional containment is important to staying with conflict.

We are not likely to change a volatile personality into a mellow one or a repressed disputant into an emotionally open person. That too is the realm of therapy, and it doesn't often happen there either. But we can help disputants develop a strategic sense about the expression and containment of emotion in conflict. We can help them think through for themselves how to take time out, find appropriate places for venting, monitor the effect that someone else is having on them emotionally, and gain some control over how they want to express their own feelings. We can also help them to understand the emotional needs and expressions of others and to develop a strategic and yet kind response to these. This is not about supplying them with a silver bullet for emotional management but about encouraging them to think and talk about these issues.

Conflict can be like a pressure cooker. If there is not some contained release of pressure, the whole thing can blow. But just opening the lid can also lead to things blowing up in your face. Sometimes the best action we can take in the middle of a heated interchange is simply to slow things down, in effect (and sometimes literally) to ask people to breathe. By the same token, sometimes the best thing we can do with the overall flow of emotional interchange is to try to slow the pace. We can do this by controlling the pace of our own communication, by the way we structure the interaction among disputants, and by encouraging disputants to slow their own responses to one another. Of course we also need to recognize when some expression is necessary and containment is neither possible nor advisable. At times it is useful to help people distinguish between their feelings and emoting itself.

What is appropriate with regards to the expression and containment of emotions is of course dependent on cultural context. In some contexts, overt, direct, and dramatic expressions of certain emotions are acceptable, common, and even expected. In others, such a display would be a serious breach of cultural norms and might lead to both a significant loss of face and a rupture in a relationship. The terms we use to discuss emotions (for example, *aloof*, *volatile*, or *repressed*) are often laden with cultural assumptions and norms. Sometimes these norms are obvious, but at other times they are more subtle, depending for example on gender, status differentials, age, and context. Conflict specialists need to refine their understanding of these norms when they are working in different cultures and often when working in their own as well.

How Can Disputants Replenish Emotional Energy?

The work of expressing and containing emotions in an enduring conflict can be extremely depleting. When people's emotional energy is depleted, they withdraw, make poor decisions, escalate ineffectively, and in general have difficulty finding a path to constructive engagement. No matter how effective disputants are in their approach to enduring disputes, emotional replenishment and revitalization are essential to their ability to stay with conflict.

What works for disputants is of course as varied as they are themselves. As we talk with disputants in enduring conflict, we need to ask them in one way or another, What do you need to do to take care of yourself over time? What works for you to reenergize yourself, to recharge your batteries? What are your sources of sustenance, and where can you get some safe space away from the dispute?

Our main goal in initiating this discussion is to raise the importance of reenergizing and help disputants attend to this aspect of sustainability. The answers people arrive at are amazingly diverse: meditation, music, travel, cooking, food, exercise, children, nature, church, art, gardening—and so on. One of the most interesting and not all that rare answers I have received is conflict itself—just a different, less exasperating, more manageable conflict. And sometimes the answer is simply time. Sometimes replenishment can be found in the conflict itself. A labor relations specialist in the middle of an extended dispute once told me that the most healing thing he can do is to pick a particular aspect of the conflict that can be worked on and to forget the larger picture and focus on that.

Groups and organizations also need an approach to replenishing their emotional resources. This can be done within the group structure or outside it, in relationship to a conflict or separately from it. I have often worked with community groups who seem to turn their meetings into community celebrations with pictures, food, music, and picnics. One of the purposes of demonstrations, marches, rallies and the like, beyond giving public voice and exerting pressure for change, is that they can be energizing, fun, and sometimes healing.

How Should Disputants Respond to Others' Emotions?

Often disputants are less concerned about managing their own emotional response to conflict than they are about dealing with others' emotional energy. Being enmeshed in a long-term relationship with someone who is volatile, passive aggressive, emotionally abusive, depressed, or in a constant state of denial about significant problems is challenging at best. Maintaining a constructive approach in the face of such emotions is extremely difficult and sometimes impossible. Yet that is what enduring conflict often involves. Consider the advice you might want to give a disputant who is engaged in a long-term conflict with someone who is volatile and emotionally aggressive. We might suggest certain principles for handling the dynamics of this conflict:

- *Respect the truth of what others have to say.* People may be volatile and at times irrational and yet still have an important message and some truth in that message. Even if this truth is hard to discover, considering it is a reasonable thing to do—and moreover, perhaps surprisingly, it can be healing. One way to respond to others' emotionality is to hear the real message behind it. This does not mean denying one's own truth of course.

- *Put limits on abusive behavior.* No one should have to take abusive behavior, especially not in the name of constructive conflict engagement. Finding a way to put boundaries, or limits, on behavior is not always easy but it is usually possible. For example, it's almost always possible to end a conversation—by ending a phone call, not responding to an e-mail, leaving the room, or simply remaining silent. Usually, the best way to do this is to ask for a behavior to stop, explain that if it does not the conversation will need to end, and then follow through. Being very clear (in as nonpejorative a way as possible) about one's reasonable limits is always justified and almost always wise.

- *Make sure that the boundaries created are reasonable and enforceable.* Reacting to abusive behavior is important; overreacting is a trap. People are often tempted to make counterthreats and set unreasonable boundaries or limits—a trap that many adolescents are masterful at putting their parents in (think about how parents threaten to ground their children for far longer than is either reasonable or possible—and then have to back off).

- *Look for structures for communicating that are less vulnerable to explosive behavior.* Mediation or facilitated communication is one such durable communication structure. But there are others such as the use of intermediaries, written or electronic communications, or determining when in the rhythm of interaction communication might work best. Or consider involving a different kind of third party—a mutual friend, pastor, or colleague, for example. In several cases I have mediated, the agreement to copy a third party on all communications helped moderate the tone of interchanges.

- *Avoid resorting to the "crazy," "evil," or "stupid" characterizations as an excuse for avoidance (see Chapter Three).* As tempting as it is to apply a pathological label to volatile or explosive behavior, it's seldom helpful. The best way to deal with volatile disputants is to take their concerns seriously, validate their feelings, and put limits on their behavior.

- *Reinforce constructive communication.* When disputants do express themselves constructively, even if they are not agreeing on substantive issues, this should be reinforced by listening, acknowledging, and encouraging further discussion.

- *Express your own feelings—directly, cogently, appropriately.* One problem disputants often experience when faced with intense emotionality is the temptation either to clam up or to respond in kind. Instead, each disputant needs to find her own voice in a conflict relationship—one that is authentic, genuine, and reflective of her values about communication as well.

- *Don't expect perfection of yourself or others.* If a disputant loses control or resorts to sarcasm, put-downs, patronizing comments, or other nonproductive communication approaches, life will go on. We are all human, and even if we are genuine, caring, open, and honest, we will sometimes also behave in ways that we don't always like. Disputants should not expect themselves to behave in an optimal manner all the time, and they should offer others the same leeway. Of course it is always helpful if disputants can acknowledge responsibility for times when they have acted in a less than helpful way.

- *Pay attention to timing and rhythms.* There is never a perfect time, but there are some times that are better than others—for all involved. Consider the rhythms discussed earlier. Time-outs are often helpful, sometimes essential.

- *Be realistic but don't give up (too quickly).* It's important to be realistic about the fact that things may not change easily or quickly and that disputants may face a long road ahead of them. But they should not give up. Things can improve, and it's important to keep trying if the relationship, organization, or issues are important. If the cost is too great to a disputant, he or she may have to withdraw for a while, and sometimes giving up on a specific issue may be necessary. But giving up on one's efforts to promote important concerns and work on significant relationships is usually neither healthy nor viable.

- *Letting go is sometimes necessary.* There are of course times when the healthiest thing to do is to let a relationship go, at least for the time being. Staying with conflict does not mean never letting go of an abusive or unhealthy relationship. As discussed in Chapter Three, avoidance is occasionally necessary. Sometimes the only way to create the boundaries or safety essential for staying with conflict is to end a relationship. However, some relationships (for example, with a sibling, parent, or child) are not so easy to end and sometimes letting go means simply withdrawing from contact, at least for a while, and giving up on trying to improve the interaction. As much as the focus of staying with conflict is on constructive engagement, constructive disengagement is sometimes also necessary.

These considerations can inform the discussions we have with disputants or the support we give to them for responding to the emotions of others. This is not about telling people what they should do or feel because we don't know that. We have to trust our clients to know what is best for them or we cannot be effective. But these considerations can form the outline of our discussion and frame any advice we might give. When we have access to the other disputant, the one who is perceived to be emotionally out of control, the work we do with him or her is likely to be framed by very similar considerations.

Often both parties feel that they are dealing with volatile or uncontrolled emotions. Managing the emotional dimension in an effective and realistic way is very hard, but it is essential to enduring conflict. No one always does it well. Everyone is sometimes very adept at it. The challenge of sustaining disputants through an enduring conflict demands that attention be paid to it. Learning to manage emotions effectively and to respond to others is essential to developing a sustainable approach to ongoing conflict. Support systems can be essential to this effort. I turn to that subject next.

RESOURCES AND SUPPORT SYSTEMS

Disputants often cannot go it alone over extended periods. They need support. Conflict specialists can be one source of that support, but disputants also need resources that are naturally part of their everyday lives, particularly resources that have some connection to the conflict itself. We can help them to recognize, access, and develop potential sources of support in their lives as they engage in a protracted conflict. We can also encourage them to recognize that going it alone is not necessarily a sign of strength and that everyone needs support.

Elements of Support

Various forms of support are needed to stay with conflict, and some will be more difficult to nurture than others. Sometimes it may be easier to find sources of emotional support than financial or political support, and at other times the reverse may be true. In general, disputants need support that is robust and durable and allows them to remain clear, centered, effective, and ethical—the fundamental building blocks of constructive engagement (see Chapter Two). More specifically, disputants often need the following types of support:

- *Protective.* Disputants need at a minimum to feel safe and protected. They need to feel there are systems in place that can protect them physically and emotionally. Knowing that there is a safe place to go to if things seem to be getting out of hand, someone to call on if one feels at the end of one's emotional resources, or an organization that will provide protective resources (the police, a social agency, a safe house, or a crisis line, for example) is often essential if people are to engage conflict productively.

- *Safe havens.* Disputants need a place to get away from the stress and anxiety associated with a conflict. This can be a physical location, a friendship, an activity, a group, a quiet time (meditating, for example), or even a set of ground rules to specify times when discussing a conflict is out of bounds. This is not necessarily about protecting disputants or providing emotional support but rather about finding a place or activity that is nurturing and separate from the conflict. Providing a retreat center for long-term participants in ethnic conflicts (for example, in Northern Ireland and South Africa) has frequently proved important in sustaining those individuals.

- *Allies.* Disputants do not want to feel alone in their struggle, and they also want additional sources of power and influence. Allies are people or systems who will take a disputant's side in a conflict, who are either committed to advancing the disputant's interests or who share enough of the same interests that they will join the disputant in the conflict. Allies can also help disputants think through their choices, make sense of what is going on, suggest a different approach, or take a few steps back to gain perspective. Union representatives, community organizers, attorneys, or conflict coaches are people who act formally in the ally role, but informal allies such as friends, sympathetic colleagues, partners, and family members also offer important resources for sustainability.

- *Emotional.* As discussed previously, managing emotions is essential for sustainability in conflict. Disputants need people to talk to who will listen to them and help them deal with the emotional ups and downs of conflict engagement. This support too may come from formal systems (offering therapy, personal coaching, or pastoral support, for example). But more often, it will be found in less formal family, community, and friendship systems.

- *Material resource assistance.* Enduring in conflict requires material resources as well as psychological support. Material resources may be financial or they may take the form of equipment, housing, offices, computers, technical assistance, transportation, and so forth. Foundations, advocacy organizations, and professional organizations are sometimes sources of such support. Sometimes the collective resources of an affected community are essential if a conflict is to continue effectively.

- *Procedural.* Disputants need support in choosing, planning, conducting, and supporting their engagement in different conflict processes, both formal and informal. Ombudsman, human resource professionals, corporate counsel, dispute system managers, and collaborative practitioners are examples of procedural support resources.

- *Accountability.* Most people need some guidepost or anchor that can pull them back if they stray too far from their own values and that can affirm they are behaving appropriately as well. This is not about being judged but about being held accountable to one's own best beliefs, which is essential to sustaining oneself through conflict. Religious institutions, respected elders, political organizations, or even cultural icons sometimes serve this purpose, as of course do good friends and family members.

Although many resources can provide more than one kind of support, seldom can one person or group provide all the needed support. We often talk generically with disputants about their systems of support, which is useful. But it is even more important to help them think through the specific kind of support system they need and where might they find it.

Recognizing, Accessing, and Developing Support

Disputants involved in enduring conflict need to recognize and access support systems they already have and develop new systems as needed. Among those systems already in place, some may be dormant or in need of revitalization. Disputants often feel alone and a natural corollary of that is to feel powerless and scared. The more powerless and vulnerable people feel, the more likely they are to act as if their survival is at stake, which means resorting to fight or flight responses, all-or-nothing tactics, and a short-term view. These are just the opposite of the responses needed to promote a durable approach to constructive engagement.

When disputants feel very vulnerable, it is especially important to work with them on connecting to the genuine support systems they have. This, more than any reassurance we give or strategies we suggest, can help them behave constructively and achieve a sustainable platform from which to operate. Even when disputants are not feeling cornered or alone, helping them discover and access support systems will assist them to function more constructively in sustained conflict.

People often have more support than they realize. As allies or conflict specialists, we can often help disputants to see and access that support by asking them to think about whom or what they naturally turn to during a crisis. For example, we can ask:

- "Whom do you turn to when you need advice?"
- "Where can you go when you want to avoid dealing with this conflict?"
- "Who really understands where you are coming from?"
- "Whom would you like to go to in order to discuss how to handle this when it comes up again?"

These questions and others like them can reinforce or foster a more sustainable approach to conflict.

We can also give disputants the task of identifying in a more formal way the potential sources of support they have, and we can ask them to develop a plan for reaching out to these individuals or groups. I often ask disputants to consider whom they can go to for advice, support, and assistance over the course of a long-term conflict. Often their initial response is to minimize the support systems they have. But as we talk about where they have gotten support in the past, whose support they would find useful, and what systems of support they would like to access, the picture begins to change. The task then becomes developing a plan for contacting these support resources and soliciting or making use of their assistance.

Even when we do not feel we can or should raise the issue directly, disputants are likely to talk about their sources of support, sometimes anecdotally. During these times we can and should point these resources out to them. This proved to be a critical factor in a highly protracted and contentious fifteen-year-old personnel dispute that I mediated a couple of years ago.

Aaron had been pursuing an equal opportunity grievance against the OT Corporation and had settled a suit that led to his reinstatement, some back pay, and guarantees of protection against further discrimination or harassment. This settlement led in turn to multiple other complaints about whether the settlement was being carried out properly, and eventually I was brought into the case.

During our meetings, Aaron presented himself as being completely alone and occasionally made statements that sounded as though he were slightly suicidal. At the same time, he seemed to have plenty of allies whom he had periodically brought in to support him by providing advice, attending meetings with management or his lawyers, and helping to debrief contentious interchanges. At one point he mentioned Kim, a retired OT official who had been helpful to him. I expressed curiosity about this person.

The next time we had a private meeting, Aaron brought Kim with him. As we talked I found out that there was a whole community of people who felt Aaron had been badly treated (although they also said he could be his own worst enemy). I suggested Aaron and Kim think of ways of getting together more often, and the two of them did discuss how this might happen. After our final meeting Aaron seemed increasingly willing to think of new support options in the future.

At times it is necessary for disputants to develop completely new sources of support. For example, as a result of the conflict, they may have lost their major sources of support. After a divorce, whole family systems and social networks may no longer be available. Disputants may exacerbate their sense of isolation by trying to gain access to systems that are no longer appropriate or available to them. Our task in these circumstances is to help people recognize the loss of a meaningful support system, and then to work with them on figuring out how they might begin to develop new ones.

We cannot find new families, partners, or social networks for disputants, but we can ask them to think about where they might begin to develop such opportunities. If they are really stuck, we can refer them to potential resources and new avenues of support. I have often referred families to family resource agencies, educational consultants, financial advisers, or parent support groups because I knew they needed kinds of support I could not provide. Many mediators stock their waiting rooms with brochures about resources for the same reason.

Everyone has resources, but no one ever has enough. It is certainly a common experience for people to alternate between feeling blessed by their friends and allies and awfully alone. Aside from empathizing, we can help people develop sustaining resources by strategizing effective approaches to resource development.

CONFLICT ENGAGEMENT AND CONFLICT ENCAPSULATION

The key to sustainability is balance. Disputants need to find balance in their lives. Intense and enduring conflicts can disrupt this equilibrium. Enduring conflict disrupts the balance between people's sensitivity to others and their advocacy of their own interests, between their ability to live in the present and their capacity for planning and foresight, between their analytical and emotional approaches to the challenges of the world.

In our work with enduring conflict, our emphasis is usually on helping people learn to engage in conflict. We focus on how to help disputants confront their avoidance in all its myriad forms, become more intentional about communication, handle and

respond to power, make effective use of agreements, create align-
ments, and in general do the work of engaging more effectively.
But it is possible to overemphasize engagement and thereby lose
one of the most important sources of sustainability—encapsulation.
As much as disputants need to learn to engage, they also need to
be able to lead a rich life outside of the conflict.

Encapsulation involves putting some boundaries around a conflict so it does not become all consuming, overwhelming every
aspect of a disputant's life. As you might expect, it's not always
easy to encapsulate a conflict. However, this can be critical to sustaining people through conflict, as was the case with a family I
consulted with a few years ago.

> Rebecca and Larissa, adult sisters, were in a long-term and highly
> contentious conflict about the appropriate care for their mother,
> Noreen, who was exhibiting symptoms of Alzheimer's. This was an
> all-consuming issue, particularly for Larissa, who lived with Noreen
> and was her primary caretaker. Almost every spare minute of
> Larissa's life was taken up with dealing with Noreen's needs or con-
> tending with her sister. We took multiple approaches to dealing with
> these issues, but one critical need was to give both sisters, but par-
> ticularly Larissa, some help in ensuring that this conflict did not con-
> sume their existences. This required putting boundaries around the
> times when Larissa and Rebecca would talk about Noreen, encour-
> aging Larissa to pursue other interests, and providing a mechanism
> for Larissa to receive more help with Noreen, which among other
> things allowed Larissa to go on a vacation for the first time in five
> years.

At times of high engagement, a conflict might appear to be all
consuming to participants. But high engagement should be balanced with low engagement, using time-outs, safe havens, and
other means of getting some distance from the conflict. As Emma
Goldman, the famous anarchist, told Vladimir Lenin in response

to his view that devotion to revolution should be the consuming focus of an activist's life: "If I can't dance, I don't want to be in your revolution."

Conflict specialists should work with disputants to find ways for them to take time out from their conflict and ways to encapsulate it. For example they can

- Ask people to go on a walk or get some food in the middle of a mediation.
- Schedule more time between meetings.
- Start a group meeting by asking disputants to discuss something that is not directly related to the conflict.
- Encourage disputants to get involved in activities unrelated to conflict.
- Negotiate safe zones or safe times when disputants promise not to contact each other.
- Identify anchors, such as family pictures, organizational mission statements, or cultural symbols, to remind people of what is important to them beyond the conflict.
- Encourage people to get exercise, go to concerts, pursue their art, watch sports, and so forth, so that the conflict is put in perspective.

PREPARING FOR THE LONG HAUL

Sometimes conflict seems, and perhaps at moments is, all pervasive. Conflict can seem to dominate disputants' existence. But even in the midst of the most difficult conflicts, people usually find ways to experience more normal aspects of living—friendship, family, work, hobbies, and so forth. This ability to lead a normal life in the face of conflict and danger is a healthy survival strategy—one that we should nurture and help disputants access as they work their way through a long-term dispute.

All our efforts to encourage sustainability—whether they are about working with the rhythms of conflict, emotional management, or support systems—are essentially about helping people to encapsulate the conflict experience or, more precisely, assisting them in finding the balance between engagement and encapsulation that will help them sustain themselves through the long course of conflict. In fact, almost everything we do with enduring conflict is related to helping people establish this balance because it is key to staying with conflict.

Enduring conflicts pose enormous challenges to maintaining a balanced approach to life, but this balance is essential. In the final chapter I focus on the variety of specific roles conflict specialists play to help disputants find a balanced and constructive approach to engaging in enduring conflict.

9

Conflict Specialists and Enduring Conflict

For growth to occur, conflicts must be effectively managed, resolved, transformed, or engaged. Conflict engagement is what takes place between the extremes of avoidance or confrontation; it can lead to dynamism, creativity, and growth.
Jay Rothman, 1997, p. 7

The prevalence of enduring conflict offers a tremendous opportunity to the conflict field. By taking up the challenge of helping disputants stay with conflict, we can greatly increase the reach and relevance of our work. The problem we face in rising to this challenge is not one of opportunity but of vision. We already face many opportunities to work with disputants on conflicts that are likely to be around for a long time. These are the foundation of the more specific disputes in which we are normally involved. But we often do not see and therefore cannot convey to disputants how we can help them work on the long-term dimensions of their struggle.

When we focus on what disputants need to do to stay strategically, intentionally, and constructively engaged over time, we can open many new doors for ourselves and our clients. But to do so we need to think about how we define our purpose, how we approach this purpose from the perspective of the variety of roles we normally play in conflict, and how we promote the use of services that offer our expanded purpose.

CONFLICT RESOLUTION, TRANSFORMATION, AND ENGAGEMENT

If we are to realize our potential for helping people to stay with conflict, we have to deal with both conceptual and practical challenges. On the conceptual level we have to understand how this work fits in with our self-definition, sense of purpose, and intervention strategies. On the practical level we have to consider, from the perspective of the various roles we assume in conflict, how we can develop the necessary skill sets, market this approach to our work, and offer specific services.

How we identify ourselves is not just a matter of semantics. The purpose of our efforts is characterized by how we name our field, and that purpose creates a narrative that both guides our work and limits it. For years the dominant identifiers of purpose in the conflict field have been the terms *dispute resolution* and *conflict resolution*. This is reflected in the names of many of our professional organizations (for example, Association for Conflict Resolution, Dispute Resolution Section of the ABA, Network for Conflict Resolution (Canada), Australian Dispute Resolution Association, and formerly, Society of Professionals in Dispute Resolution). Where conflict resolution has not been the identifying theme, our third-party role has been (for example, Academy of Family Mediators, Family Mediation Canada, International Academy of Mediators, and International Ombudsman Association).

Conflict transformation has been suggested as an alternative formulation. This concept was central to the work of a number of scholar practitioners who organized a graduate program in conflict transformation at Eastern Mennonite University (Lederach, 2003). Later, in quite a different spirit, Bush and Folger (1994) advocated the use of the term *transformative mediation*. Whereas Lederach emphasizes how the nature of a conflict can be transformed, Bush and Folger focus on how disputants themselves can experience a transformation.

In *Beyond Neutrality* (2004) and again in this book, I have promoted the concept of *conflict engagement* as the defining focus of our field, and I have urged that we think of ourselves as conflict specialists or conflict engagement practitioners. Others have suggested this formulation as well (for example, see Rothman, 1997; Nelson, 2008). Each of these identifiers has implications for the work we are doing, and each carries with it advantages and problems.

Conflict Resolution

Conflict resolution is probably the easiest identity to market and explain. Resolution speaks to what most people want (even if they know it is unrealistic). A common bit of marketing wisdom suggests that one should "sell the sizzle, not the steak" (that is, the benefits of a product or service rather than its features or methodology). If the steak is our services as coaches, strategists, third parties, or system designers and the skills we bring to help disputants communicate, negotiate, and problem solve, the sizzle is that we help people resolve their conflict, deal with their problem, and cope with unpleasant situations and people. The term *conflict resolution* speaks to at least part of this sizzle—disputants' hopes that a conflict can be ended, preferably on terms favorable to them.

Conflict resolution also sounds more tangible than transformation or engagement, and it does suggest an end to something painful. But even this name is more abstract than many people can handle, as most practitioners have experienced when they try to explain in casual conversation what their line of work is. If we say we work in conflict resolution, we are likely to get a glazed or uncomprehending look.

Because of this, it is tempting to explain our work in terms of our role—as mediator, coach, advocate, or ombudsman, for example. Identifying our work with a particular role offers a more tangible articulation of what we do. But a field of practice is more than a specific role or intervention tactic. By identifying our work in such a narrow way (which would be analogous to saying that one's profession is litigation rather than law, or marriage counseling rather than psychotherapy), we ignore the diversity of approaches that we can bring to conflict and minimize the potential breadth of our field.

At the 2004 annual conference of the Association for Conflict Resolution, I participated in a panel titled "If Mediation Is Our Position, What Is Our Interest?" The title speaks for itself—although mediation is a process that is useful under the right circumstances, we should be taking a broader view of our field of practice or professional orientation. We don't want mediation to be the hammer that makes everything look like a nail needing third-party intervention. (For a fuller discussion of these issues, see Golten, Smith, and Woodrow, 2002; Mayer, 2004.)

The more profound problem with conflict resolution as the organizing definition of the conflict field is that it suggests a limited purpose and one that often seems unrealistic. As discussed earlier in this chapter and throughout this book, resolution is just one part of the conflict process that disputants need assistance with. Moreover, in many and perhaps most conflicts, resolution is not the most troublesome or difficult part people need to work on. Disputants know that many elements of their conflict will not be readily resolved and often believe that the work of conflict resolvers is therefore either irrelevant or naïve. As a result, disputants either limit their use of conflict specialists to those relatively few situations or aspects of a conflict that they feel are amenable to resolution but that still require the help of third parties, or they redefine their conflict to fit it into a resolution framework. More often, they decline to use conflict specialists at all. When we are candid with disputants about the unlikelihood of obtaining a long-term solution, and suggest that they instead need assistance in working on a conflict over time, they are often more likely to appreciate the relevance of our services.

Conflict Transformation

Conflict transformation offers a different vision. It suggests that with our assistance disputants can transform the nature of the conflict or the conflictual relationship and in the process change themselves. This is a very uplifting and broad mission. Like this book, conflict transformation recognizes that people's purpose in conflict should not be limited to resolution and that significant conflicts do not readily lend themselves to resolution.

But there are several potential pitfalls here as well, particularly with the transformational approach to mediation. One is that disputants have not necessarily come to us to be transformed. They normally come to us because they want help with a conflict with which they are struggling. A second and perhaps more significant pitfall is that we are not very likely as a matter of course to transform either people or conflicts. Transformation is a rather rare occurrence and requires a confluence of external factors allowing and promoting transformation, an internal readiness for transformation to occur, and a process that allows people to realize the transformative potential. We can have some control over the process but not over the external factors or internal readiness.

Transformative moments do at times occur in mediation and other conflict interventions. Insights or "aha" moments occur, breakthroughs happen, and conflicts are fundamentally transformed when disputants are ready and circumstances favorable. We open doors that can allow this to happen, but we encounter a paradox in doing this—if we are specifically trying to transform or are too exclusively focused on transformation, we can provoke resistance or defensiveness that makes it harder for people to see the doors and walk through them.

If transformation is our purpose, disputants either have to buy into a rarely achieved and very abstract goal in order to use our services or we have to be content in having a different mission than our clients have. Having a different mission is not necessarily a major problem if our purposes are transparent and at a minimum compatible with the disputants' goals. But there is the potential for a contradiction between having a goal of achieving as good an outcome as possible and transforming the nature of the conflict.

Conflict Engagement

Conflict engagement may be, paradoxically, the most abstract and yet most viable and tangible goal of all. Disputants often just want a conflict to go away, but if they are involved in some intentional conflict process, then some form of engagement is clearly necessary, and assistance with that engagement is what we are really about. Conflict engagement has the advantage of speaking to what people most need assistance with. It offers the potential of breakthroughs in relationships or disputes, but its immediate goal is more modest and therefore we can be more credible about what it is we are offering.

Still, engagement is an abstract concept and that is a problem. Engagement lacks some of the drama or pizzazz of transformation and the results-oriented attractiveness of resolution. We may eventually settle on a more appealing and descriptive term, but it will likely have to evolve from our practice and experience rather than market-oriented, creative brainstorming.

Despite the limitations of conflict engagement as a marketing tool, it has the critical advantages of accuracy, modesty, and openness. We need a descriptor that encourages us to take on the essential services that our background, experience, and training prepare us for and that people in conflict need. We also need a self-definition that accurately reflects what we can actually accomplish when we work with people in conflict. Simply put, our field is conflict, our overarching purpose is constructive conflict engagement. We work in the conflict field as engagement specialists.

This does not mean that we resist working on conflict resolution. As I discussed in Chapter Seven, working on agreements to the degree possible and appropriate is an important part of what we do, but we have to see this as a part of a larger purpose and not as the be all and end all of what we are about. We should also be open to both the potential and the opportunity for transforming the nature of a conflict and of conflictual relationships.

I believe the surest way to do this, without getting out of step with disputant needs and expectations and without promising something that we can only occasionally deliver, is to focus our efforts and our self-definition on how people can engage in conflict—both in its immediate challenges and its long-term requirements—effectively, powerfully, constructively, and wisely. For all these reasons I believe the concept of conflict engagement provides the most flexible, accurate, and inclusive way to understand our essential goal as conflict specialists.

MEDIATING IN THE SHADOW OF ENDURING CONFLICT

Throughout this book I have been focusing generically on the role of the conflict specialist. As I see it, there are three fundamental roles we can play as conflict specialists: third-party, ally, and system roles (see Mayer, 2004, chap. 7, for a full discussion of these choices). Many of the challenges presented to us are the same whatever role we are enacting. However, there are certain challenges specific to each role as well. If we are to be successful in helping people stay with conflict, we need to think about how we can approach this task not only generically but also from the specific role we are playing. Because mediation is still the most prevalent role conflict professionals play in conflict, I will focus on that first.

Enduring conflict presents some very specific challenges to the mediator in the areas of role specificity, neutrality, agreement focus, and short-term involvement. Each of these challenges offers both opportunities and obstacles for the mediator to help people stay with conflict.

Role Specificity

The power of the mediator's role is related to its limits. Because mediators are not normally engaged to render a decision, conduct a therapeutic process, offer expert substantive advice, or enforce laws or social norms, they are in position to receive confidential information and focus on the process of negotiation and communication. Many in conflict are willing to take a chance with mediators and mediation precisely because mediators do not have the power to enforce an outcome.

As a result of these role expectations, mediators are often in an ideal position to help disputants stay with conflict but are limited in how they can do this as well. They often are called in to deal with long-term disputes but are asked to focus on immediate issues. Mediators are in a position to observe the emotional and cognitive dimensions of conflict but are often asked to focus on forging immediate agreements, and this focus can constrain their ability to work on emotional dynamics or underlying belief systems.

Mediators cannot force parties to take a long-term view, but they can usually encourage people to think about the long-term ramifications of immediate decisions. They can do this by the questions they ask, the time they allocate for reflection and decision making, and the way they frame the issues being raised, concerns being expressed, and suggestions being made. Furthermore, by being transparent about wanting to craft a robust and durable agreement, mediators encourage a long-term perspective. For example, when mediators ask what will happen when future conflicts arise, as conflicts do all the time, they are essentially asking disputants to think about the enduring nature of their conflict. When mediators frame an issue in terms of how people will approach a task or advocate for a cause over time, they are working on staying with conflict. When one party suggests a process for making a particular decision, mediators often pose this as an example or precedent for ongoing decision making.

Neutrality and Impartiality

Mediators normally present themselves as being neutral and impartial. Although there may be conceptual problems in how this quality is defined, implemented, or presented, the underlying ethical commitment is clear—mediators commit to not intentionally advocating for one party's essential interests at the expense of those of another party.

The problem in enduring conflict is that a long-term focus may be in one party's interest but not in the other's. Typically, the disputants with the most power do not feel they need to worry about anything but the immediate agreement and are quite willing to take their chances about the long-term ramifications. Or disputants may be able to push through an agreement with long-term ramifications (and advantages for them) without these consequences being thoroughly vetted.

Mediators may feel constrained from pushing an enduring view too heavily if it might align them with one side of the conflict and raise issues that one or both parties would rather avoid. However, when the enduring view is not emphasized that may allow the mediation process itself to be used to the disadvantage of one side, often the weaker one. The ability of the mediator to balance these competing needs can be crucial to the way an enduring conflict plays out. I experienced this in a case about a looming smokestack:

"Is this [huge] smokestack an issue in this process," I asked the project coordinator overseeing the cleanup and redevelopment of a toxic site that had formally been a large smelter. "No," the coordinator said, "that is not our problem." "It will be," I predicted—perhaps, given my role as a mediator, inappropriately but very accurately. After a complex cleanup and redevelopment agreement had been reached among different government entities, present property owners, and the original smelter operator, it turned out that the smokestack was in fact laden with toxic materials and likely to come down in an earthquake. It had to be removed and the very expensive cleanup could not proceed without that step.

The problem was that a nearby small trailer park would have to be evacuated for seventy-two hours during the removal. The trailer park residents were very poor, and the trailers too old to move. Eventually, the trailer park would have to be closed permanently for the redevelopment to occur. I was called back in to mediate an agreement between the developer—a huge corporation—and the trailer park residents about the procedure for this seventy-two-hour evacuation. The developer wanted to focus only on the agreement about how to proceed with the evacuation, but this was the one time in the whole process when the trailer residents had some leverage over the corporation. Their agreement was essential if the demolition were to proceed in a timely way. This was an opportunity for them to ask for some assistance with their longer-term needs. However, the residents were poorly represented, stressed in many ways, and the immediate incentives being offered them (some cash and a weekend at a nice hotel) looked awfully attractive.

My challenge was how much to push the longer-term issues— how to ask for a discussion of how the whole process leading to the ultimate closure of the trailer park would flow, what ongoing role the residents would have in the decisions about the trailer park, and what the larger picture and long-term future would look like for them. The residents were easily distracted into a discussion about the evacuation, and the more I raised the longer-term issues, the more I was forsaking a commitment to remaining impartial. In the end an agreement was worked out that set up some resources for the final relocation and a process for requesting additional help if neces- sary. The brief evacuation and demolition went forward, and when the long-term relocation occurred there was some short-term assis- tance for the residents.

In many circumstances, mediators are forced to walk a line between ensuring that a process offers an adequate perspective on the enduring conflict and maintaining their commitment to neutrality. To walk this line effectively, mediators have to face the enduring aspect of the challenge and articulate it, at least for themselves. If emphasizing the enduring dimension favors one of the parties, ignoring that aspect of the conflict favors the other party. In these situations, mediators generally need to find a way of raising a question about the ongoing challenges disputants will face and framing the long-term dimension in a way that allows disputants to talk about it if they choose. But mediators cannot and should not force disputants to take on this discussion. The art is to provide an effective narrative for considering the long-term context but to respect the purpose that brought the disputants to mediation.

Agreement Focus

In *The Promise of Mediation*, Bush and Folger (1994) argue that a settlement orientation is precisely what prevents mediators from realizing the transformational potential of the process. Others have argued that this orientation encourages an overly directive, evaluative, and rights-based approach to mediation (Alfini, 1991; Sander, 1995). I believe it can distract us from understanding or focusing on the challenge and opportunity of enduring conflict. But whatever one thinks about an agreement focus, the fact is that mediators are very often engaged to help disputants reach an agreement and the time frame for doing this is usually limited.

As mediators we are constantly engaged in a process of negotiation with our clients about our role, process, focus, timing, and communication, among other issues. We can and must negotiate our role, but we cannot dictate it. As a result we are obligated by both business realities and ethical considerations to take the desire of disputants to arrive at immediate agreements very seriously and to commit ourselves to this goal.

But we can also insist that in doing this everyone be given time to consider the long-term ramifications of the decision. If we are genuinely committed to helping our clients reach the agreements they seek, we are in a strong position to raise the questions that will help them think about the enduring conflict. We can do this, for example, by asking disputants to think about the long-term implications of the agreement, by raising what-if questions, by suggesting that they consider identifying the structures of communication that will be necessary between them over time, and by framing any agreement as a step within a long-term process. We can also suggest that no agreement can cover all future issues and ask the parties to consider principles for handling other disputes they may have.

Short-Term Contract

Occasionally mediators are engaged or appointed to take on a long-term role in a conflict. Labor mediators are sometimes assigned for years to the same collective bargaining unit. Family mediators may play a role in a case over many years, sometimes by the voluntary decision of a family, sometimes by binding agreement or court order. Over the years, I have been involved in a number of conflicts or projects that spanned multiple years. But for the most part, as mediators, we are hired for a time-limited task. This means that we are only available to work on a particular manifestation of an enduring conflict.

Although this is a limiting role it is nonetheless a very important one, and when we undertake it our understanding of the dynamics of enduring conflict is critical to our effectiveness in helping people stay with conflict. The fact that our role is time limited does not mean we should take only a time-limited perspective or discourage disputants from thinking about the long-term challenge. We are often in an ideal position to promote a long-term view, because our work deals with the kinds of problems that disputants are likely to be dealing with for many years. If we play into denial, short-term framing, or an immediate agreement focus, we enable a limited and often counterproductive approach. But if we remain alert to the long-term challenge, we will find many opportunities to offer, even as short-term interveners, significant assistance to disputants with long-term problems. Our whole way of thinking and intervening in conflicts needs to change. Instead of asking ourselves, How can this conflict be settled? we should be asking, Given the enduring nature of the underlying conflict, what is the most important work that can be done now?

Frequently, we are asked back repeatedly by a particular set of clients to assist them with new conflicts (which are often manifestations of the same enduring conflict). An organization may ask us back often (or give us a contract) to assist with grievances, workplace disputes, and contract negotiations. We may work in a policy arena (for example, land use, water, or transportation conflicts) that repeatedly involves us with the same set (or overlapping sets) of players. Or a large organization may ask us to work on a single set of issues in multiple settings. In doing this, we gradually build up the relationships, the expertise, and the access to give us an entry into the enduring conflicts that generate these short-term issues.

We also have another alternative, one that we should develop and promote, and that is to offer our services for the long haul. This can either mean contracting for a long-term involvement (which requires rethinking our role and marketing it accordingly) or agreeing to play a short-term role with a long-term focus, that is, to undertake conflict intervention with a strategic focus. We can also suggest an on-call arrangement for dealing with future issues. When we are faced with a conflict that has been going on for a long time and is likely to continue in one form or another, we can advocate for a long-term role. We can do this out of a commitment to the genuine demands of the situation. Of course people might not be willing to consider this or, worse, may be concerned that we are mostly advocating for our own financial interests. We should check our perceptions of what is needed against this possibility, but if we sense that a long-term intervention is what is needed, we should be willing to raise that issue.

The assistance that can be offered to enduring conflict disputants by the mediator and related third-party roles is potentially significant. Mediators are sometimes the best placed of all practitioners to help a conflict system recognize and address the challenge of staying with conflict. Because mediators have a role to play with all the key participants in a conflict, have a confidential relationship with all the parties, and are not expected to promote the interests of one party at the expense of another, they can also play a big role in fostering constructive engagement.

CONFLICT ALLIES IN ENDURING CONFLICT

Because of the limits on the role of the third party, we are often most likely to have access to enduring conflict when we are in the role of *conflict allies*. Coaches, strategists, advocates, consultants, and organizers are examples of ally roles we might play. Even as allies we are often asked for advice on a short-term conflict, but effectiveness in the ally role almost always requires that we understand the enduring context. The key challenge for the ally is determining how to help disputants understand and engage in the enduring aspect of conflict while at the same time focusing on the immediate issues that form the context of most disputant discussions. Meeting this challenge requires clarity about our contract, a viable format for working with disputants, and an effective set of intervention tools.

Contracting for Staying with Conflict

Our ability to assist with enduring conflict is dependent on what people are asking from us, how we present ourselves, and the specific contract we work out that defines our role. Consider these two requests I received for assistance with long-term conflicts.

> "I am going to have to negotiate a new agreement with my business partner, because we just are not getting along and I want him out. I want your advice."

> "Morale around here stinks and so does communication. We need to fix this problem."

Both of these requests display an implicit understanding of my role but also a lot of room for confusion about what my focus should be. When I inquired further about the conflict history, it became clear that in each situation there had been conflicts of some sort for a long time and there would be some ongoing connection or interdependence in the future. It was clear that no single agreement could end either of the conflicts because they were embedded in the structure of the relationships and the personal styles and values of the participants.

In the first request the assumption was that my focus would be on a one-off negotiation that would end a long-term business relationship. As I explored this further with the disputant (I'll call her "Michelle"), three things became clear:

1. The most appropriate role for me to play would be Michelle's conflict coach.

2. Negotiating an end to the partner relationship seemed necessary and probably doable.

3. Ending the partner relationship would not necessarily end the business relationship. Michelle and her partner would still have to interact around past work and mutual associates, clients, and friends.

Once I had this information, I agreed to focus on how to conduct the immediate negotiation but was clear that this needed to be done with an eye to its effect on future interactions, which could easily be conflictual. I also felt that Michelle and I should spend some time considering how to approach those interactions.

In response to the second request, I set up a two-stage contract for services. In the first stage my focus was on data gathering and situation assessment; the second stage involved implementation of the recommendations that came out of the assessment. During the assessment phase, it became clear that two kinds of assistance were needed—management training and coaching on how to deal with conflicts and difficult employees, and a facilitated dialogue among staff and management. Although there are times when the same intervener can fulfill both roles, this can be tricky. To fully ally oneself with the managers' interests, as called for in the coaching role, and then to be completely dedicated to the facilitative role, with an equal commitment to all participants, would be difficult, particularly when I believed that the problem was an enduring one. In these circumstances I felt the long-term challenge was the most essential one. I suggested that I work with the top managers on the enduring issues, and I suggested other practitioners who could serve as facilitators of a large-group interaction focused on more immediate concerns.

In both of these circumstances the contracting was complicated because of the potential multiple focuses that could lead to more than one role. Each situation required some sort of initial assessment, one more formal than the other. The suggestions I made for the role I negotiated were critical to the eventual direction of my work and the degree to which I could focus on enduring conflict.

Developing a Format for Intervention

Through the contract we negotiate, we arrive at a format (or arena or platform) for our work. Formats can involve training, coaching, advocacy support, facilitating dialogues, mediation, dispute system design, or strategic planning. Not all these formats allow us to work on staying with conflict. For example, conflict specialists are often asked to provide training to disputants on dealing with conflict when the real concern is working on a particular conflict situation. Training in conflict skills can of course be very valuable, but it is not the same as working on a specific conflict. Sometimes we work with disputants whose role is short term and time limited and who are not the actual carriers of the enduring conflict (for example, we may be asked to work at an organization level where the turnover is high but the sources of the enduring conflict behind this problem are at a different level of the organization).

Arriving at an optimal intervention arena and process is critical to our efforts. When we can focus on the key issues, interact with the key players, and work on immediate problems with a view to the long-term context, our ability to help disputants engage constructively increases. One interesting example of this occurred when I was asked to help with improving the climate of student and administration relationships at a private university.

As student activism increased around the issues of the war in Iraq and globalization, I was approached by the administration of a midsized university to help the school develop a constructive approach to student political activity. I had previously worked with this university on faculty administration relationships and on a number of intradepartmental disputes. I was immediately concerned about being used to disempower students or to undercut the impact of their protests. I said that I would agree to take on this project only if the idea was to create a constructive atmosphere in which students and administrators could deal with their conflicts, and to enable students to have an effective and constructive voice about the issues that concerned them.

Several approaches to this work seemed possible. I could suggest a joint meeting that I could facilitate with students and administrative representatives. Conflict resolution training was an option. I could offer to sit in with administrators on negotiations with student leaders, and I could work with the university on preparing for an upcoming week when student protests were planned. Although these were not necessarily mutually exclusive approaches, resources were limited, and it seemed important to pick a particular venue or format. I decided to work in a coaching role primarily with the dean of students and with an assistant to the president who was very involved in planning the university's response to student protests. We decided to set up regular monthly meetings to which others could be invited as necessary. We also could increase or decrease the frequency of these meetings as events dictated. We maintained this arrangement for about five years, during which relations between students and administration were not perfect, but were mostly constructive.

I found that the format of my work—regular meetings with two top administrators—was critical to the success of this effort. I had decided on this focus for three reasons—stability, influence, and focus. The dean of students and the assistant to the president were likely to be involved over a number of years with this issue, whereas student leaders and some staff were likely to be gone in three years. The two administrators had the influence to shape the university's approach and could bring in others (such as the university president, the vice president-academic, the vice president-business, the chief of police, and legal counsel) as necessary, which they did. I also thought this format would best allow us to focus on the general issue of the relationship between activists and administration over time. Although we looked at specific events, we always did so in the context of the longer-term and larger picture.

Choosing Effective Intervention Tools

The whole range of tools that I have discussed in previous chapters of this book—dealing with avoidance, framing the narrative, working on long-term patterns of communication, power, escalation, and agreements—is at the core of the interventions we use in staying with conflict. But we also need to think about some specific ways of working with disputants as allies. The range of tools we can use here is also very broad. We can elicit disputants' own insights, role-play, offer our best advice, provide specific training, observe disputants in action (directly or through a video or audio setup) and provide feedback, and occasionally work with them as advocates or representatives. The specific tools we intend to use should be discussed as we contract for the intervention.

Here are three approaches that I have found especially useful for enduring conflict when working as an ally—the reflective method, role playing, and scenario mapping. Variations of each of these can be used by third parties as well, but they are especially useful to allies acting as coaches, consultants or strategists.

The Reflective Method

The reflective method (Schön, 1983; Lang and Taylor, 2000) encourages practitioners to develop an ability to reflect on the actual impact of what they are doing, as an ongoing discipline. The particular goal of this activity is to help practitioners become reflective about what they are doing, why they are doing it, what the embedded assumptions are in the approach they are taking, what the results of their approach are, and how they might want to change that approach.

The reflective method is also very useful for disputants in an enduring conflict. For example, we can use it to help them review specific conflict interactions. I might ask a disputant to discuss a particular interchange and to focus on a particular moment that was "poignant" to him or her, meaning stressful or perhaps productive and effective. I then ask five focused questions:

- Why was it poignant?
- What did you do or say at that moment?
- Why did you do that?
- What was the response you received?
- What can you learn from this?

Each of these questions can open up an interesting and meaningful discussion, and each can be difficult for disputants to answer. But the cumulative effect of these questions is that people begin to look at the assumptions and reasoning that underlie their actions and to generalize the impact. Perhaps paradoxically, this focused approach to a specific conversation almost always leads to a discussion of the enduring elements of a conflict, precisely because it encourages an in-depth of analysis of what is happening.

Role Playing with a Long-Term Perspective

Most conflict professionals are well acquainted with role playing as a teaching and intervention technique. We create simulations so that trainees can practice mediation, negotiation, facilitation, coaching, or other interventions. We sometimes ask disputants to role-play the way in which they might like to approach someone they are in conflict with or to try to reenact a problematic interaction. Sometimes we might ask people to play their own role in a situation, but at other times we might suggest they try someone else's role—perhaps that of their adversary. We are in essence using role playing to help people rehearse for upcoming interactions.

Role playing can be a very effective—although for some intimidating—way to practice new skills and gain insight into conflict. Perhaps the most frequent comment on training programs that I have conducted over the past thirty years amounts to this: "I hate role playing and dreaded what it was going to be like, but it was essential to my learning, the most valuable part of the course, and I especially appreciated the individual coaching I received."

Although many people may resist role playing, when done effectively it is very powerful and the individual feedback is critical to helping people practice new skills. When using role-playing techniques with disputants involved in enduring conflict, it is important that we follow their lead in focusing on the interaction they are concerned about. But we can also consider with them what implications for a long-term process they see in the interaction they are playing out. If I am coaching a parent in dealing with an ex-spouse and we are role playing an interaction about appropriate educational programs for a child with learning disabilities, I want to ask that parent to play out the interaction not simply with a view to finally resolving the issue but with an understanding that she and her ex-spouse are likely to be engaging in one version or another of this interaction for many years. By doing this, participants can experience in a direct and tangible way the nature of their long-term challenge and can begin to consider in practical terms what it will take to stay with conflict.

Scenario Mapping

Scenario mapping is a process for considering the long-term implications of the choices people make in conflict situations. This is accomplished through a structured set of questions about the responses and counter-responses that are likely to occur to different approaches that individuals or groups may take to conflict. This can involve sequential role playing but more often is done by asking disputants to use their best knowledge of the different parties involved to anticipate the range of responses they are likely to get to different actions. They are then asked to consider their own range of likely counter-responses and the reactions these might create. The facilitators of this effort may propose certain external considerations that might intervene—an economic downturn or new legal ruling, for example. After several interchanges of this nature have occurred, participants in this effort are asked to consider the conclusions this experience suggests for their approach to a long-term conflict.

Scenario mapping (sometimes called the *alternative futures approach*) can be quite technical and is often used for long-range forecasting or looking at broad policy questions. It is generally applied to large group conflicts (often international conflicts) involving multiple players and complex interaction patterns. I have participated in mapping efforts, for example, about how to deal with potential regional water crises and how to respond to potential terrorist incidents. In a less formal way, it can also be used with individuals or small groups as well. It promotes a more strategic, long-term view of how to approach conflict, and it helps people realize how hard it is to predict a likely course of events. This in turn encourages participants to focus more on sustainable and fluid approaches to conflicts that can be adapted to changing circumstances rather than on a more fixed or inflexible approach. This can be an effective alternative to more deterministic approaches to strategic planning.

Disputants in long-term conflicts are often torn between very different approaches—for example, between giving in or escalating, ending a relation or increasing communication, imposing sanctions or offering concessions. Rather than work with these choices through a rational discussion of the pros and cons of each choice or through recommending a particular approach, we can use mapping to help disputants consider and experience multiple approaches.

In considering how to respond to a very talented but difficult coworker, for example, a disputant might feel that he wants nothing to do with that person ever again and therefore seek to insulate himself from all interactions. He might also, however, think that imposing some consequences or trying yet again to work things out would be wiser approaches. We can use mapping to imagine how this would work. We might ask: How does having nothing to do with this person look? What do you have to do to make that happen? What response to those steps might you encounter? Are there future events that are likely to make your insulation difficult, and how might you handle this? What does your interaction look like several years down the line? We could ask a similar set of questions for different potential consequences or various approaches to working things out. We might also be tempted to ask him to consider the costs of taking these various approaches, but we lose some of the power of the mapping process if we get into a cost-benefit analysis rather than sticking to the construction of alternative scenarios that is the heart of mapping. If someone carefully imagines what particular approaches might realistically look like, those costs will become obvious. We would then ask him to consider what this suggests for the fundamental strategies he might want to take with respect to communication, rewards, sanctions, escalation, avoidance, and negotiation (among other considerations).

The point is not to argue for one approach or another but to help people experience as directly as possible the real implications of their choices and to focus them on the long-term implications. Our role in this intervention is to ask questions, keep it specific, keep it moving, and not allow people to get bogged down in details that cannot be known.

All three of these approaches to acting in the ally role are examples of how to make an abstract challenge—engaging in conflict constructively over time—tangible, specific, and doable. As allies to enduring disputants, we are often in a particularly advantageous position to work over time on enduring conflict issues. But it is important that we focus on specifics. We have to help disputants arrive at particular approaches to changing the nature of their engagement so that staying with conflict seems possible and not too daunting.

SYSTEM ROLES FOR ENDURING CONFLICT

As system designers and system managers, conflict specialists are naturally directed toward sustainable approaches to conflict. Dispute system designers work with organizations or communities to set up approaches to handling the repeating disputes that a group faces. Typical system examples are grievance systems, consumer complaint protocols, and citizen boards to review community-police issues.

As we do with almost all conflict specialist roles, when designing systems we generally focus on short-term, resolution-oriented procedures. This is a result of the questions we are asked to address and how we understand the task ourselves. But changing the nature of the way conflicts are conducted is in fact the underlying goal of most dispute systems and is a logical place from which to work on enduring conflict.

Effective grievance systems, for example, are in part about decreasing the tension in the workplace and solving immediate complaints quickly and effectively. But they also involve a recognition that conflict will be ongoing, and the goal is to create a constructive approach for dealing with them as they inevitably arise. The question facing system designers and managers is how to build a focus on or sensitivity to the enduring element of conflict into the process itself. For instance, in creating an approach to harassment complaints in the workplace, it is important to move beyond a case-by-case approach and consider how to work on the overall culture of organizations. In looking at how to create a discrimination complaint system, it is important to consider how a community can provide individual redress and also to look at the wider challenge of promoting better relations in the community among different ethnic, gender, religious, or other groups.

The system design process offers an important mechanism for attending to enduring conflict, and system designers have tackled it in many creative ways. For example, among many possible approaches, systems design might include

- *Review panels* to take a look at complaints in aggregate, identify patterns and systemic problems that need addressing, and make recommendations on ways to address them

- *Community or organizational communication procedures* (for example, newsletters, regular meetings, processes for providing feedback and reaction to proposals, interactive Web sites, or groups formed to address particular problems) designed to address systemic concerns

- *An internal neutral* whose responsibilities include looking beyond individual complaints to organizational conflicts and systemic sources of disputes, and suggesting processes for dealing with conflicts

- *Periodic organizational or community surveys or inventories* to evaluate the health of communication and conflict processes and the overall state of relationships and morale

- *Evaluation and monitoring procedures* to measure the degree to which important issues are engaged, not just the number of settlements reached (see, for example, Bingham, 2003)

System managers (for example, ombudsmen, corporate counsel, human resource directors, state offices of dispute resolution) are also well positioned to examine and raise awareness about the nature of enduring conflict in a system and how it might be approached. This can be done through establishing direct processes, such as those suggested previously, and also through the protocols that set out how interveners are trained and how they conduct their work. If the expectation and the basis of evaluation for grievance or equal employment mediators, for example, is that they will settle as many cases as possible, as quickly as possible, then a significant disincentive for staying with conflict has been built into the system. However, mediators and other interveners can also be trained and evaluated on the basis of how effective they are in engaging disputants in a constructive discussion about their genuine concerns and differences, and they can be encouraged to prepare disputants for the challenge of dealing with these issues over time. Constructing effective evaluation procedures to do this poses methodological challenges, but these are not insurmountable. This was accomplished, for example, in Project Redress, the massive mediation programs initiated in the U.S. Postal Services in the 1990s. In this project mediators were evaluated based on their success in engaging clients in the mediation process and not on the basis of how many agreements were reached (Bingham, 2003).

None of this is to suggest that the resolution of grievances or other disputes on a case-by-case basis does not have value and should not proceed. That will continue to be an important element of conflict systems work, but it does not have to be the only one. System creation and maintenance offer an important opportunity to encourage a constructive approach to enduring conflict.

A MARKETING APPROACH TO STAYING WITH CONFLICT

Inevitably the marketing question arises—how do you sell a service that asks people to stay with something they would rather avoid or at least move past as quickly as possible? There is a big difference between a need for a service or product and a market for it. As important as it may be to help people with enduring conflicts, how can we make that our work? How can we make a living helping people to stay with conflict? Related to this is the question of how to structure our practices and find or develop institutional structures to support this approach?

I believe that if there is a genuine need, the market will ultimately follow. But the path can be tortuous and long. If we hone our understanding of the challenge and our skills in responding to it, we will find increasing opportunities to offer services related to enduring conflict. This, more than effective marketing or advertising, is how the practice of mediation has grown. I believe that the deepest meaning of marketing is to identify the real needs of our potential client base, to develop services that genuinely answer those needs, and to articulate or frame those services in a way that speaks to potential users. But more traditional approaches to marketing might also help us translate a need into a market smoothly and quickly, and I think there are several things that we can do to promote the process of market development.

1. We can continue to refine and articulate exactly what need we are addressing and what service we are offering. I have

tried to do that in this book, but I believe successive iterations of this will be necessary and inevitable.

2. We can recognize what we are already doing that is helping people to stay with conflict, and we can use these experiences to leverage more work along these lines. For example, my experience in bringing workers and managers together to discuss how they will handle ongoing and inevitable differences pushed me to offer that specific service more broadly and encourage others to use it.

3. We can include these services in our marketing material—our brochures, Web sites, résumés, and advertisements. Listing "Assistance with Ongoing Conflict" is a start. More robust descriptions should also be used. For example, in a brochure for a family conflict intervention program we might say:

"Differences about how to parent are natural when couples are married and they are natural after marriages end as well. When parents handle these differences wisely, children benefit. The answer is not pretending these differences don't exist or letting one parent's approach dominate. Instead, parents need help in learning how to raise their concerns and how to listen to each other so that they can continue to work together as parents, even when they disagree. Family Conflict Services supports separated and divorced parents in the ongoing challenge of working together."

I think it is a worthwhile exercise to try to write out a description like this for each arena in which we practice. In doing that we will be pushed to find language that is user friendly. We can imagine similar statements for organizational, labor-management, community, commercial, environmental, educational, public policy, and international dispute resolution programs. Many organizations already offer descriptions of their work that are close to this in spirit. For example, the following statement was found on the Web site of Search for Common Ground (2008): "Founded in 1982, Search for Common Ground works to transform the way the world deals with conflict—away from adversarial approaches and towards collaborative problem solving. We work with local partners to find culturally appropriate means to strengthen societies' capacity to deal with conflicts constructively: to understand the differences and act on the commonalities."

4. We can present our experiences in working on enduring conflicts at conferences and in professional articles that we write. This may not seem like direct marketing, but it is an important way in which we get new approaches understood, accepted, and disseminated. And when we articulate our experience and the lessons we have learned for others, we refine the way we frame and present our approach.

5. We can develop research and evaluation processes to measure the effect of this work—again an important tool that gets to the essence of marketing—and we can develop effective services that meet this essential need to engage conflict. This could also involve market research on how people experience the need for assistance with long-term conflict and what language works best for them when discussing it.

6. In answering RFPs (requests for proposals), we can propose services that include staying with conflict.

7. We can develop training programs for staying with conflict or incorporate our approaches into existing programs.

8. We can clearly recommend to clients that they put resources into the long-term conflicts they face.

Of course, many other approaches can be taken as well, but all involve one simple challenge—being willing to take some risks. If we are unwilling to push the envelope on how we market ourselves, then it is unlikely our program of services will change and an important opportunity will be lost. We are not asking disputants to accept a reality of which they are unaware. Most people know quite well that the most significant issues they face will not readily go away, and speaking to that kind of awareness is what marketing is all about.

We will also have to consider internal marketing, that is, within our own organizations. If we work as a corporate ombudsman, we have an internal job of marketing to do to create an awareness of a new potential dimension for our work. If we work for a conflict resolution firm, we will have to make a case with our colleagues. As professors in conflict resolution programs, we have to market our concepts about engaging in enduring conflict to our colleagues, create relevant courses, and work with curriculum development committees to promote them. We also have to market our concepts to our professional organizations so that they increasingly include them in their conferences, publications, professional development seminars, and professional service categories.

Marketing sometimes seems to professionals to be an activity that is not quite as serious or prestigious as the delivery of services. I see marketing, in its most essential form, as an integral part of service delivery and professional development. Marketing involves an ongoing two-way communication between professionals and their clients. It is a creative, constructive, and essential part of the service delivery system. As we market staying with conflict, we will become increasingly clear about what we mean, what our clients' needs are, and how we can best meet them.

For innovations in practice and in our orientation to our work to take hold, they have to speak to our personal capacities and interests, effectively address a genuine need, appeal to our client base, and be accessible to those clients. In a sense marketing is what ties all this together. For marketing to result in work, it has to speak to the need and perceptions of consumers of our service and has to make a case for our ability to address this need in a user-friendly way. The real test of an innovative approach is not whether it sounds intriguing or convincing but whether it can be translated into actual services to be used by actual disputants. I believe that the need people have for assistance with enduring conflict is significant, widespread, and inadequately addressed. But I don't believe disputants often think in these terms, nor do professionals. That is why a concerted effort at presenting a broader vision of services is so essential.

The heart of the marketing challenge is also the heart of the challenge of staying with conflict—we need to raise the issue of enduring conflict in a way that speaks to disputants and that suggests that constructive and meaningful work can be done on long-term disputes even though they are unlikely to be resolved. This is the work of constructive conflict engagement. Conflict engagement builds on the insights and skills of conflict resolution but is different and broader. The future of the conflict specialist will build on the past but will necessarily involve a broader view of conflict and a broader approach to our role and task as conflict professionals. As we become more oriented to the call of long-term conflict, we will not abandon the work we do on more immediate disputes. In fact we will become better at that work because we will have a richer context for it. But we will also be opening up much broader arenas for our efforts. I believe this will strengthen our understanding of conflict, our practice, and our field.

Epilogue

The Dynamic Nature of Enduring Conflict

Every enduring conflict is an evolving, changing, dynamic process. Staying with conflict does not mean adopting a set strategy for an unchanging and intractable conflict. Nor does it imply that disputants are stuck in a process they cannot escape. Conflicts endure because they are embedded in the values, identity, and structures of people's lives. But they are also the means by which these structures, values, and identity grow, change, and adapt to new circumstances.

Disputants need to take a dynamic approach to a dynamic process. That is, they need to adapt their approach as the conflict evolves. The work we do with disputants in long-term conflict is largely about how to explore new strategies in the face of an ongoing but constantly changing effort. The challenge can seem daunting, but it is also energizing and necessary.

The central element of the challenge is one of imagination. Can those of us who work in the conflict field envision for ourselves a new role, one that incorporates the work we have always done and then expands on it? Can we change our focus in conflict from prevention, management, and resolution to anticipation, support, and engagement? Can we see within the many roles we already play the opportunities to work with disputants on the enduring element of conflict, not just the transient or stubborn elements? Can we change how we frame our larger role so that we are more than conflict resolution practitioners and are in fact conflict engagement specialists? I believe we can do this because of the experience we bring to the table and the insights we have developed about conflict. And I believe that if we do this, we will find many new vistas opening up for us—and for our clients.

If we can develop the imagination we need to envision this new role, then many things will begin to fall into place. We will find many opportunities within the work we already do to focus on enduring conflict. We will see new opportunities for offering our services. Even in our more limited role as facilitators of resolution efforts, we will find that a perspective that maintains a focus on enduring conflict will help us be more effective in our immediate tasks because we will be operating from a more realistic context.

When working with disputants in an enduring conflict, we will always face the six specific challenges that I have discussed in this book:

- Confronting avoidance
- Framing the enduring elements of conflict
- Promoting sustainable approaches to communication
- Supporting people in using power wisely
- Recognizing the role of agreements in long-term disputes
- Helping disputants develop systems of support

We need to recognize the different faces of avoidance—denial, minimization, misdirection, escalation, and premature problem solving. We need to help disputants face their avoidant decisions and understand the implications of avoidance and what their alternatives really are. In doing so, we always have to honor the decisions that people make and to recognize that sometimes avoidance is appropriate or even necessary. But over the course of a long-term conflict, avoidance interferes with progress on the most important issues that people face.

Once we have begun to reconstruct our own narratives about the nature of conflict and our role in it, we can help disputants begin to adopt a different frame for conflict—one that incorporates the challenge of engaging with enduring conflict with both realism and optimism. We need to help disputants think through the narratives they have created and begin to change those narratives so that they leave room for the perspectives of others as well.

We should always support people in their efforts to communicate, and the communication skills that we are always encouraging—good listening, artful framing, participating in dialogue, effective questioning, and raising difficult issues, among others, are very relevant to enduring conflict. But we also need to look at the long-term patterns of interaction in a conflict and help disputants establish multiple durable channels of communication. We need to help disputants recover from destructive interchanges and learn how to deal with people who are persistently negative in their approach to communication. Finally, we need to understand that at different times during the life of a conflict, different approaches to communication make sense. Sometimes it is best to pull back, and at other times it is wisest to assertively pursue direct communication.

As much as we might like to think that good communication, good problem solving, and good intentions are the main keys to constructive engagement, we must also look at the use of power. Conflict involves power exchanges. Furthermore, it is sometimes necessary to escalate a conflict in order to put limits on destructive behavior or to insist that significant concerns be addressed. Disputants need help in understanding the dynamics of power in conflict so they can grasp the true nature of their own power and then use that power effectively. They also need assistance in understanding and responding wisely to the power that others exert. The goal is not to prevent the application of power but to encourage a constructive, reciprocal, and sustainable pattern of power exchange.

A focus on enduring conflict does not mean that we are not interested in helping people resolve conflicts or achieve agreements on nagging issues. We have an important contribution to make in this arena, and we ought not to sacrifice this important part of our work to our focus on enduring conflict. But we also need to understand the role of agreements in enduring conflict. They memorialize progress that has been achieved and create new and, we hope, more constructive platforms from which to continue the conflict engagement process. As we work with disputants on resolving issues in the course of an enduring conflict, we need to keep in mind—and help disputants to understand—that resolving issues does not end an enduring dispute.

Disputants cannot engage in long-term conflict alone if they are to remain effective and constructive. They need support and assistance. One of our tasks is to help disputants think through the type of support they need and the sources of support that they have. In part this involves encouraging people to ask for help—and to see this request as a sign of strength and not of weakness—but it also involves connecting people with systems of support that either already exist or need to be developed.

These six challenges are the heart of the strategic approach to enduring conflict that is the subject of this book. Each of them requires that we become clear about the challenge and the goal. Each of them draws on the skills conflict specialists have already developed and apply all the time. We do this from the perspective of being third parties, allies, or system interveners. Each of these roles offers particular opportunities for working with enduring conflict, and of course there are limitations in each role as well. Part of what we need to do is to assert this dimension of our work in how we present ourselves to the public, to our potential clients, and to ourselves. Developing an understanding that in our new role we are conflict engagement specialists can give us an overall umbrella for this effort.

But in this field we are also all clients, disputants ourselves. The challenge of staying with conflict, of finding a constructive approach to enduring disputes, is a challenge that we all face as well, every day of our lives. Most of us have had the experience of people looking incredulously at us at some point when we ourselves were involved in a conflict, and clearly thinking (or saying), "Aren't you supposed to be an expert in conflict?" Our knowledge about conflict, communication, and collaboration is at the core of the skills we bring to disputants, but that does not mean we have mastered applying it in our own lives.

It is to be hoped that working in this field can help us improve our own skills in handling conflicts, particularly enduring ones. That is one of the genuine benefits of working as conflict specialists. But we struggle in the same way everyone else does with conflict. As we consider how to help other disputants take a new approach to enduring conflict, it makes sense for us to think about the role of conflict in our own lives as well.

Conflict is the vehicle through which we all engage the major issues of our lives, as individuals, groups, and communities. Although it can seem at times that we are caught in an intractable conflict, at an impasse, or stuck, those descriptions define our feelings about conflict more accurately than they define conflict's true nature. In fact, conflict causes us to adapt to others and to adjust to changing circumstances continuously. When we try to apply old strategies to new situations for which they are inappropriate or ineffective, conflict is the vehicle that lets us know the limitations of our approach.

I have avoided using the terms *intractable conflict* or *impasse* in this work. Instead I have talked about *enduring conflict* or *long-term disputes*, but I could also have discussed *evolving conflict* or *dynamic ongoing conflict*. We need to get away from thinking of long-term conflict as a trap from which escape would be desirable but impossible. Instead we have to see enduring conflict as not only inevitable but essential, an opportunity to grow, to confront life's biggest challenges, and to give fuller meaning to our lives. This is true whether we are disputants or conflict interveners.

Many enormous and difficult issues confront us as a society— climate change, increasing demands for energy, income disparities, poverty, contentious race relations, gender inequality, religious and ethnic conflict, family violence, globalization, war, and organized violence against civilians, for example. As individuals, most people face a variety of personal, organizational, or familial struggles. Our most significant social and personal challenge is to engage effectively with these issues. We cannot do this if we are unwilling to enter into a process that will necessarily be conflictual at times. We can aim for a collaborative approach. We can look to build consensus. We can promote dialogue and problem solving. But if these strategies turn into mechanisms for avoiding conflict, rather than delving into it, we will be acting in a counterproductive way. Our ability to engage over time in conflict for which there is no easy solution, and to do so with energy, élan, optimism, and realism, is essential to our capacity to work effectively on the big issues of our lives and our times.

Conflict specialists alone will not change the world. But we can be a vital part of helping people and organizations address what appear to be the ever more complex dilemmas everyone faces. In doing so, we do not have to claim to have the magic bullet to address the big issues, to oversell our potential contribution, or to insist that we are the sine qua non for dealing with major disputes. There is no magic bullet. We are just one group among many groups of players who have a potential contribution to make.

But we do not have to undersell what we have to offer either. We have the capacity, and perhaps the obligation, to enhance people's effectiveness in facing the most significant struggles of their lives. We should not be afraid to develop this capacity and to promote it. We can, should, and I believe will take on the meaningful challenge of helping people develop dynamic, evolving, and constructive approaches to staying with conflict

References

Abraham Path Initiative. "About the Initiative." http://www
.abrahampath.org/about.php?lang=en, accessed January 23,
2008.

Adler, P. *Eye of the Storm Leadership: 150 Ideas, Stories, Quotes,
and Exercises on the Art and Politics of Managing Human
Conflicts.* http://www.mediate.com, 2008.

Alfini, J. "Trashing, Bashing, and Hashing It Out: Is This the End
of 'Good Mediation?'" Florida State University Law Review.
19 (1991): 47–75.

Allred, K. G. "Anger and Retaliation in Conflict: The Role of
Attribution." In *The Handbook of Conflict Resolution: Theory
and Practice,* edited by P. T. Coleman, M. Deutsch, and E. C.
Marcus, 236–255. San Francisco: Jossey-Bass, 2000.

Andrews, J., and Zarefsky, D., eds. *American Voices: Significant
Speeches in American History 1640–1945.* New York: Long-
man, 1989.

Axelrod, R. *The Evolution of Cooperation.* New York: Basic Books,
1984.

Baris, M. A., Coates, C. A., Duvall, B. B., Garrity, C. B., Johnson,
E. T., and LaCrosse, E. R. *Working with High-Conflict
Families of Divorce: A Guide for Professionals.* Northvale, NJ:
Aronson, 2001.

Benjamin, R. D. "Guerilla Mediation: The Use of Warfare Strategies in the Management of Conflict and Pursuit of Peace." http://www.mediate.com, October 1998.

Berger, P. L., and Luckmann, T. *The Social Construction of Reality: A Treatise in the Sociology of Knowledge*. New York: First Anchor Books, 1966.

Bingham, L. B. *Mediation at Work: Transforming Workplace Conflict at the United States Postal Service*. Arlington, VA: IBM Endowment for the Business of Government, 2003.

Blake, R. B., and Mouton, J. *Solving Costly Organizational Conflicts*. San Francisco: Jossey-Bass, 1984.

Bush, R.A.B., and Folger, J. P. *The Promise of Mediation: Responding to Conflict Through Empowerment and Recognition*. San Francisco: Jossey-Bass, 1994.

Coleman, P. T. "Power and Conflict." In *The Handbook of Conflict Resolution: Theory and Practice*, edited by P. T. Coleman, M. Deutsch, and E. C. Marcus, 108–130. San Francisco: Jossey-Bass, 2000.

Coleman, P. T., Bui-Wrzosinska, L., Vallacher, R. R., and Nowak, A. "Protracted Conflicts as Dynamical Systems." In *The Negotiator's Fieldbook: The Desk Reference for the Experienced Negotiator*, edited by C. Honeyman and A. K. Schneider, 61–74. Washington, DC: ABA Section on Dispute Resolution, 2006.

Constantino, C. A., and Merchant, C. S. *Designing Conflict Management Systems: A Guide to Creating Productive and Healthy Organizations*. Hoboken, NJ: Wiley, 1995.

Coser, L.A. *The Functions of Social Conflict*. New York: Free Press, 1956.

Covey, S. R. *The 7 Habits of Highly Effective People*. New York: Simon & Schuster, 1989.

Crum, T. *The Magic of Conflict: Turning a Life of Work into a Work of Art*. New York: Simon & Schuster, 1987.

Diamond, J. *Collapse: How Societies Choose to Fail or Succeed*. New York: Penguin, 2005.

Ellis, D., and Stuckless, N. "Separation, Domestic Violence, and Divorce Mediation." *Conflict Resolution Quarterly* 23, no. 4 (2006): 461–481.

Etzioni, A. *A Comparative Analysis of Complex Organizations*. New York: Free Press, 1975.

Everitt, A. *Augustus: The Life of Rome's First Emperor*. New York: Random House, 2006.

Fisher, R., and Ury, W. *Getting to Yes: Negotiating Agreement Without Giving In*. New York: Penguin, 1981.

Follett, M. P. "*Dynamic Administration*." *The Collected Papers of Mary Parker Follett*, edited by H. C. Metcalf and L. Urwick. New York and London: Harper & Brothers, 1940.

Freytag, G. *The Technique of the Drama: An Exposition of Dramatic Composition and Art*. Translation by E. J. MacEwans. Chicago: S. C. Griggs & Company, 1984.

Gadlin, H., Schneider, A. K., and Honeyman, C. "The Road to Hell Is Paved with Metaphors." In *The Negotiator's Fieldbook: The Desk Reference for the Experienced Negotiator*, edited by C. Honeyman and A. K. Schenieder, 29–36. Washington, DC: ABA Section on Dispute Resolution, 2006.

Gamson, W. A. *Power and Discontent*. Homewood, IL: Dorsey Press, 1968.

Garrity, R. *Mediation and Facilitation Training Manual: Foundations and Skills for Constructive Conflict Transformation*, 4th ed. Akron, PA: Mennonite Conciliation Service, 2000.

Goleman, D. *Emotional Intelligence: Why It Can Matter More Than IQ*. New York: Bantam Books, 1995.

Golten M. M., Smith, M., and Woodrow, P. "Hammers in Search of Nails: Responding to Critics of Collaborative Processes." Hewlett-ACR-EPP White Papers, 2002. http://Consenus .fsu.edu/ epp/hammers.html.

Grillo, T. "The Mediation Alternative: Process Dangers for Women." *The Yale Law Journal* 100, no. 6 (1991): 1545–1610.

Hale, K. "The Language of Cooperation: Negotiation Frames." *Mediation Quarterly* 16, no. 2 (1998): 147–162.

Harper, G. *The Joy of Conflict Resolution*. Gabriola Island, BC: New Society, 2004.

Honeyman, C. "Using Ambiguity." In *The Negotiator's Fieldbook: The Desk Reference for the Experienced Negotiator*, edited by C. Honeyman and A. K. Schenieder, 461–466. Washington, DC: ABA Section on Dispute Resolution, 2006.

Honeyman, C., Macfarlane, J., Mayer, B., Schneider, A., and Seul, J. "The Next Frontier Is Anticipation: Thinking Ahead About Conflict to Help Clients Find Constructive Ways to Engage Issues in Advance."*Alternatives to the High Cost of Litigation* 25, no. 6 (June 2007), 99–103.

Honeyman, C., and Schneider, A. K. eds. *The Negotiator's Fieldbook: The Desk Reference for the Experienced Negotiator*. Washington, DC: ABA Section on Dispute Resolution, 2006.

Johnson, C. H. *Creating Short Screen Plays That Connect*, 2nd ed. St. Louis: Focal Press, 2005.

Johnstone, G., and Van Ness, D. *Handbook of Restorative Justice*. Portland, OR: Willan, 2007.

Jones, E. E., and Davis, K. E. "From Acts to Dispositions: The Attribution Process in Person Perception." In *Advances in Experimental Social Psychology*, edited by L. Berkowitz, 219–266. Vol. 2. Orlando: Academic Press, 1965.

Kelley, H. H. "Attribution Theory in Social Psychology." In *Nebraska Symposium on Motivation*, edited by D. Levine. Morristown, NJ: General Learning Press, 1967.

Lang, M., and Taylor, A. *The Making of a Mediator*. San Francisco: Jossey-Bass, 2000.

Lax, D., and Sebenius, J. *The Manager as Negotiator*. New York: Free Press, 1986.

Le Guin, U. K. *Steering the Craft: Exercises and Discussions on Story Writing for the Lone Navigator or the Mutinous Crew*. Portland, OR: Eighth Mountain Press, 1998.

Le Guin, U. K. *The Wave in the Mind: Talks and Essays on the Writer, the Reader, and the Imagination*. Boston: Shambhala, 2004.

Lederach, J. P. *The Little Book of Conflict Transformation*. Intercourse, PA: Good Books, 2003.

Lederach, J. P. *The Moral Imagination: The Art and Soul of Building Peace*. New York: Oxford University Press, 2005.

Levi-Strauss, C. *Structural Anthropology*. New York: Basic Books, 1963.

Lewicki, R. J., and Wiethoff, C. "Trust, Trust Development, and Trust Repair." In *The Handbook of Conflict Resolution: Theory and Practice*, edited by P. T. Coleman, M. Deutsch, and E. C. Marcus, 86–107. San Francisco: Jossey-Bass, 2000.

Macfarlane, J. *The New Lawyer: How Settlement Has Transformed the Practice of Law*. Vancouver: University of British Columbia Press, 2008.

Mao Zedong. *On Guerrilla Warfare*. Translated by Samuel B. Griffiths II. Chicago: University of Chicago Press, 2000. Originally published 1937.

Mayer, B. "The Dynamics of Power in Mediation and Conflict Resolution." *Mediation Quarterly* 16 (Summer 1987): 75–86.

Mayer, B. *The Dynamics of Conflict Resolution: A Practitioner's Guide*. San Francisco: Jossey-Bass, 2000.

Mayer, B. *Beyond Neutrality: Confronting the Crisis in Conflict Resolution*. San Francisco: Jossey-Bass, 2004.

Mayer, B., Ghais, S., and McKay, J. *Constructive Engagement Resource Guide: Practical Advice for Dialogue Among Facilities Workers, Communities, and Regulators*. Washington, DC: U.S. Environmental Protection Agency, 1999.

Mnookin, R. H., Peppet, S. R., and Tulumello, A. S. *Beyond Winning: Negotiating to Create Value in Deals and Disputes*. Cambridge, MA: Bellnap Press, 2004.

Monk, G., and Winslade, J. *Narrative Mediation: A New Approach to Conflict Resolution*. San Francisco, Jossey-Bass, 2000.

Moore, C. *The Mediation Process: Practical Strategies for Resolving Conflict*. San Francisco: Jossey-Bass, 2003.

Morris, E. *Theodore Rex*. New York: Modern Library, 2001.

Nelson, G. *Gini Nelson's Engaging Conflicts*. [Blog.] http:// engagingconflicts.com (accessed August 14, 2008).

Olson, K. B., and Ver Steegh, N. eds. "Domestic Violence." Special issue, *Family Court Review* 46 (July 2008).

Raiffa, H. *The Art and Science of Negotiation*. Cambridge, MA: Harvard University Press, 1982.

Ricci, I. *Mom's House, Dad's House: Making Two Homes for Your Child*. New York: Simon & Schuster, 1997.

Ross, L. *Barriers to Conflict Resolution*. Edited by R. H. Mnookin, K. J. Arrow, L. Ross, A. Tversky, and R. Wilson. New York: Norton, 1995.

Rothman, J. *Resolving Identity-Based Conflict in Nations, Organizations, and Communities*. San Francisco: Jossey-Bass, 1997.

Sander, F. "The Obsession with Settlement Rates." *Negotiation Journal* 11, no. 94 (1995): 329–332.

Schneider, A. K. "Shattering Negotiation Myths: Empirical Evidence on the Effectiveness of Negotiation Style." *Harvard Negotiation Law Review* 7 (Spring 2002): 143–233.

Schön, D. *The Reflective Practitioner: How Professionals Think in Action*. New York: Basic Books, 1983.

Search for Common Ground, Home page. http://www.sfcg.org/ sfcg/sfcg_home.html (accessed May 7, 2008).

"Serenity Prayer Attributed to Niebuhr, Reinhold." Queries and Answers. *New York Times Book Review* (August 2, 1942): 19.

Shell, R. G. *Bargaining for Advantage: Negotiation Strategies for Reasonable People*. New York: Penguin, 2000.

Sun Tzu. *The Art of War*. Translated by Lionel Giles. El Paso, TX: El Paso Norte Press, 2005. Originally published 6th century B.C.E.

Tannen, D. *That's Not What I Meant: How Conversational Style Makes or Breaks Relationships*. New York: Ballantine Books, 1986.

Tesler, P., and Thompson, P. *Collaborative Divorce: The Revolutionary New Way to Restructure Your Family, Resolve Legal Issues, and Move On with Your Life*. New York: Regan Books/HarperCollins, 2006.

Thomas, K. W., and Kilmann, R. H. *Thomas-Kilmann Conflict Mode Instrument*. Tuxedo, NY: Xicom, 1974.

Ury, W. *Getting Past No*. New York: Bantam, 1991.

Ury, W. *The Power of a Positive No: How to Say No and Still Get to Yes*. London: Hodder & Stoughton, 2007.

Ury, W. L., Brett, J. M., and Goldberg, S. B. *Getting Disputes Resolved: Designing Systems to Cut the Costs of Conflict*. San Francisco: Jossey-Bass, 1988.

Victor, D. G. *The Collapse of the Kyoto Protocol and the Struggle to Slow Global Warming*. Council on Foreign Relations Book. Princeton, NJ: Princeton University Press, 2001.

Vonnegut, K. *Slaughterhouse Five*. New York: Delacorte Press, 1969.

Walton, R. E., Cutcher-Gershenfeld, J. E., and McKersie, R. B. *Strategic Negotiations: A Theory of Change in Labor-Management Relations*. Boston: Harvard Business School Press, 1994.

Wilde, O. *The Importance of Being Earnest*. New York: Bone and Liveright, 1919.

About the Author

Bernard Mayer, a professor at the Werner Institute for Negotiation and Dispute Resolution, Creighton University, and a partner in CDR Associates, has been working in the conflict field since the late 1970s as a mediator, facilitator, trainer, researcher, program administrator, and dispute system designer. He has worked on many complex environmental conflicts, organizational and labor-management disputes, interpersonal conflicts, planning and development issues, public decision-making processes, and ethnic disputes. He has an extensive background in family and child welfare mediation as well.

Bernie has worked with corporations; labor unions; Native American governments and associations; federal, state, and local agencies; public interest groups; professional associations; schools; child welfare programs; mental health services; and universities. He has consulted on conflict and conflict intervention throughout the United States and Canada and has extensive experience working internationally as well.

He has been recognized as a leader in applying mediation in new arenas such as mental health, child welfare, and disputes between public agencies and involuntary clients. He has also been recognized for his work in bridging the gap between theory and practice in conflict intervention.

Bernie received his Ph.D. degree from the University of Denver, his M.S.W. from Columbia University, and his B.A. from Oberlin College. He is the author of *The Dynamics of Conflict Resolution: A Practitioner's Guide* (Jossey-Bass, 2000) and *Beyond Neutrality: Confronting the Crisis in Conflict Resolution* (Jossey-Bass, 2004), which received the 2004 annual book award from the CPR International Institute for Conflict Prevention & Resolution, as well as many other writings about conflict. He lives in Kingsville, Ontario, and Boulder, Colorado, with his wife, Julie Macfarlane, and family.

Index

when refusing to negotiate, 46–47; and using agreements strategically, 47–48; and using power constructively, 44–45

Belfast Agreement (1998), 182

Beliefs, 35. *See also* Values

Benjamin, R. D., 149

Berger, P. L., 88

Beyond Neutrality: Confronting the Crisis in Conflict Resolution (Mayer), 8, 38, 239

Bingham, L. B., 261

Blake, R. B., 73, 74

Blake, William, 55

Boomers and Weiners (case), 208–209

Bosnians, 22

Boulder, Colorado, 10–11

Boundary creation, 192–193, 223

Brett, J. M., 152, 194

Bridge building, 190–192

Bui-Wrosinska, L., 31

Bulgaria, 200

Bulgarian Foundation on Negotiation and Conflict Resolution, 200–202

Bully pulpit, 154

Bush, R.A.B., 190, 238, 247

C

Camp David talks, 188

Carol and Paul (case), 127

Carrie and Karenna (case), 168–169

Casino Royale (movie), 114

Catholics, 22, 29, 46, 182

Cats (musical), 98

Causal crutches, 63–64

CDR Associates, 200

Charles (case), 135–137

China, 140, 182

Christianity, 116. *See also* Catholics; Protestants

Clarity, 142, 174

Clinton administration, 188

Clinton, Bill, 80, 188

Coates, C. A., 126

Cognitive dissonance, 37

Cold War, 125

Coleman, P. T., 31, 71, 153

Communication: adopting flexible approach to, 135–137; avenues of contact in, 124–130; dealing with persistently dysfunctional, 137–140; ebb and flow of, 132–137; in enduring conflict, 119; and finding effective voice, 133–135; and finding right fit, 129–130; and guerrilla communicator, 148–150; how to reestablish direct, 140; identifying effective avenues of, 127–128; intentional avenues of, 125–127; lines of, 45–46; and recovering from destructive interaction, 147–148; and speaking through conflict,